A COLLECTION OF SIMPLEST AND MOST POTENT

URDU GHAZALS

(ROMAN & HINDI SCRIPT WITH ENGLISH TRANSLATION)

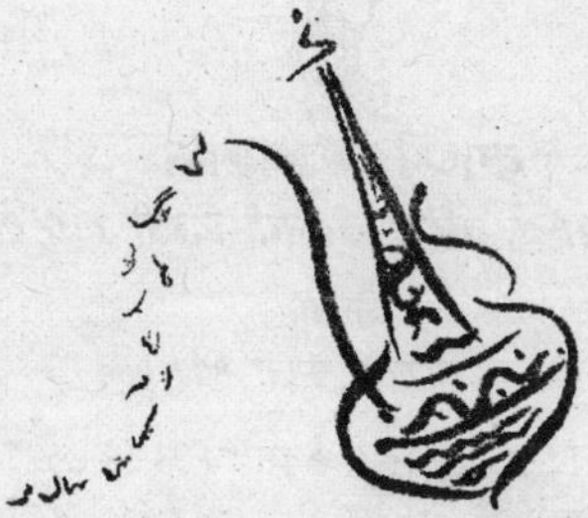

Gaagar Mein Saagar - II

Compiled and translated by
Commander IN (Retd) Rajesh Sharma

वाणी प्रकाशन

वाणी प्रकाशन

4695, 21-ए, दरियागंज, नयी दिल्ली 110 002

शाखा

अशोक राजपथ, पटना 800 004

फ़ोन : +91 11 23273167 फ़ैक्स : +91 11 23275710

www.vaniprakashan.in
vaniprakashan@gmail.com
sales@vaniprakashan.in

GAAGAR MEIN SAAGAR-II
Compiled and translated by Commander in (Retd) Rajesh Sharma

ISBN : 978-93-5229-128-1
Collection of Ghazals

संस्करण 2010
आवृत्ति संस्करण 2016

मूल्य : ₹ 450

एशियन प्रिंटर्स, दिल्ली-110 093 में मुद्रित

वाणी प्रकाशन का लोगो मक़बूल फ़िदा हुसेन की कूची से

Dedicated to
all those poets
whose work has figured in this collection.

Preface

This volume comes in the wake of **'Gaagar mein Saagar'** which was a collection of most quotable Urdu couplets. This one is a collection of the simplest and most potent ghazals picked up by me in the slow lane of life during the last 45 years or so. Each Ghazal is a gem by itself. The criteria for selection remains unchanged i.e simplicity, originality, spontaneity, sensibility, dexterity, serenity, lucidity, freshness, romanticism, imagery, innovation, longevity, topicality and last but not the least quotability.

The collection has about 200 Ghazals covering varied subjects like humanity, self-respect, God, mysticism, friendship, betrayal, morality, loyalty, wine, love, hope, dejection, joy, sorrow, tranquility, revenge, mercy et al.

All Ghazals have been translated into simple English prose preceded by Roman and Hindi script in order to share the bliss of Urdu poetry with as many sections of readers as possible.

This compilation is more from heart rather than the brain so the readers are requested to refrain from examining this from pure scholarly angle.

For the successful completion of this gigantic task, I owe special thanks to literati like **Shri Khushwant Singh, Dr Bashir Badr, Prof. Waseem Bareilivi and Dr. S.S Bhatti (Ta'meer Chandigarhi)** for providing me with the inspiration, encouragement and impetus.

I also take this opportunity to thank **Mr. S D Singh** of **Akshay Media** for his personal interest and professional advice which have greatly contributed towards the compilation and publication of this book.

J-132, Sector 25
Noida (U.P.), Pin-201301
Tele - 95120-2444780

Rajesh Sharma

Introduction

This volume is a sequel to 'Gaagar Mein Saagar'. Any introduction to this volume will not be complete without reproducing the introduction to the first volume. It follows as under (verbatim albeit with minor corrections):-

A collection of Urdu couplets, coming from a person who has no Urdu background, who does not know how to read and write Urdu and on top of that who has spent thirtyfive years of his life in the Indian Navy, for sure needs some explaining. Here it goes —

God has been kind to me by blessing me with the gift of memory and a keen sense of picking up the best from a thick volume. At the age of nine, I had surprised my parents and neighbours by reciting the entire Radheyshyam's Ramayana. I had learnt or shall we say crammed the volume by heart. I had started cramming up all kind of poems in order to excel in the game of Antaakshri. I became a natural favourite in the game and had no rival in my age group in my city i.e. Meerut.

My first introduction to Urdu poetry was through my father. I vividly remember the day I was scolded by him for some misdemeanour on my part and I had talked back to him. He flared up and said, "Son, don't ever be disrespectful to your elders, remember, बेअदब, बेनसीब, बाअदब, बानसीब".

At that time I could not understand the true import of the quote but later, on my asking, he told me the meaning:-

बेअदब, बेनसीब।

बाअदब, बानसीब।

Beadab, benaseeb.
Baaadab, baanaseeb.

(one) Without respect (is) without luck.
Respectful (is) full of luck.

Good forty years have passed. This quote has remained with me for its sheer brevity, simplicity and lasting impact. It won't be out of context to reproduce here three of his favourite quotes,

देर आयद, दुरुस्त आयद

Der aayad, durust aayad
Late awakening (is) right awakening

(Better late than never)

कभी भूल कर किसी से, न करो सलूक ऐसा,
अगर कोई तुमसे करता, तुम्हें नागवार होता।

Kabhee bhool kar kisee se na karo salook aisa,
Agar koee tumse karta tumhein naagawaar hota.

Don't even by mistake, behave with anyone in such a manner that,
If someone were to do likewise to you, you would have felt hurt.

'ज़फ़र' आदमी उसको न जानिऐ, हो वो कैसा भी साहिबे-फ़हमो-ज़का,
जिसे ऐश में यादे-ख़ुदा न रही, जिसे तैश में ख़ौफ़े-ख़ुदा न रहा।

'Zafar' aadmee usko na jaaniye, ho wo kaisa bhee saahibe-fahmo-zaka,
Jise aish mein yaade – khudaa na rahee, jise taish mein khaufe-khuda na raha.

O! 'Zafar', don't consider him a human being,
however intelligent and sagacious he may be,
The one who doesn't remember God amidst luxuries
and when in rage, doesn't fear the wrath of God.

Whether it was the influence of such quotes or the availability of plenty of cheap Urdu couplets, or the combination of both which drew me towards the Urdu poetry, I am not sure. There was this elderly chronic bachelor of our Mahalla (colony) who used to gather us young boys and recite third rate Urdu couplets with a claim that those couplets were the best stuff by which one could impress and win the love of any damsel. I was nearing my adolescence and was really fascinated by those naughty couplets. Here are few examples of the most decent ones of the lot:-

आँखों में लाल डोरा, कानों में बालियाँ,
हमको ग़रीब जान के देती हो गालियाँ।

Aankhon mein laal dora, kaanon mein baaliyaan,
Humko ghareeb jaan ke detee ho gaaliyaan.

(With) Red streak in the eyes (and) golden rings in the ears,
considering me a destitute, you are abusing me.

शीशी भरी गुलाब की, पत्थर पे तोड़ दूँ,
तेरे हुस्न की ख़ातिर, दुनियाँ को छोड़ दूँ।

Sheeshee bharee gulaab kee, patthar pe tod doon,
Tere husn kee khaatir, duniyaan ko chod doon.

I wish to break the bottle full of rosewater on the stone,
For the sake of your beauty, I am willing to leave this world.

आता हूँ दौड़-दौड़ कर, करता हूँ गदाई,
लानत है ऐसे हुस्न पर, जो भीख भी ना पाई।

Aataa hoon daud – daud kar, karta hoon gadaaee,
Laanat hai aise husn par, jo bheekh bhee na paaee.

I keep coming running to you and keep begging,
Fie on such beauty that could not be obtained even by begging.

I do confess that I managed to cram up hundreds of such couplets and became a sort of hero in the eyes of local boys. It is another matter that I could never gather enough guts to recite any of such couplet in front of any damsel. Even today I am unable to erase any of those couplets out of my mind.

"Bad things, at times, lead to good things in life", came true for me on the day I was proudly reciting this variety of my collection to a motley crowd of young roadside romeos of our mahalla. We did not know that a dignified old man (popularly known as Baabaa jee) was eavesdropping. That evening I got the thrashing of my life at my father's hands. Next day I was directed to visit Babaa jee regularly for an hour for a discourse on good things in life. I was angry and scared but in the first meeting itself, I found that the old man was full of wisdom and was in fact very interesting. He started with praising me for my memory but ended up by childing me for my choice and taste. His exact words, "Son, on one hand you know the Ramayana by heart, on the other hand you cram up this rubbish. God has given you talent, choose and retain the right stuff. You are interested in Urdu poetry, all right, there is so much good in Urdu poetry that you will be surprised to know. I know a little bit of Urdu and shall tell you what I know about the poetry".

Baabaa jee was no poet himself but he had a very interesting way of reciting and narrating. He had a very good sense of humour too. He started with couplets on humanity, self-respect, God, mysticism, friendship, morality, loyalty etc. Once he knew that I was really liking what I was getting, he got down to other topics befitting my age. Most ofthe couplets he recited to me had a story attached to the origin of an individual couplet. It was thus impossible not to get interested in what he said. Here are a few examples:-

There was this poet (he didn't know the name) once, who was engrossed while trying to write some new couplets under the candle-light one dark night. The fatal attraction of the moth towards candle-light is well known the world over. So, sure enough some moths started hovering over the candle. Their shadows kept disturbing the poet and he was unable to concentrate. However, he didn't give up and kept at it but the menace continued unabated. He tried to shoo them away but in vain. Lo! and behold! one big moth got burnt and fell right on top of the flame and extinguished it. It became pitch dark and no matchbox was ready at hand. The poet got wild and started cursing loudly and in that state of his, he did create the best couplet of his life. The couplet was:-

इलाही! आग ही लग जाए इस जज़्बे-मोहब्बत को,
जले कोई, मरे कोई, है ज़ुल्मत मेरी महफ़िल में।

Ilaahee! aag hee lag jaaye is jazbe-mohabbat ko,
Jale koee, mare koee, hai zulmat meree mehfil mein.

O! God, let the fire consume this sentiment of love,
(Wherein) Someone burns and someone else dies, causing darkness in my assembly.

Now, this one he told me about a blind poet and his adversary. One night in his unlit room, the blind man was trying hard to add a line to his incomplete couplet, but was not getting the right words. In his desperation he was thumping his feet and was loudly repeating the one line which he had already composed. The line was:-

शबे हिज्राँ मिसाल इक गेसूए-दीजूर की सूझी

Shabe-hijraan misaal ik gesooye-deejoor kee soojhee,
On the night of separation, the simile of black tresses came to mind

The poet had no idea that his adversary was standing outside next to his window and was eavesdroppoing. He continued repeating his line, and in sheer frustration was getting louder and louder. Suddenly he heard the voice of his adversary completing the couplet. The line added was:–

कि अँधे को अँधेरे में, बड़ी ही दूर की सूझी।

Ki andhe ko andhere mein, badee hee door kee soojhee.
The blind man, in the darkness has thought of a thing far too distant.

Now the complete couplet read thus:-

शबे-हिज्राँ मिसाल इक गेसूए-दीजूर की सूझी,
अँधे को अँधेरे में, बड़ी ही दूर की सूझी।

Shabe-hijraan misaal ik gesooye-deejoor kee soojhee,
Andhe ko andhere mein, badee hee door kee soojhee.

On 'the night of separation', the simile of black tresses came to mind,
The blind man, in the darkness has thought of a thing far too distant.

And this one is about the genius of a poet, 'Naasikh' (if I remember the name correctly) who was once challenged to add a line to the second line of an incomplete couplet. The second line was:-

नातवाँ हूँ, कफ़न भी हो हलका।

Naatwaan hoon kafan bhee ho halka.

The line he added was:-

डाल दे साया अपने आचँल का,

Daal de saaya apne aanchal kaa,

The complete couplet now read as:-

डाल दे साया अपने आचँल का,
नातवाँ हूँ, कफ़न भी हो हलका।

Daal de saaya apne aanchal kaa,
Naatwaan hoon, kafan bhee ho halkaa.

Cast the shadow of your hem (on my dead body),
I am a weakling, the shroud too has to be light.

He also told me the story about late Pt. Daya Shankar 'Naseem' (popularly known as Pandit jee) who, in his times, was acclaimed to be the greatest living Urdu poet. He was also an exponent in the art of improvisation and could create verses impromptu on any subject. He was held in high reverence by Hindus and Muslims alike, both for his poetic skills and secular approach. However, a small group of petty-minded fanatics did not like the renown and respect being enjoyed by the poet. They were particularly jealous of his poetic talents and abhorred the idea of a Hindu excelling in Urdu poetry. They were in the lookout for an opportunity to pull the carpet from under his feet in full public view.

They got their chance on a day when Pandit jee was presiding over a big 'Mushaaira'. It was a full house and a lot of celebrities were in attendance. One after another people were giving topics of their choice to Pandit jee for creating on the spot couplets and he was obliging much to the delight of the capacity crowd. Suddenly, one member of this group appeared on the stage and challenged the poet to add a line to an unfinished couplet which would be given by him to the poet. Pandit jee accepted the challenge and asked for the line. The man announced that there was a condition attached to his challenge. The poet said that any condition was acceptable to him. The man then announced that if Pandit jee failed to complete the couplet then he would have to give up writing the Urdu poetry. Without batting an eyelid Pandit jee readily accepted the challenge. The man then gave the line of the unfinished couplet to him. It was:-

बन्दे वो काफ़िर है, जो क़ायल नहीं इसलाम के

Bande wo Kaafir hain, jo qaayal naheen islaam ke

Those people, who do not believe in 'Islaam' (Muslim religion), are infidels

Pandit jee was horrified and crestfallen. He did not know, what hit him. There was a pin-drop silence amongst the audience as well as on the stage. Pandit jee was in a quandary ... "If I complete the couplet, the religion is gone, if I don't, then the 'shaairy' is gone. After some wait, people observed, relief returning to Pandit jee's face. He requested his challanger to provide him with a blackboard, a piece of chalk and a pointer. This was arranged. Pandit jee placed the blackboard on a high stool, facing the crowd and wrote the Urdu letter 'Laam' in a large size on the board with the help of the chalk. The letter 'Laam' appeared to the public thus ل.He then took the pointer and pointed it on to the letter 'Laam' and completed the couplet reading it at the top of his voice:-

लाम के मानिन्द हैं गेसू मिरे घनश्याम के,
बन्दे वो काफ़िर है, जो क़ायल नहीं इस–'लाम' के।

'Laam' ke maanind hain gesoo mire Ghanshyaam ke,
Bande wo Kaafir hain, jo qaayal naheen is- 'Laam' ke.

Like the 'Laam' are the tresses of my 'Lord Krishna',
Those people, who do not believe in this 'Laam', are infidels.

Within about six months of our association, Baabaa jee left for his heavenly abode. He had taught me a lot. He had introduced me to the world of Kabir, Rahim, Ghalib, Iqbaal, Meer and the like. I had noted down all the stuff he had recited to me and was in the lookout for more. I wasn't partial to Urdu. I wanted to collect good poetry in Hindi and English too. Thus started a hot pursuit in the form of visits to Libraries,

Mushaairaas and Kavisammelans. My personal collection of choicest of verses was getting bigger and bigger. No one was available to tell if I was collecting the right stuff or not. I was going on with a missionary zeal. That, I did have an uncanny sense of picking up the right stuff, was proved to me by the Providence itself. Readers please bear with me.

I was in the eleventh standard then. There was a Mushaaira in our city. The elder brother of a friend of mine was the Executive Officer in the municipality. Through him I managed a place for myself on the stage itself. So there I was sitting amongst the poets, with a brand new notebook and a pen. Soon, oblivious of the poets sitting around me I became totally engrossed in noting down whatever I was liking. I must have noted down some 20 odd couplets in about two hours of time. Suddenly, through my peripheral vision I could feel that the elderly person, sitting next to me, was watching me intently. I started feeling uneasy.

The watcher must have realised my nervousness. He patted me on the back reassuringly and said, "Son, I have been watching you for quite some time. It's obvious to me that you do not know how to write Urdu but at the same time I have realised that you do understand it quite well." I nodded my head in mute silence. He went on, "Son, I have observed that you have missed noting down many of those couplets which got lot of applause". I said, "Sir, I have noted down only those ones, which I liked". He said, "Applause and reputation of a poet means nothing to you", I said, "You are right sir, what matters to me is poetry and nothing else". He looked quite pleased and patted me once more and said, "God bless you son, you do not know what gift God has blessed you with. Keep it up, don't ever give up what you are doing. Remember my words. Carry on, I don't want to disturb you any further". I continued with my noting. After a while, I realised that the man had left his place. I felt relieved and at ease as I was no more being watched. After about midnight, I sat up in rapt attention. The most sought-after poet of those days, one of my favourites (I had never heard him in person before, though I had read lot of his work) was being invited on the mike for recital. Yes, Janaab Khumaar Barabankvi was being invited. I was keen, indeed very keen to see this great poet. Lo! and behold ! who else but the elderly man talking to me a little while ago was holding the mike. I cannot describe the state of my mind and heart. I was dumb struck, awe-struck or what. It turned out to be Khumaar Barabankvi's night. No other poet got so much applause as he did. And by God, didn't he deserve every bit of it? I haven't seen him after that night either in person or on TV. But I can never forget that night and the couplet on which he had received the maximum applause and was forced to repeat it many a time. The couplet was:-

रात बाक़ी थी, जब वो बिछड़े थे,
कट गई उम्र, रात बाक़ी है।

Raat baaqee thee jab wo bichhade the,
Kat gaee umr, raat baaqee hai.

Night was still remaining when she had parted from me,
Life has been spent, night still remains.

My obsession with the poetry allowed me no time for studies, as a result of which I failed miserably in my twelfth standard. Consequently, all my books and notes on the subject were withdrawn and locked away. I wasn't allowed to attend any Mushaaira and Kavisammelan. I had no choice but to study for my career. I managed to clear my twelfth following year. Much against the wishes of my father, I changed over to Art's side and opted for English literature as one of the subjects in BA. Thus, I had an opportunity to go through and admire the works of Keats, Shelley, Wordsworth, Shakespeare, Browning and Milton to name a few. I did my graduation in1965 and joined the Indian Navy in 1967 while I was in the final year of MA English literature.

Joining the Navy, was it the final good-bye to the world of poetry? While leaving the house I had requested all at home to take care of my books and notes. Navy was a different ball game. Where was the time for poetry? First four years were real tough and busy. It was only after two years or so that I was able to visit home on some leave. On my return, to my horror, I was told that all my books and notes had to be thrown as the termites had destroyed them. It was a personal tragedy. I felt so depressed and helpless. Seething with impotent anger I made my way back to the Navy. Next 33 years were the naval years far from the world of poetry. But I kept my interest alive by reading an odd book and by listening to the tapes of Jagjit Singh, Mehdi Hasan, Ghulaam Ali, etc. An odd piece of a Mushaaira or Kavisammelan on the TV used to be like a boon. Surprisingly in the Navy I did find lot of officers who were interested in serious poetry and at times at the bar I used to entertain like-minded people by reciting couplets on wine, beauty and love. Many who did not understand Urdu /Hindi used to ask me for a simple translation in English. I was surprised to find that most of the stuff consumed by the termites was still alive in my memory.

A part of my obsession was revived while I was on posting to Delhi in late-80s. One evening an old friend had dropped in and over a drink, he casually mentioned that the famous Urdu poet Dr Bashir Badr was in town for a couple of days and was staying next door to his house in Noida. I had watched Dr Badr on TV a number of times and had developed a liking for him. I requested my friend if he could arrange a short interview for me. He said that he would try. Next day I received a call informing me that Dr Badr had agreed to meet me at my friend's place on the same evening. It was a real honour to meet him. We chatted for good two hours or more. I found him very humble and down-to-earth. He was so famous and much sought after but he had no airs about himself. During the chat he asked me which of his couplet was liked by me most. I told him that I had not read him extensively but still my favorite one was:-

उन्हीं रास्तों ने, जिन पर मेरे साथ तुम चले थे,
मुझे रोक-रोक पूछा, तेरा हमसफ़र कहाँ है?

Unheen raaston ne, jin par mere, saath tum chale the,
Mujhe rok-rok poochha, tera humsafar kahaan hai?

The tracks, on which you had walked with me,
Repeatedly stopped me and asked, "your companion, where is she?"

Dr Badr smiled and told me that I had the couplet all wrong and that the original was:-

उन्हीं रास्तों ने, जिन पर कभी तुम थे साथ मेरे,
मुझे रोक-रोक पूछा, तेरा हमसफ़र कहाँ है?

Unheen raaston ne, jin par kabhee tum the saath mere,
Mujhe rok-rok- poochha, tera humsafar kahaan hai?

The tracks, on which you had been with me once upon a time,
Repeatedly stopped me and asked, "your companion, where is she?"

However, he was quick to add, "Doesn't matter, the meaning is same, you haven't got the meaning wrong. And now look at my audacity, I quipped back, "Dr Saahib, this shair has been in my mind for the last 15 years or so and I would like to retain it in its same form because I still feel that it reads and sounds better in the format in which I have remembered it".

Having said that, I immediately regretted and worriedly awaited his reaction. Dr Badr kept quiet for a minute or so as if he was humming something within, then be burst into a laughter, held my hand softly and said, "OK!, I give up, I agree with you that your version of the shair has more weight, I am thankful to you for your unintentional mistake". He went on to add further, "Next time, when I read this Shair in a Mushaaira, it will be in your format". I do not know whether he did that or not but that was the day this gem of a human being bought me forever. Subsequent to our meeting, I wrote an article on him and his poetry. The article was published by The Sunday Herald on 19 February 1989. The article was well received. A lot of friends and well wishers advised me to write more on the subject. In fact, the editor himself asked me to write articles on other contemporary poets like Waseem Bareilvi, Gopal Das Neeraj, Nida Fazli, et el. I did have the inclination but no time. However, I had promised myself that one day I would restore my lost treasure and put it in a book form.

That day came but came after thirteen years. Immediately after my retirement from the Navy on 30 June, 2002, I decided that it was time for me to exercise my memory and rebuild my collection which had been consumed by the termites way back in the late -60s. Thus, started the long grind. At bit by bit I started jotting down the lost treasure from the memory bank. Large number of newly-procured books and cassettes on the subject and exchange of notes with lovers of poetry also helped.

Perhaps I have used the wrong word 'grind', for there was never a dull moment. The more I concentrated on the job, the more pleasure it gave to me. I was able to re-build the collection of about ten thousand couplets out of which I have picked up the choicest 1000 and odd for this book. I have included very few couplets from the old masters like Ghalib, Meer, Momin, Zauq, Iqbal etc and I have my reasons for doing so. With all due respect to the great poets of yore, I find their Urdu rather difficult and out of reach of a person who is not well versed in Urdu. Secondly, their work has already been covered by so many books and so many authors. Thirdly, I wanted readers to enjoy the couplets which are simpler to recite, remember and quote. I enjoy reading the poetry which is closer to being Hindustani in tone and tenor rather than belonging exclusively to a particular language. Fourthly, there is so much first-rate poetry created by the modern and not-so-old poets that there is hardly any need to repeat and re-repeat the old masters. I find that the modern poets are too humble and refuse to acknowledge their own creation as a great work. For instance take the case of Janaab Muzaffar Waarsi who is the creator of such wonderful couplets:-

शोला हूँ, भड़कने की गुज़ारिश नहीं करता,
सच मुँह से निकल जाता है, कोशिश नहीं करता।
हमदर्दि-ए-अहबाब से डरता हूँ 'मुज़फ़्फ़र',
मै ज़ख़्म तो रखता हूँ नुमाइश नहीं करता।

Shola hoon, bhadakne kee guzaarish naheen karta,
Sach muhn se nikal jaata hai, koshish naheen karta.
Humdardi-a-ehbaab se darta hoon 'Muzaffar',
Main zakhm to rakhta hoon numaaish naheen karta.

I am a flame, (I) do not ask permission to flare-up,
Truth comes out from the mouth by itself, I don't try.
I am afraid of the sympathies of friends, O! 'Muzaffar',
I do possess wounds, but do not hold exhibition.

On the one hand, he composes such powerful verse and, on the other, he goes on to say:-

सर्राफ़े में कौन 'मुज़फ़्फ़र' तुझ से लेगा ठीकरियाँ,
इस बाज़ार के जरग़र है ग़ालिब, इक़बाल, अनीस, नज़ीर।

Sarraafe mein kaun 'Muzaffar' tujh se lega thheekriyaan,
Is baazaar ke jarghar hain Ghalib, Iqbal, Anees, Nazeer.

O! 'Muzaffar', in the gold market who will buy trinkets from you,
This market has (great) goldsmiths (like) Ghalib, Iqbal, Anees, Nazeer (etc).

Tell me isn't it over – humility and gross understatement?

And lastly, I wanted to bring the work of little-known poets to light. Every poet, worth his salt, in his life-time does produce 3 – 4 couplets which are unbeatable but for various reasons their work remains unknown. I shall cite the case of a relatively unknown yet a real good poet whom I had heard in a small mushaaira some forty years back. Till date his poetry and his tarannum (melody) haunt my memory. I am talking about a blind poet from a remote corner Khatauli (a village near Muzaffar Nagar, U.P.). I had heard 'Saleem' Khataulvi when I was 18 year old and at 58 now I wish I could listen to him again and again. Check this one from him:-

ये क़हक़हे तो मेरी बात का जवाब नहीं,
सलीक़ा चाहिए फूलों को, गुफ़्तगू के लिए।
ये हमसे पूछ, कि कितनी हसीं बहारों का,
हुआ है ख़ून, गुलिस्ताँ में रंगो बू के लिए।

Ye qahqahe tau meree baat ka jawaab naheen,
Saleeqa chaahiye phoolon ko guftgoo ke liye.
Ye humse poochh ki kitnee haseen bahaaron ka,
Hua hai khoon gulistaan mein rango-boo ke liye.

These guffaws are no answer to my query,
Flowers need to observe etiquettes while talking.
Ask me how many beautiful springs have been,
Sacrificed for providing the colour and fragrance to the garden.

On the day I had finished selecting the couplets, a friend dropped in and gave me a rude shock. This friend has no interest in poetry or for that matter in any literary work. He casually inquired as to what I was doing. I told him about my preoccupation. He started laughing and said, "What do you know of Urdu, don't waste your efforts, why go into the uncharted waters, a book on Urdu poetry, you must be joking, come out of your fool's paradise …. and so on". I tried to convince him that I was quite capable of doing what I intended to do but be wouldn't budge. I tried my penultimate argument, "look here, to be a critic, one doesn't have to be a novelist first". But bull–headed as he was, he wouldn't buy such a logical argument either. However, he was stumped and did a vanishing act immediately after I told him this, "Look friend, I am not a hen so I cannot lay eggs yet you cannot deny the fact that I am better qualified than the hen to comment upon the quality of an Omelette".

Vanish, he did but he left me thinking. Earlier I was too sure of what I was doing and now suddenly I wanted reassurance from someone. I stopped further work and started looking for some authority who could advise me on the subject. Suddenly, I thought of Dr Bashir Badr but did not know his whereabouts. My cousin from Meerut University managed to trace Dr Badr's address and passed on to me. In the night I rang up Dr Badr at his Bhopal's residence and quite hesitatingly re-introduced myself. To my surprise, he could recollect our meeting and also referred to the article which I had done on him and his poetry. I told him about my intention and dilemma. He said that whatever little he knew about me was enough to make him believe that I would do a good job. He advised me to send the copy of the selected couplets to him and that he would come back to me. The very next day I sent the copy to him through the courier. His response was not only reassuring but great. He said that the collection was quite good but it needed certain corrections in some couplets. He added that he would take some time in going through the entire lot and on completion the copy would be sent to me. He was kind enough to do the needful and handed over the copy to me on his next trip to Delhi. Grateful, am n't I?

Having finalised the selection, I got down to the challenging and daunting task of translating these into English prose for the benefit of those who are unfamiliar with Urdu and Hindi. The verses in this book will appear first in Hindi script followed by Roman script and the translation in simple English.

I am no Saahir Ludhiyaanvi hence I can not say-

दुनियाँ ने तर्जुबात-ओ-हवादिस की शक्ल में,
जो कुछ मुझे दिया है, वो लौटा रहा हूँ मैं।

Duniyaan ne tajurbaat-O-hawaadis kee shakl mein,
Jo kuchh mujhe diya hai, wo lauta raha hoon main.

Whatever, the world has given to me in the form of experience and mishaps,
I am returning the same to it.

I can only say that whatever pleasure these verses have given to me, I am offering the same to the readers for sharing. I request the readers not to read this book in one go or in a hurry. Every couplet is worth savouring for days and calls for some real pondering.

Depending upon the response, I shall dig more into my memory and come back to you with more heady wine of Urdu poetry for sharing it by offering the intoxicant to the readers. As a poet has said-

ये तो चन्द क़तरे है, जो छलक आए है,
रंग अभी और है दिल के गुलिस्ताँ में मेरे।

Ye tau chand qatre hain, jo chhalak aaye hain,
Rang abhee aur hai, dil ke gulistaan mein mere.

These are only a few droplets which have spilled out,
There is lot more colour in the garden of my heart.

Till then thank you and happy reading

Well, Well, Well, so that was it. Now to the introduction part to this volume. I am not the one for name(s) dropping, Yet I can not help but reproduce what reverend **Khushwant Singh** had said about the first volume. Here it goes-, ***"Thanks for 'Gaagar mein Saagar'. I will keep it by my pillow for solace".*** Such honour bestowed upon the book by him and overwhelming response from varied strata of readers had left me with no choice other than to try and produce a sequel to the main volume. I am truly exhausted yet quite happy in the hope that "Gaagar Mein Saagar II" will also be received with the same love and admiration.

Happy reading once again

ज़रा सा क़तरा कहीं आज अगर उभरता है,
समन्दरों ही के लहजे में बात करता है।
खुली छतों के दिये कब के बुझ गये होते,
कोई तो है, जो हवाओं के पर कतरता है।
शराफ़तों की यहाँ कोई अहमियत[1] ही नहीं,
किसी का कुछ न बिगाड़ो तो कौन डरता है।
यह देखना है कि सहरा[2] भी है समन्दर भी,
वह मेरी तश्नालबी[3] किस के नाम करता है।
तुम आ गये हो तो कुछ चांदनी सी बातें हों,
ज़मीं पे चांद कहां रोज़-रोज़ उतरता है।
ज़मीं की कैसी वकालत, हो फिर नहीं चलती,
जब आसमाँ से कोई फ़ैसला उतरता है।

वसीम बरेलवी

1.महत्ता 2.मरूस्थल 3.प्यास

Zara sa qatra kaheen aaj agar ubharta hai,
Samandaron hee ke lahje mein baat karta hai.
Khulee chhaton ke diye kab ke bujh gaye hote,
Koee tau hai, jo hawaaon ke par katarta hai.
Sharaafaton kee yahaan koee aihmiyat hee naheen,
Kisee ka kuchh na bigaadho tau kaun darta hai.
Yah dekhna hai ki sahra bhee hai samandar bhee,
Wah meree tashnaalabee kis ke naam karta hai.
Tum aa gaye ho tau kuch chaandnee see baatein hon,
Zameen pe chaand kahaan roz-roz utarta hai.
Zameen kee kaisee wakaalat, ho phir naheen chaltee,
Jab aasmaan se koee faisla utarta hai.

These days even if a mere droplet gains a little bit of height,
It talks only in the tone and tenor of the oceans.
The earthen lamps on the open roofs would have got extinguished long back,
There sure is someone, who has been clipping the wings of the winds.
Humility has no importance over here,
Unless you harm someone, who is scared of you.
Desert too is here, so is the ocean, let us see,
Whom she assigns my thirst to.
Once you have come, then let us have some moonlit conversation,
It is not every day that the moon comes down to the earth.
Whatever may be the pleas of the earth, it doesn't work,
When some verdict comes down from the heavens.

Waseem Bareilvi

दिल को अब यों तेरी हर एक अदा लगती है,
जिस तरह नश्शे की हालत में हवा लगती है।
रत-जगे ख़्वाबे-परेशाँ से कहीं बहतर हैं,
लरज़ उठता हूँ अगर आँख ज़रा लगती है।
ऐ रगे-जाँ के मकीं[1], तू भी कभी ग़ौर से सुन,
दिल की धड़कन तेरे क़दमों की सदा लगती है।
गो दुखी दिल को बहुत हमने बचाया फिर भी,
जिस जगह ज़ख़्म हो वाँ चोट सदा लगती है।
शाख़े-उम्मीद पे खिलते हैं तलब के गुंचे,
या किसी शोख़ के हाथों में हिना लगती है।
तेरा कहना कि हमीं रौनक़े-महफ़िल हैं 'फ़राज़',
गो तअल्ली[2] है मगर बात ख़ुदा-लगती[3] है।

अहमद फ़राज़

1.निवासी 2.अतिशयोक्ती 3.सच्ची

Dil ko ab yon teree har ek ada lagtee hai,
Jis tarah nashshe kee haalat mein hawa lagtee hai.
Rat-jage khawwaabe-pareshaan se kaheen bahtar hain,
Laraz uthhta hoon agar aankh zara lagtee hai.
Aye rage-jaan ke makeen, too bhee kabhee ghaur se sun,
Dil kee dhadkan tere qadmon kee sada lagtee hai.
Go dukhee dil ko bahut hamne bachaaya phir bhee,
Jis jagah zakhm ho waan chot sada lagtee hai.
Shaakhe-ummeed pe khilte hain talab ke gunche,
Ya kisee shokh ke haato mein hina lagtee hai.
Tera kahna ki hameen raunqe-mahfil hain 'Faraaz',
Go t-allee hai magar baat, khuda lagtee hai.

Now a days the heart is so captivated by every charm of yours,
Like in an intoxicated state a person getting swayed by the breeze.
Remaining awake through the night is better than the nightmares,
I start trembling the moment the eyes try to take even a wink.
O, dweller in my breath ! sometime you too should litsten attentively,
(My) Heartbeat sounds like the beat of your footsteps.
Even though I do try a lot to safeguard my miserable heart,
Yet every time it gets hurt where it has the wound.
On the branch of hope, are these the blooming rose-buds of desire,
Or henna is being applied on the palms of some beauty.
O, 'Faraaz'! your claim that you alone are the light of the assembly,
Though is a hyperbole, yet it sounds true.

Ahmed 'Faraaz'

आँखों में रहा, दिल में उतर कर नहीं देखा,
कश्ती[1] के मुसाफिर ने समन्दर नहीं देखा।
बेवक़्त[2] अगर जाऊँगा, सब चौंक पड़ेगें,
इक उम्र हुई, दिन में कभी घर नहीं देखा।
जिस दिन से चला हूँ, मेरी मंज़िल पे नज़र है,
आँखो ने कभी मील का पत्थर नहीं देखा।
ख़त ऐसा लिखा है कि, नगीने से जड़े हैं,
वो हाथ कि जिसने कभी ज़ेवर[3] नहीं देखा।
ये फूल मुझे क्या कोई विरासत[4] में मिले हैं,
तुमने मेरा काँटों भरा बिस्तर नहीं देखा।
पत्थर मुझे कहता है, मेरा चाहने वाला,
मैं मोम हूँ, उसने मुझे छूकर नहीं देखा।

बशीर बद्र

1.नाव 2.बिना समय 3.गहना 4.पुरखों की सम्पत्ती

Aankhon mein raha, dil mein utar kar naheen dekha,
Kashtee ke musaafir ne samandar naheen dekha.
Bewaqt agar jaaoonga, sab chaunk padheinge,
Ik umr huee, din mein kabhee ghar naheen dekha.
Jis din se chala hoon, meree manzil pe nazar hai,
Aankhon ne kabhee meel ka patthar naheen dekha.
Khat aisa likha hai ki,nageene se jadhe hain,
Wo haath ki jisne kabhee zewar naheen dekha.
Ye phool mujhe kya koee wiraasat mein mile hain,
Tumne mera kaanton bhara bistar naheen dekha.
Patthar mujhe kahta hai, mera chaahne waala,
Main mom hoon, usne mujhe chhookar naheen dekha.

(She) Remained in the eyes, did not get down into the heart,
The traveller in the boat did not have a look at the ocean.
Everyone at home will be startled if I reach at odd time.
(For), It has been ages since I saw home during day light hours.
The destination has been in my eyes from the day I started my journey.
These eyes never saw a milestone (enroute),
The letter is such as if it has been studded with jewels by her hands.
Those hands which have never seen an ornament.
(You think) These flowers have been given to me in inheritence.
You have not seen my bed riddled with thorns.
The one, who loves me, calls me a stone,
I am all wax, she has not felt me by touching.

Bashir Badr

इस दर्जा[1] बदगुमाँ[2] हैं खुलूस[3]-ए-बशर[4] से हम,
अपनों को देखते हैं पराई नज़र से हम।
.गुचों[5] से प्यार करके ये इज़्ज़त[6] मिली हमें,
चूमे क़दम[7] बहार ने, गुज़रे जिधर से हम।
वल्लाह तुझसे तर्क-ए-तअल्लुक[8] के बाद भी,
अकसर गुज़र गए हैं तेरी रहगुज़र[9] से हम।
सिदक़-ओ-सिफ़ा[10]-ए-क़ल्ब[11] से महरूम[12] है हयात[13],
करते हैं बन्दगी[14] भी जहन्नुम के डर से हम।
अकबा[16] में भी मिलेगी यही ज़िन्दगी 'शकील',
मर कर भी छुट न पाएंगे इस दर्द-ए-सर[17] से हम।

'शकील' बदायूनी

1.अधिक 2.अविश्वास होना 3.मोहब्बत 4.इन्सान, मनुष्य 5.अधखिले फूल 6.सम्मान 7.पाँव 8.सम्बन्ध विच्छेद 9.रास्ता 10.सच्चा, साफ़ 11.दिल 12.वंचित 13.जीवन 14.पूजा 15.नर्क 16.मृत्यु के बाद का जीवन 17.सर का दर्द।

Is darja badgumaan hain khuloose-bashar se ham,
Apnon ko dekhte hain paraaee nazar se ham.
Gunchon se pyaar karke ye izzat milee hamein,
Choome qadam bahaar ne, guzre jidhar se ham.
Wallaah tujhse tark-e-taalluk ke baad bhee,
Aksar guzar gaye hain teree rahguzar se ham.
Sidaq-o-sifa-e-qalb se mahroom hai hayaat,
Karte hain bandghee bhee jahnnum ke dar se ham.
Akba mein bhee milegee yahee zindgee 'Shakeel',
Mar kar bhee chhuthh na paayeinge is dard-e-sar-se ham.

I am so much sceptical about the human love ,
That I look at my near and dear ones with a strange eye.
For loving the half-bloomed flowers, I have been honoured thus,
That the spring has kissed my feet, whichever way I have passed through.
Look at it ! even after the break up with you,
I have often passed through you street.
The life is bereft of a true and clear heart,
Even the worship which I do, I do it because of the fear of hell.
O, 'Shakeel' ! even after the death I will receive the same life,
Despite of being dead, I will never be able to get rid of this headache.

'Shakeel' Badayooni

ख़ुद बना लेगा ज़माना अपना अफ़साना[1] मुझे,
आप फ़रमाऐं तो फिर मुस्कुरा के दीवाना मुझे।
फूँक डाला है मुझे इक शम्मा-रुख़[2] के इश्क़ ने,
क्यूँ न देखे रश्क़[3] से महफ़िल में परवाना मुझे।
ये क्या कम एहसान है मुझ पर जुनूने-इश्क़[4] का,
देखता है क़द्र[5] की नज़रों से वीराना मुझे।
मैनें देखी तक नहीं, पीना तो पीना है 'सलीम',
जाने क्यूँ कहती है दुनियाँ पीरे-मयख़ाना[6] मुझे।

सलीम खतौलवी

1.कहानी 2.शम्मा जैसी सुन्दरी 3.जलन 4.प्रेम का पागलपन 5.इज़्ज़त 6.शराबखाने का बुजुर्ग

Khud bana lega zamaana apna afsaana mujhe,
Aap farmaayein tau phir muskura ke deewaana mujhe,
Phoonk daala hai mujhe ek shamma-rukh ke ishq ne,
Kyoon na dekhe rashq se mehfil mein parwaana mujhe.
Ye kya kam aihsaan hai mujh per junoone-ishq ka,
Dekhta hai qadr kee nazron se weeraana mujhe.
Maine dekhee tak naheen, peena tau peena hai 'Saleem',
Jaane kyoon kahtee hai duniyaan peere-maikhaana mujhe.

The world on it's own, will fabricate a tale out of me,
The moment you smilingly pronounce me a 'Madman'.
The love of a candle-faced beauty has burnt me down,
Why shouldn't the moth give me an envious look in the gathering?
This is no small a favour done to me by the madness of love,
Because of which the ruins too give me an admiring look.
O! 'Saleem' I have not even seen (the wine) leave alone drinking,
Why then this world hails me as 'the veteran' of the bar.

Saleem Khataulvi

ख़ुद की खातिर ना ज़माने के लिए ज़िन्दा हूँ,
क़र्ज़[1] मिटटी का चुकाने के लिए ज़िन्दा हूँ।
किसको फ़ुर्सत, जो मेरे ज़ख़्म गिने बात़ सुने,
ख़ाक[2] हूँ, ख़ाक उडाने के लिए ज़िन्दा हूँ।
रूह[3] आवारा ना भटके ये किसी की ख़ातिर,
सारे रिश्तों को भुलाने के लिए ज़िन्दा हूँ।
लोग जीने के ग़रज़मन्द[4] बहुत है लेकिन,
मैं मसीहा को बचाने के लिए ज़िन्दा हूँ।

मुमताज राशिद

1.उधार 2.धूल 3.आत्मा 4.इच्छुक

Khud kee khaatir na zamaane ke liye zinda hoon,
Qarz miththi ka chukaane ke liye zinda hoon.
Kisko fursat, jo mere zakhm gine baat sune,
Khaak hoon, khaak udhaane ke liye zinda hoon,
Rooh aawaara na bhatke ye kisee kee khaatir,
Saare rishton ko bhulaane ke liye zinda hoon.
Log jeene ke gharazmand bahuat hain lekin,
Main Maseeha ko bachaane ke liye zinda hoon.

I am alive neither for myself nor for the world's sake,
Am alive for the sake of repaying the loan of the soil.
Who has time for counting my wounds (or) for listening to my woes,
(I am) Mere dust, I am alive for scattering the dust.
(So that) The soul of mine may not wander in quest of some one,
I am alive to forget all relationships.
People (here) are very desirous of living,
I am alive for the sake of saving the prophet (christ/healer).

Mumtaaj Raashid

बाग़बा ने यह अनोखा सितम[1] ईजाद[2] किया,
आशियाँ[3] फूँक के पानी को बहुत याद किया।
दरेजिन्दाँपै[4] लिखा है किसी दीवाने ने ----
''वही आज़ाद है, जिसने इसे आबाद किया''।
जिसपर अहबाब[5] बहुत रोए, फ़क़त इतना था,
घर को वीरान किया,, कब्र को आबाद किया।
इसको नाक़दरिये-आलम[6] का सिला[7] कहते है,
मर चुके हम, तो ज़माने ने बहुत याद किया।

'चकबस्त' लखनवी

1.अत्याचार 2.आविष्कार 3. घोंसला 4. जेल के द्वार पर 5. मित्र, रिश्तेदार
6. गुणी व्यक्ति के प्रति संसार की उपेक्षा 7. बदला, उपहार

Baaghbaa ne yah anokha sitam eejaad kiya,
Aashiyaan phoonk ke paanee ko bahut yaad kiya.
Darezindaanpai likha hai kisee deewaane ne,
"Wahee aazad hai, jisne ise aabaad kiya".
Jispar ahbaab bahut roye faqat itna tha,
Ghar ko weeraan kiya, qabr ko aabad kiya.
Is ko naaqadriye-aalam ka sila kahte hain,
Mar chuke hum, tau zamaane ne bahut yaad kiya.

The gardener has invented this strange violence,
Having setfire to the nest, he remembered the water a lot.
On the entrance of the prison, some madman has written this----
"Only he is free, who has inhabited this (prison)".
Only on this non-event, the near and dear ones wept a lot,
(I) Deserted the home (and), inhabited the grave.
This is called the gift from the world indifferent to talented lot,
After I was dead, the world remembered (me) a lot.

'Chakbast' Lucknavi

रंजिश[1] ही सही, दिल ही दुखाने के लिए आ,
आ फिर से मुझे छोड़ के जाने के लिए आ।
कुछ तो मेरे पिंदारे-मुहब्बत[2] का भरम रख,
तू भी तो कभी मुझको मनाने के लिए आ।
पहले से मरासिम[3] न सही फिर भी कभी तो,
रस्मो-रहे-दुनिया[4] ही निभाने के लिए आ।
किस-किस को बताएगें जुदाई का सबब[5] हम,
तू मुझ से ख़फा है, तो ज़माने के लिए आ।
इक उम्र से हूँ लज्ज़ते-गिरियाँ से भी महरूम[7],
ऐ, राहते-जाँ[8] मुझको रुलाने के लिए आ।
अब तक दिले ख़ुश-फ़हम[9] को तुझसे हैं उमीदें,
यह आख़िरी श्म्एँ भी बुझाने के लिए आ।

अहमद फ़राज

1.दुश्मनी, कड़वाहट, 2.प्रेम का घमंड 3.संबधं 4.रिवाज, प्रथा 5.कारण 6. रोने का सुख 7.रिक्त 8.जीवन की शांती 9. अच्छा भम्र

Ranjish hee sahee, dil hee dukhaane ke liye aa,
Aa phir se mujhe chhodh ke jaane ke liye aa.
Kuchh tau mere pindaare-muhabbat ka bharam rakh,
Too bhee tau kahbee mujhko manaane ke liye aa.
Pahle se maraasim na sahee phir bhee kabhee tau,
Rasmo-rahe-duniyaan hee nibhaane ke liye aa.
Kis-Kis ko bataayeinge judaaee ka sabab hum,
Too mujh se khafa hai tau zamaane ke liye aa.
Ek umr se hoon lazzate-giriyaan se bhee mahroom,
Aye raahte-jaan mujhko rulaane ke liye aa.
Ab tak dile khush-faham ko tujhse hain umeedein,
Yah aakhree shamein bhee bujhaane ke liye aa.

Enmity not withstanding, at least come for hurting the heart,
Come, for deserting me once again.
Do give some due to my illusion in the pride of love,
some time you too must come to cajole me.
Agreed (our) relationship may not be what it used to be, even then,
Come atleast for the sake of maintaining worldly tradition.
To whom all, shall I explain the cause of our break up,
If you are angry with me, then come for the sake of the world.
For ages I have even been bereft of the bliss of weeping,
O, peace of soul! come for making me cry.
Till now the heart under happy illusion has hopes from you.
Come, for extinguishing these last candles (of hope) too.

Ahmed 'Faraaz'

कुछ और बढ़ गए अँधेरे तो क्या हुआ,
मायूस तो नहीं हैं तूलिए-सहर[1] से हम।
ये माना कि ज़मीं को ना गुलज़ार[2] कर सके,
कुछ ख़ार तो कम कर गए, गुज़रे जिधर से हम।
ले-देके अपने पास फ़क़त इक नज़र तो है,
क्यों देखें किसी को किसी की नज़र से हम?
ये कब कि आपने हम्हें अपना बना लिया,
ये आरज़ू[3] थी आपको अपना बनाएँ हम।
ऐ, दोस्त! तूने तो बहुत आज़मा[4] लिया, हम्हें,
वो दिन ख़ुदा करे कि तुझे आज़माएँ हम।

'ना मालूम''

1.सुबह का आगमन 2.बाग़-बाग़ 3.इच्छा, कामना 4.परिक्षा लेना

Kuchh aur badha gaye andhere tau kya hua,
Maayoos tau naheen hain tooliye-sahar se hum,
Ye maana ki zameen ko na gulzaar kar sake,
Kuchh khaar tau kam kar gaye, guzre jidhar se hum.
Le-deke apne pass faqat ik nazar tau hai,
Kyon dekhein kisee ko kisee kee nazar se hum?
Ye kab ki aapne humhein apna bana liya,
Ye aarzoo thee aap ko apna banaaein hum.
Aye, dost! toone tau bahut aazma liya humhein,
Wo din khuda kare ki tujhe aazmaayein hum.

If the darknesses have increased a bit more, then so what,
I am not (yet) hopeless about the arrival of the morning.
Agreed, I could not turn the world into a garden,
(At the same time) I did consume some thorns from whichever way I passed.
After all give and take, I have been left only with eyes,
Why should I perceive someone from someone else's eyes?
When it was, that you made myself your own,
it was (my) desire that i should make you mine.
O, friend! you have tested me enough,
May God bring the day when I too should test you.

Unknown

मिलना था इत्तिफ़ाक़[1], बिछड़ना नसीब[2] था,
वो इतनी दूर हो गया, जितना क़रीब था।
मैं उसको देखने को तरसती ही रह गई,
जिस शख़्स की हथेली में मेरा नसीब था।
दफ़ना दिया गया मुझे चान्दी की क़ब्र में,
मैं जिसको चाहती थी वो लड़का ग़रीब था।
बस्ती के सारे लोग ही आतिश-परस्त[3] थे,
घर जल रहा था मेरा और समन्दर क़रीब था।

अन्जुम रहबर

1.अचानक 2.भाग्य 3.अग्नी के पुजारी

Milna tha ittifaaq bichhadhna naseeb tha,
Wo itnee door ho gaya, jitna qareeb tha.
Main usko dekhne ko tarastee hee rah gayee,
Jis shaksh kee hatelee mein mera naseeb tha.
Dafna diya gaya mujhe chaandee kee qabr mein,
Main jisko chaahtee thee wo ladhka ghareeb tha.
Bastee ke saare log hee aatish-parast the,
Ghar jal raha tha mera aur samandar qareeb tha.

(Our) Meeting was just a chance, parting was (our) destiny,
He went away as far, as he was close.
I was left craving for a look at the one,
Who had my destiny in his palms.
I was made to get buried in the silver grave.
The boy whom I wanted was a poor sod.
All residents of (my) settlement were worshippers of fire,
My house was on fire and the sea was next door.

Anjum Rahbar

शमा के जलते ही, ऐ दोस्त! भर आए आँसू।
कल तुझे मैनें बहुत याद किया शाम के बाद।
मैं ख़तागारे-मुहब्बत[1] सही लेकिन ऐ दोस्त।
ज़िन्दगी और निखर आई हर इल्ज़ाम[2] के बाद।
है यही हासिले-मिराजे़-मुहब्बत[3] शायद,
अब कोई नाम नहीं लब पे तेरे नाम के बाद।
मुझको अक्सर हुआ आदाबे-जुनूँ[4] का एहसास[5],
कभी आग़ाज़[6] से पहले कभी अजांम[7] के बाद।
वादा-ए-इश्क़[8] मे इतना था सरूर[9] ऐ 'जौहर',
उम्र भर होश ना आया मुझे एक जाम के बाद।

जौहर बिजनौरी

1.प्रेमका दोषी 2.लाँछन 3.प्रेम की पराकाष्ठा का फल 4.पागलपन का आदर 5.अनुभव 6.शुरूआत 7.अंत 8.प्रेम के दौरान 9.नशा

Shama ke jalte hee, aye dost! bhar aaye aansoon,
Kal tujhe maine bahut yaad kiya shaam ke baad.
Main khataagaare-muhabbat sahee lekin aye dost!
Zindagee aur nikhar aaee har ilzaam ke baad.
Hai yahee haasile-meeraaze-muhabbat shaayad,
Ab koee naam naheen lab pe tere naam ke baad.
mujhko aksar hua aadaabe-junoon ka aihsaas,
Kabhee aaghaaz se pehle kabhee anjaam ke baad.
Waadaa-e-ishq mein itna tha saroor aye 'Johar',
Umr bhar hosh na aayaa mujhe ek jaam ke baad.

With the lighting of candle O! friend, tears welled up,
Yesterday I remembered you a lot after the onset of dusk.
I may be guilty for indulging in love, O, friend! but,
Life has brightened even more after every accusation.
Perhaps this is the ultimate limit of love,
Where I don't have any other name on my lips after your name.
Often I have had the feeling of respect towards the madness,
Sometime before the beginning, sometime after the end.
There was so much intoxication in the wine of love, o! 'Johar',
(that) After the first drink, I never regained consciousness throughout the life.

Johar Bijnori

बुझ गया दिल हयात[1] बाक़ी है,
छुप गया चाँद रात बाक़ी है।
हाले-दिल[2] उनसे कह चुके सौ बार,
अब भी कहने की बात बाक़ी है।
रात बाक़ी थी जब वो बिछड़े थे,
कट गई उम्र रात बाक़ी है।
इश्क़ में हम समझे सबसे,
एक ज़ालिम हयात बाक़ी है।
रहमते-बेपनाह[3] के सदक़े[4],
एक मौजे-निजात[5] बाक़ी है।
न वो दिल है, न वो शब ऐ 'ख़ुमार'!
किस लिये अब हयात बाक़ी है?

'ख़ुमार बाराबंकवी'

1.जीवन 2.हृदय की हालत 3.अनन्त दया 4.कुरबान 5.छुटकारों की लहर

Bujh gayaa dil hayaat baaqee hai,
Chup gaya chaand raat baaqee hai.
Haale-dil unse kah chuke sau baar,
Ab bhee khane kee baat baaqee hai.
Raat baaqee thee jab woh bichhude the,
Kat gayee umr raat baaqee hai.
Ishq mein hum samjhe sab se,
Ek zaalim hayaat baaqee hai.
Rahmate-bepanaah ke sadqe,
Ek mauje-nijaat baaqee hai,
Na wo dil hai, na wo shab, aye 'Khumaar'!
Kis liye ab hayaat baaqee hai?

The heart has been doused, life remains,
The moon has hidden, night remains.
State of heart has been told to her hundred times,
(Yet) The thing which was to be told still remains.
When she had departed, night was remaining,
Life has been spent, (yet) the night remains.
In course of love I have sorted out everything,
Only the cruel life remains (to be tackled).
(I am) Extremely grateful for the unlimited benevolence,
Only good riddence from life is awaited.
O! 'Khumaar', neither that heart nor that night is there (with me),
Why then this life continues to remain?

'Khumaar' Barabankvi

तेरी आरज़ू बहुत है, तेरा इन्तिज़ार कम है,
ये वो हादिसा[1] है जिस पर मेरा अख़्तियार[2] कम है।
ये हवादिसे-ज़माना[3] बड़ी दूर ले गए हैं,
मुझे अपनी ज़िन्दगी से ये नहीं कि प्यार कम है।
मैं गुनाहग़ार भी हूँ, मैं गुनाहग़र भी लेकिन,
मुझे ऐसा कोई टोके जो गुनाहग़ार कम है।
मेरे रहबरों[4] से कह दो, मुझे रास्ता दिखायें,
मेरी ज़िन्दगी के चेहरे पे अभी गुबार कम है।
मैं 'वसीम' शेर कहने को तरस रहा हूँ,
कई दिन से आँख मेरी अभी अश्क-बार[5] कम है।

वसीम बरेलवी

1.दुर्घटना 2.अधिकार, बस 3.सासॅारिक दुर्घटनाएँ 4.रास्ता दिखानेवाले 5.आसूँ भरी

Teree aarzoo bahut hai, tera intizaar kam hai,
Ye wo haadisa hai jis par mera akhtiyaar kam hai.
Ye hawaadise-zamaana badee door le gaye hain,
Mujhe apnee zindagee se ye naheen ki pyaar kam hai,
Main gunaahghaar bhee hoon, main gunaaghar bhee lekin,
Mujhe aisa koee toke, jo gunaahghaar kam hai.
Mere rahbaron se kah do, mujhe raasta dikhaayein,
Meree zindagee ke chehre pe abhee gubaar kam hai.
Main 'Waseem' shair kahne ko taras raha hoon,
Kayee din se aankh meree abhee ashk-baar kam hai.

Longing for you is excessive, wait for you is less.
This is that mishap over which I have no control.
These worldly mishaps have taken me too far,
It is not that I love my life any less.
(Ok) I am guilty also, I am guilt-maker too,
(But) Only that one should point at me, who is any less guilty.
Ask my guides to show me the way,
(For) Till now there is less dust on the face of my life.
O, 'Waseem'! I have been tantalized to recite couplets,
For the last few days my eyes have been less tearful.

Waseem Bareilvi

मैं बैठा हूँ बज़्मे-तमन्ना[1] सजाए,
मगर क्या भरोसा वो आएँ न आएँ।
नई मंज़िलें ढूँढने तो चले हो,
मगर मशग़ले-अज़्म[2] बुझने न पाए।
वहीं मेरे तारे-नफ़स[3] टूट जाना,
जहाँ अज़्मते-इश्क़[4] पर आँच आए।
राहे-इश्क़ में हमसफ़र थे हज़ारों,
मगर दो क़दम साथ चलने न पाए।
ये रस्मे-मोहब्बत[5], अरे तौबा-तौबा,
कोई याद रख्खे, कोई भूल जाए।
वहीं तक चराग़े-वफ़ा[6] जल गए हैं।
जहाँ तक पड़े हैं शबे-ग़म[7] के साए।
बुझा दो-बुझा दो, ये शम्में बुझा दो,
मेरे हाय दाग़े-जिगर[8] मुस्कराए।
उजालों की तज़दीद[9] क्या-क्या हुई हैं,
'रज़ा' जब पड़े हैं शबे-ग़म के साए।

रज़ा रामपुरी

1.इच्छाओं की महफ़िल 2.इरादों की परिपाटी 3.साँस का तार 4.प्यार की इज़्ज़त 5.प्रेम करने का रिवाज 6.वफ़ा के दिए 7.दुख की रात 8.हृदय के घाव 9.अन्त

Main baithha hoon bazme-tamanna sajaaye,
Magar kya bharosa wo aayein na aayein.
Nayee manzile dhoondhne tau chale ho,
Magar mashgale-azm bujhne na paaye.
Waheen mere taare-nafas toot jaana,
Jahaan azmate ishq par aanch aaye.
Raahe-ishq mein humsafar the hazaaron,
Magar do qadam saath chalne na paaye.
Ye rasmë-mohabbat are tauba-tauba,
Koee yaad rakhkhe, koee bhool jaaye.
Waheen tak charaaghe-wafa jal gaye hain,
Jahaan tak pade hain shabe-gham ke saaye.
Bujha do-bujha do, ye shammein bujha do,
Mere haai daaghe-jigar muskuraaye.
Ujaalon kee tazdeed kya-kya huee hai,
'Raza' jab pade hain shabe-gham ke saaye.

Having adorned the assembly of desire, I have been waiting,
But there is no surety, she may come, may not come,
While you have started off in search for new destinations,
Do make sure that the customary resolution does not get extinguished.
O, The thread of my breath ! You must break,
The moment the dignity of love is under fire.
There were thousand odd co-travellers on the track of love,
But they could not accompany me (even) for two steps.
Oh ! This (strange) tradition of love, never again,
Someone remembers (you), someone forgets (you).
The earthen-lamps of faithfulness have continued burning to the same extent,
The extent to which the shadows of the night of sorrows have stretched.
Let us extinguish all these candles,
Now since the scars of my heart have started smiling.
O, 'Raza'! What a sad end the brightness has met,
Under the shadows of the night of sorrows.

Raza Rampuri

दीवारों से मिलकर रोना अच्छा लगता है,
हम भी पागल हो जाएगें, ऐसा लगता है।
दुनिया भर की यादें हमसे मिलने आती हैं,
शाम ढले, इस सूने घर में मेला लगता है।
कितने दिनों के प्यासे होगें सारों सोचो तो,
शबनम का क़तरा[1] भी जिनको दरिया लगता है।
किसको 'कै़सर' पत्थर मारो, कौन पराया है,
शीशमहल में इक-इक चेहरा अपना लगता है।

'कै़सर'

1.बून्द

Deewaaron se milkar rona achchha lagta hai,
Hum bhee paagal ho jaayeinge, aisa lagta hai.
Duniyaan bhar kee yaadein humse milne aatee hain,
Shaam dhale, is soone ghar mein mela lagta hai.
Kitne dinon ke pyaase honge, yaaron socho tau,
Shabnam ka qatra bhee jinko dariya lagta hai.
Kisko 'Qaisar' patthar maaro kaun paraaya hai,
Sheeshmahal mein ik-ik chehra apna lagta hai.

(I) Relish embracing the walls and (then) crying,
It appears as if I too will become insane (soon).
Memories of the entire world come to meet me,
In the wake of sunset, in this desolate house assembles a fair.
O, friend! do give it a thought, for how long they have remained thirsty,
To whom a mere drop of dew tastes like a river.
O, 'Qaiser'! who do i pelt with stone, who is not my own here,
In the palace of mirrors every face appears to be own.

Qaiser

मै अपने आपको तेरी तरह समझता हूँ,
मेरी नज़र में मेरा एतबार[1] कम कर दे।
वो हाथ काट दिए जायेगें, जो लिखते हैं,
ख़ुदा से एक दुआ हैं, उन्हें क़लम[2] करदे।
यहाँ लिबास[3] की क़ीमत है आदमी की नहीं,
मुझे गिलास बड़े दे, शराब कम कर दे।

बशीर बद्र

1.विश्वास 2.काट दे 3.पोशाक

Main apne aapko teree tarah samajhta hoon,
Meree nazar mein mera aitbaar kam kar de.
Wo haath kaat diye jaayeinge, jo likhte hain,
Khuda se ek dua hai, unhein qalam kar de.
Yahaan libaas kee qeemat hai, aadmee kee naheen,
Mujhe gilaas badhe de, sharaab kam kar de.

I consider myself (just) like you,
Reduce my confidence in my own eyes.
Those hands which write, will be cut off (one day),
There is this prayer to God, please chop them (hands) off (now).
Here attire has value, man has none,
Give me bigger glasses, (never mind) reduce the quantity of wine.

Bashir Badr

ऐ, जज़्बाए-दिल[1]! ग़र मैं चाहूँ, हर चीज़ मुक़ाबिल[2] आ जाए,
मंज़िल के लिए दो गाम[3] चलूँ, और सामने मंज़िल आ जाए।
ऐ, शम्मा क़सम परवाने की इतना तो मेरी ख़ातिर कर,
उस वक़्त चमक कर गुल[4] होना, जब रंग पे महफ़िल आजाए।
हाँ याद मुझे तुम कर लेना, आवाज़ मुझे तुम दे लेना,
इस राहे-मुहब्बत में कोई, दरपेश[5] जो मुश्किल आ जाए।
आता है तूफ़ाँ तो आने दे, कश्ती का ख़ुदा ख़ुद हाफ़िज़[6] है,
मुमकिन है कि उठती लहरों में, बहता हुआ साहिल[8] आ जाए।
इस जज़्ब-ए दिल के बारे में एक मश्वरा[9] तुझसे लेता हूँ,
उस वक़्त मुझे क्या लाज़िम[10] है, जब तुझ पे मेरा दिल आ जाए।

बहज़ाद लखनवी

1.दिल की तीव्र इच्छा 2.सामने 3.क़दम 4.बुझना 5.सामने 6.रक्षक 7.सम्भव 8.किनारा 9.राय 10.उचित, बाध्य

Aye, jazb-e-dil! ghar main chaahoon, har cheez muqaabil aajaaye,
Manzil ke liye do gaam chaloon, aur saamne manzil aajaaye.
Aye, shamma! qasam parwaane kee, itna tau meree khaatir kar,
Us waqt chamak kar gul hona, jab rang pe mahfil aajaaye.
Haan yaad mujhe tum kar lena, aawaaz mujhe tum de lena,
Is raahe-muhabbat mein koee, darpesh jo mushqil aajaaye.
Aata hai toofan tau aane de, kashtee ka khuda khud haafiz hai,
Mumqin hai ki uthhtee lahron mein, bahta hua saahil aajaaye.
Is Jazb-e-dil ke baare main, ek mashwara tujh se leta hoon,
Us waqt mujhe kya laazim hai, jab tujh pe mera dil aajaaye.

O, Passion of heart! if I wish, everything will appear right infront,
(If) I were to take two steps towards the destination, the destination would come right infront.
O, Candle! for the sake of the moth, at least do this much favour to me,
Do brighten up and get extinguished, the moment the assembly comes in full bloom.
Yes, do remember me, do call me up, should you encounter any difficulty on this path of love.
If the storm is in the offing, let it come, God himself is the protector of the boat,
It is (Quite) possible that the shore may arrive in the flow of the rising waves.
About this passion of heart, I wish to take an advice from you,
What is mandatory for me, once my heart falls for you.

Bahzaad Lucknavi

दर्द सीने से उठा, आँख से आसूँ निकले,
रात आई तो ग़ज़ल कहने के पहलू[1] निकले।
दिल का हर दर्द यूँ शैरों में उभर आया है,
जैसे मुरझाते हुए फूलों से खुशबू निकले।
जब भी बिछड़ा है कोई शख़्स, तेरा ध्यान आया,
हर नये ग़म से तेरी याद के पहलू निकले।
अश्क उमड़े तो सुलगने लगीं पलकें 'राशिद',
ख़ुश्क[2] पत्तों को जलाते हुए जुगनू निकले।

मुमताज 'राशिद'

1.दृष्टीकोण 2.सूखे

Dard seene se uthha, aankh se aansoon nikle,
Raat aaee tau ghazal kahne ke pahloo nikle.
Dil ka har dard yoon shairon mein ubhar aaya hai,
Jaise murjhaate huye phoolon se khusboo nikle.
Jab bhee bichhdha hai koee shaks, tera dhyaan aaya,
Har naye gham se teree yaad ke pahloo nikle.
Ashk umdhe tau sulagne lageen palkein 'Raashid',
Khusk patton ko jalaate huye jugnoo nikle.

Pain rose from heart, tears came out of the eyes,
With the onset of night, emerged subjects for composing poems.
Every pain in the heart has emerged out of couplets in a way,
Like the fragrance emanating from the withering flowers.
Whenever someone has parted, your thought has come (to the mind),
From every new sorrow came out excuses for remembering you.
O, "Raashid"! when the tears welled up, the eyelids started smouldring,
Fire flies came out burning the dry leaves.

Mumtaaj "Raashid"

ख़िंजा[1] में भी भरा रगें-बहारे-गुलसिताँ[2] हमने,
बनाए बिजलियों की ज़द[3] में अकसर आशियाँ[4] हमने।
चमन में जब कभी छेड़ी है अपनी दास्ताँ[5] हमने,
गुलों[6] से छीन ली है शोखिये हुस्ने-बयाँ[7] हमने।
परेशाँ बाल, लब पर सर्द आहे, आँख में आसूँ,
उन्हे किस हाल में देखा नसीबे-दुशमना[8] हमने।
हमारे दम से बाबिस्ता[9] हैं शायद गर्दिशे-दौराँ,[10]
वहीं ये भी चली आईं क़दम रखखा जहाँ हमने।
सहर[11] की रौशनी में ओस बनकर उड़ गई वो भी,
लिखी थी आसुओं से रात भर जो दास्ताँ हमने।

नज़र बाराबकंवी

1.पतझड़ 2.बंसत ऋतु के बाग का रंग 3.निशाना 4.घोसले 5.कहानी 6.फूलों 7.सुन्दरता बयान करने की चातुरता 8.दुर्भाग्य ग्रस्त 9.जुड़ी हुई 10.सासाँरिक दुर्घटनाएँ 11.सुबह

Khijaan mein bhee bhara range-bahaare-gulsitaan humne,
Banaaye bijlion kee zad mein aksar aashiyaan humne
Chaman mein jab kabhee chhedee hai apnee daastaan humne,
Gulon se chheen lee hai shokhiye-husne-bayaan humne.
Pareshaan baal, lab par sard aahein, aankh mein aansoo,
Unhein kis haal mein dekha naseebe-dushmana humne.
Humaare dam se baabista hain shaayad gardishe-dauraan,
Waheen ye bhee chalee aayee, qadam rakhkha jahaan humne.
Sahar kee raushnee mein os bankar ud gayee wo bhee,
Likhee thee aansuon se raat bhar jo daastaan humne.

I have filled even the autumn with the colours of spring,
Often I have built the nests within the gunsight of lightning.
When ever I started narrating my tale in the garden,
I did snatch the agility of the beauty of speech from the flowers.
Dishevelled hair, cold sighs on lips, tears in eyes,
O! bad luck, in what state did I see her.
Perhaps the worldly woes exist because of me,
For, whereever I stepped, these followed.
In the brilliance of morning, even that got evaporated like dew,
The story which I had written with tears throughout the night.

Nazar Barabankvi

बुलबुल ही कोई माइले-आहों-फ़ुगाँ[1] मिले,
गुलशन[2] में ज़िन्दगी का कहीं तो निशाँ मिले।
हाथ आगए जो चाँद सितारे तो क्या हुआ,
उस आस्ताँ[3] की ख़ाक के ज़र्रे[4] कहाँ मिले।
ऐ काश! मेरे उजड़े निशेमन[5] के सामने,
ख़ामोश सर झुकाए हुए बाग़बाँ[6] मिले।
अल्लाह रे! बहार की ये धीगाँ-मस्तियाँ[7],
दामन यहाँ मिले तो ग़रेबाँ वहाँ मिले।
छोटों से यूँ बड़ो को तवक्को[8] न चाहिए,
झुक कर मिले जमीं से अगर आसमाँ मिले।
ऐ, दिल! हज़ूमे-ग़म[9] में गनीमत[10] है बेबसी,
चीखें निकल पड़ें जो कोई महरबाँ[11] मिले।
आती थी कहकहों की सदा दूर से 'हफ़ीज़',
देखा क़रीब से तो, आँसू रवाँ[12] मिले।

हफ़ीज़ मेरठी

1.रूदन ग्रस्त 2.चमन,बाग 3.द्वार 4.टुकड़े 5.घोसला 6.माली 7.किल्लोलें 8.आशा 9.दुखों के जमघट 10.सहायक 11.कृपालु 12.मिश्रित

Bulbul hee koee maaile-aahon-fugaan mile,
Gulshan main zindagee ka kaheen tau nishaan mile.
Haath aagaye jo chaand sitaare tau kya hua,
Us aastaan kee khaak ke zarre kahaan mile.
Aye kaash! mere ujadhe nisheman ke saamne,
Khaamosh sar jhukaaye huye baaghbaan mile.
Allaah re! bahaar kee ye dheenga-mastiyaan,
Daaman yahaan mile tau gharebaan wahaan mile.
Chhoton se yoon badon ko tawakko na chaahiye,
Jhuk kar mile zameen se agar aasmaan mile.
Aye, dil hazoome-gham mein ganeemat hai bebasee,
Cheekhein nikal padein jo koee meharbaan mile.
Aaatee thee qahqahon kee sada door se 'Hafeez',
Dekha qareeb se tau, aasoon rawaan mile.

Even a sole nightingale lamenting in a haunting tone will do,
(I) Must find some signs of life in the garden,
So what if the moon and stars have fallen in my lap,
Did I get the dust particles of her door ?
O! God how I wish to see the gardener standing tongue-tied
And head-down in front of my razed nest.
O! God, look at the playful assaults of the spring,
Hems were found here and collars were found there.
Big people should not expect so much from the menials,
It is the sky that has to bow down, whenever it wants to meet he earth.
O! Heart, amidst the swarm of sorrows, only saving grace is (my) helplessness,
The suppressed cries would gush out, it there were a sympathizer.
O! 'Hafeez', sound of guffaws was coming from the distance,
On reaching close it emerged that the laughter was laced with tears.

'Hafeez' Meeruthi

अब तो ये भी नहीं रहा अहसास[1],
दर्द होता है या नही होता।
इश्क़ जब तक न कर चुके रुस्वा[2],
आदमी काम का नहीं होता।
हाय! क्या हो गया तबियत को,
ग़म भी राहत-फ़ज़ा[3] नहीं होता।
वो हमारे क़रीब होते हैं,
जब हमारा पता नहीं होता।
दिल को क्या-क्या सुकून[4] होता है,
जब कोई आसरा[5] नहीं होता।

जिगर

1.होश 2.बदनाम 3.शांति देने वाला 4.शांति 5.सहारा, ठिकाना

Ab tau ye bhee naheen raha aihsaas,
Dard hota hai ya naheen hota.
Ishq jab tak na kar chuke ruswa,
Aadmee kaam ka naheen hota.
Haai! kya ho gaya tabiyat ko,
Gham bhee raahat-faza naheen hota.
Wo humaare qareeb hote hain,
Jab humaara pata naheen hota.
Dil ko kya-kya sukoon hota hai,
Jab koee aasra naheen hota.

These days even this much sensation is not there,
(To feel) If the pain is there or not there.
Unless the love has defamed him/her,
Human being is of no use.
Alas! What has happend to the mood,
Even the pain has stopped giving relief.
She remains next to me,
(Only) When I am in oblivion.
What all relief the heart feels,
When there is no succour around

'Jigar'

वो कौन हैं?जो ग़म का मज़ा जानते नहीं,
बस दूसरों के दर्द को पहचानते नहीं।
इस जर्ब्रे-मसलहत[1] से तो रुस्वाईयाँ[2] भली,
जैसे कि हम उन्हें वो हमें जानते नहीं।
कमवख़्त आँख उठी न कभी उनके रूबरू[3],
हम उनको जानते तो हैं पहचानते नहीं!
हद से बढ़े तो इल्म[4] भी ज़हर है दोस्तों!
सब कुछ जो जानते हैं वो कुछ जानते नहीं।
रहते है आक़बत[5] से वो ही लोग ऐ 'ख़ुमार'!
जो ज़िन्दगी में ग़म का मज़ा जानते नहीं।

ख़ुमार बाराबंकवी

1.जबरदस्ती की सलाह 2.बदनामियाँ 3.सामने 4.ज्ञान 5.दूरअन्देशिता

Wo kaun hain, jo gham ka maza jaante naheen,
Bas doosron ke dard ko pahchaante naheen.
Is jabre-maslahat se tau ruswaaiyaan bhalee,
Jaise ki hum unhe wo hume jaante naheen.
Kamwakht aankh uthee na kabhee unke roobaroo,
Hum unko jaante tau hain pahchaante naheen.
Had se badhe tau ilm bhee zahar hai doston.
Sab kuchh jo jaante hain wo kuchh jaante naheen.
Rahte hain aaqbat se wo hee log, aye 'Khumaar'!
Jo zindagee mein gham ka maza jaante naheen.

What kind of people are those who do not know the bliss of sorrow,
They just fail to realise the pain of others.
Even the infamies are better than this enforced counselling,
For behaving in such a way as if I don't know her and she doesn't know me.
This wretched eye could never dare to lift in front of her,
I do know her yet cannot recognize her.
If the knowledge crosses the limits, it becomes poison O! friends,
Those who know all, know nothing at all.
O! 'Khumaar', only those people live with prudence,
Who in life time do not know the bliss of sorrow

'Khumaar' Barabakvi

मेरे दिल की ग़मपसन्दी[1] तो ज़रूर कम न होगी,
मगर उनकी आरज़ू[2] है तो अब आँख नम न होगी।
मेरी आँख मे कुछ आसूँ जो बहें तो ग़म न कीजे,
ये शराब अपने साग़र[3] से छलक के कम न होगी।
मेरी मौत पर कुछ ऐसे ये चराग़ गुल हुए हैं।
मेरे बाद दुनियाँ में जैसे कभी शामे-ग़म[4] न होगी।
किसी मयकदे[5] में जाऊँ कि हरम[6] में शब गुज़ारूँ,
मगर ऐसी तश्नगी[7] है, जो 'वसीम' कम न होगी।

वसीम बरेलवी

1.दुख पसंद करने की आदत 2.कामना,इच्छा 3.शराब का प्याला 4.दुख की संध्या 5.शराबखाना 6.जनान ख़ाना 7.प्यास

Mere dil kee gham pasandee tau zaroor kam na hogee,
Magar unkee aarzoo hai tau ab aankh nam na hogee.
Meree aankh se kuchh aansoon, jo bahein tau gham na keeje,
Ye sharaab apne saaghar se chhalak ke kam na hogee.
Meree maut per kuchh aise ye charaagh gul huye hain,
Mere baad duniyaan mein jaise kabhee shaame-gham na hogee.
Kisee maikade mein jaaoon ki haram me shab guzaaroon,
Magar aisee tashnagee hai, jo 'Waseem' kam na hogee.

My heart's relish for sadness, will not dwindle in any case,
But if it is her desire, then the eyes (of mine) will not get moist henceforth.
Do not grieve, should some tears fall out of my eyes,
This wine will not get diminished after spilling from the goblet.
On my death, these earthen lamps have extinguished in such a way,
As if after my demise there will be no other evening of sorrow.
I may go to a tavern, else I may opt to pass the night in a harem,
O! 'Waseem', this thirst is such that it will never diminish.

'Waseem' Bareilvi

उदास आँखों से आँसू नहीं निकलते है,
ये मोतियों की तरह सीपियों में पलते हैं।
ये एक पेड़ है आ इससे मिलके रोलें हम,
यहाँ से तेरे-मेरे रास्ते बदलते हैं।
कई सितारों को मैं जानता हूँ बचपन से,
कहीं भी जाऊँ, मेरे साथ-साथ चलते हैं।

बशीर बद्र

Udaas aankhon se aansoo naheen nikalte hain,
Ye moteeyon kee tarah seepion mein palte hain.
Ye ek pedh hai, aa isse milke rolein hum,
Yahaan se tere-mere raaste badalte hain.
Kaee sitaaron ko main jaanta hoon bachpan se,
Kaheen bhee jaaoon mere saath-saath chalte hain.

Tears do not come out from the sorrowful eyes,
These get nurtured like the pearls in the oysters.
This is one tree, let us embrace it and weep,
From here, your and my ways part.
Many stars I know from childhood.
Wherever I go, they move with me.

Bashir Badr

कैसे कहदूँ कि मुलाक़ात[1] नहीं होती है,
रोज़ मिलते हैं, मगर बात नहीं होती है।
आप लिल्लाह[2] ना देखा करें आईना कभी,
दिल का आजाना बड़ी बात नहीं होती है।
छुप के रोता हूँ तेरी याद में दुनिया भर से,
कब मेरी आँखों से बरसात नहीं होती है।
हाले-दिल पूछने वाले तेरी दुनियाँ में कभी,
दिन तो होता है, मगर रात नहीं होती है,
जब भी मिलते हैं तो कहते हैं कि, कैसे हो शकील[3],
इससे आगे तो कोई बात नहीं होती है।

शेख़ आदम अबूवाला

1.मिलन 2.भगवान के लिए 3.सुन्दर

kaise kahdoon ki mulaaqaat naheen hotee hai,
Roz miltein hain, magar baat naheen hotee hai.
Aap lillaah na dekha karein aaeena kabhi,
dil ka aajaana badhee baat naheen hotee hai.
Chhup ke rota hoon teree yaad mein duniyaan bhar se,
Kab meree aankhon se barsaat naheen hotee hai.
Haale-dil poochhne waale teree duniyaan mein kabhee,
Din tau hota hai, magar raat naheen hotee hai.
Jab bhee milte hain tau kahte hain ki kaise ho shakeel,
Isse aage tau koee baat naheen hotee hai.

How can I say that no meeting ever takes place,
We meet every day but no coversation takes place.
For God's sake, do not ever look into the mirror,
Falling of heart in love with ownself is not a big thing/deal.
Hiding fron the entire world I weep in your remembrance,
When it is, that it doesn't rain from my eyes.
O, enquirer of my heart's plight! in your world,
Day always is there, but night never sets in.
Whenever she meets she says, "How are you handsome"?
Beyond this, no talk ever takes place.

Sheikh Aadam Aboowaala

झील में चाँद नज़र आए, थी हसरत[1] उसकी,
कब से आँखों में लिए बैठा हूँ सूरत उसकी।
एक दिन मेरे किनारों में सिमट जाएगी,
ठहरे पानी सी ये ख़ामोश मोहब्बत उसकी।
बन्द मुटठी की तरह, वो कभी खुलता ही नहीं,
फ़ासले और बढ़ा देती हैं क़ुरबत[2] उसकी।
किसने जाना है, बदलते हुए मौसम का मिज़ाज[3]
उसको चाहो तो, समझ पाओगे फितरत उसकी।

मुमताज 'राशिद'

1.इच्छा 2.सामिप्य 3.प्रकृति

Jheel mein chaand nazar aaye, thee hasrat uskee,
Kab se aankhon mein liye baithha hoon soorat uskee.
Ek din mere kinaaron mein simath jaayegee,
Thhare paanee see ye khaamosh muhabbat uskee.
Band muthhthhee kee tarah, wo kabhee khulta hee naheen,
Faaslein aur badha detee hai qurbat uskee.
Kisne jaana hai, badalte huye mausam ka mizaaj,
Usko chhaaho tau, samajh paaoge phitrat uskee.

Must see the moon in lake, was her desire,
Since long have I been preserving her face in my eyes.
One day it will snuggle into my shores,
Her silent love like still waters.
Like a close fist, she never opens up,
Her nearness increases the distances a bit more.
Who has ever understood the temperament of changing weather,
Once you start loveing her, only then you will be able to understand its true nature.

Muntaaj 'Raashid'

एक तुम ही नहीं दुनियाँ में, हैं ज़फ़ाकार[1] बहुत,
दिल सलामत है तो दिल के लिए आज़ार[2] बहुत।
हाय क्या चीज़ हैं महरू-मी-ओ-ग़म[3] के रिश्ते,
मिल गए ज़ीस्त[4] के हर मोड़ पर ग़म-ख़्वार[5] बहुत।
यादे-अहबाब[6] की खुशबू से महकती शामें,
कुछ कहो, कमवक़्त होती हैं दिलाज़ार[7] बहुत
इश्क़े-आवारा[8] कहाँ, क़ैदे-दरो-बाम[9] कहाँ,
बेनवाओं[10] के लिए साया-ए-दीवार[11] बहुत।
दिल की आवाज बदल जाती थी आवाज के साथ,
याद आता है वो पैराया-ए-गुफ़तार[12] बहुत।
वक़्त इक रोज बताएगा जुनूँ की अज़्मत[13]
यूँ तो हम लोग हैं रुस्वा-सरे-बाजार[14] बहुत।

गुलाम रब्बानी तावाँ

1.अत्याचारी 2.दुख 3.कमी और दुख 4.जीवन 5.दुखबाँटने वाले 6.दोस्तो की याद 7.लुभानेवाली 8.आवारा प्रेम 9.घर और छत की क़ैद 10.दरिद्रों 11.दीवार की छाँव 12.बात करने का सलीका 13.महत्व 14.खुले बाजार मेंबदनाम

Ek tum hee naheen duniyaan mein hain zafaakaar bahut,
Dil salaamat hai tau dil ke liye aazaar bahut.
Haai kya cheez hain mahroomee-o-gham ke rishte,
Mil gaye zeest ke har mod par gham-khawwaar bahut.
Yaade-ahbaab kee khushboo se mahaktee shaamein,
Kuchh kaho, kamwaqt hotee hain dilaazaar bahut.
Ishqe-aawaara kahaan, quaide-daro-baam kahaan,
Benawaaon ke liye, saaya-e-deewaar bahut.
Dil kee aawaaz badal jaatee thee aawaaz ke saath,
Yaad aata hai wo pairaaya-e-guftaar bahut,
Waqt ek roj bataayega junoon kee azmat,
Yoon tau hum log hain ruswa sare-baazaar bahut.

You are not the only one, the world is full of tyrants,
So long the heart is there, many pains are there for it.
Alas! Strange are the relationships between deprivation and sorrows,
On every turn of life one finds many sympathisers.
Evenings full of the fragrance of the memories of friends,
You may say anything, but these damn evenings are very captivating.
There is no comparison between vagrant love and captivity of door and roof,?
For the destitutes a mere shadow of a wall is more than enough.
The voice of heart used to change with her voice,
Today, that style of talking haunts (me) a lot.
Time one day will tell you the importance of madness,
Otherwise for the sake of it we people are quite infamous in the world-market.

Ghulam Rabbani Taawaan

जामे-तही[1] क़ुबूल न था, ग़म समो लिए,
फूलों के इन्तिज़ार में काँटें चभो लिए।
महरूमिए-दवाम[2] भी क्या लुत्फ़[3] दे गई,
ये सोच कर हँसे हैं कि इक उम्र रो लिए।
हम हैं वो सादालोह[4] कि पाकर रज़ाए-दोस्त[5],
ख़ुद अपने हाथ अपने ही ख़ून में डबो लिए,
पिछला पहर है शब का, कि है शाम का समाँ,
वो क्या बता सकेगें जो इक नींद सो लिए।
क्या जब्र[6] है, सबूते-वफ़ा[7] पेश कीजिए।
और उनका नाम आए तो फिर लब न खोलिए।

मोहसिन भोपाली

1.शराब का खाली प्याला 2.स्थायी वंचितता 3.आनन्द 4.सीधे साधे 5.दोस्त की रज़ामन्दी 6.ज़बर्दस्ती 7.वफा का प्रमाण

Jaame-tahee qubool na tha, gham samo liye,
Phoolon ke intizaar mein kaante chabho liye.
Mahroomiye-dawaam bhee kya lutf de gayee,
Ye soch kar hanse hain ki ek umr ro liye.
Hum hain wo saadaloh, ki paakar razaaye-dost,
Khud apne haath apne hee khoon mein dabo liye.
Pichhla pahar hai shab ka, ki hai shaam ka samaan,
Wo kya bata sakenge jo ek neend so liye.
Kya zabr hai, saboote wafa pesh keejiye,
Aur unka naam aaye tau phir lab na kholiye.

Empty goblet was not acceptable (to me), (hence I) filled it with sorrows,
In the wait for flowers, (I) pierced (myself) with the thorns.
Perenr.ial deprivation had given me such a strange pleasure,
That I have started laughing having realised that I had been weeping for ages.
I am such a simple soul that at the behest of beloved,
I have dipped my hands in own blood.
Whether it is the fag end of night or it is evening time?
How can they tell, those who have already finished one sleep.
What sort of compulsion is this, that (I should) submit the proof of devotion,
And when her name appears, then I should seal my lips.

'Mohsin' Bhopali

उस दिल की मुसीबत कौन सुने, जो ग़म के मुक़ाबिल[1] आ जाए,
किसने ये कहा था तिनके से, वो बिजली से टकरा जाए।
दुनियाँ की बहारों से आँखें यूँ फेर ली जाने वालों ने,
जैसे कोई लम्बे क़िस्से को पढ़ते-पढ़ते उकता जाए।
आग़ाज़े-मुहब्बत[2] है, और दिल यूँ हाथ से निकला जाता है,
जैसे किसी अल्हड़[3] का आचँल सरका जाए, ढलका जाए।
गुजरे हुए दिलकश[4] लम्हों[5] की भूली हुई याद ऐसी आई,
जैसे कोई परीतम परदेसी सोते में अचानक आ जाए।
जब पहले-पहल महसूस हुआ है हुस्न तो दिल ऐसा कापाँ,
जैसे कि दुल्हन पहली शब की आहट जो मिले थर्रा जाए।
कंधे से घनेरी ज़ुल्फ़ों में यूँ लहरे पड़ती जाती हैं,
जैसे कि धुधँलका सावन का बढ़ता जाए बढ़ता जाए।
हस्ती[6] का नज़ारा क्या कहिए, मरता है कोई, जीता है कोई,
जैसे कि दीवाली हो, कि दिया बुझता जाए, जलता जाए।
एक आस जो दिल की टूट गई, फिर दिल की ख़ुशी बाक़ी न रही,
जैसे कि अँधेरे घर का दिया, गुल हो तो अंधेरा छा जाए।
दिल है कि 'नुशूर' एक बाजा है सीने के अन्दर तारों का,
जब चोट पड़े झकाँर उठे, जब ठेस लगे थर्रा जाए।

'नुशूर' वाहिदी

1.सामने 2.प्रेम की शुरूआत 3.चंचल सुन्दरी 4.दिल लुभाने वाले 5.क्षण 6.ज़िन्दगी

Us dil kee museebat kaun sune, jo gham ke muqaabil aajaaye,
Kisne ye kaha tha tinke se, wo bijlee se takra jaaye.
Duniyaan kee bahaaron se aankhen yoon pher lee jaane waalon ne,
Jaise koee lambe qisse ko padhte-padhte ukta jaaye.
Aaaghaaze-muhabbaat hai, aur dil yoon haath se nikla jaata hai,
Jaise kisee allahad ka aanchal sarka jaaye, dhalka jaay,
Guzre huye dilqash lamhon kee bhoolee huee yaad aise aayee,
Jaise koee pareetam pardesee sote mein achaanak aajaaye.
Jab pahle-pahal mahsoos hua hai husn, tau dil aise kaanpa,
Jaise ki dulhan pahlee shab kee aahat jo mile, tharra jaaye,
Khandhe se ghaneree zulfon mein yoon laharein padtee jaatee hain,
Jaise ki dhundhalka saawan ka badhta Jaaye, badhta jaaye.
Hastee ka nazaara kya kahiye, marta hai koee, jeeta hai koee,
Jaise ki deewaalee ho, ki diya bujhta jaaye, jalta jaaye.
Ek aas jo dil kee toot gayee, phir dil ki khushee baaqee na rahee,
Jaise ki andhere ghar ka diya, gul ho tau andhera chha jaaye.
Dil hai ki ' Nushoor ' ek baaja hai seene ke andar taaron ka,
Jab chot pade, jhankaar uthe, jab thhes lage tharra jaaye.

Who will listen to the woes of the heart which faces the sorrow,
Who had told the straw to go and confront the lightning.
The departing folks turned their eyes away from the springs of the world,
Like someone who has become bored of reading a long story.
It is just the beginning of love and the heart is going out of hands,
Like the ever dangling and swaying hem of a young coquette.
The lost memory of heart warming moments of good old days came in such a way,
Like the unexpected visit by the lover from overseas during the sleep.
At the first feel of beauty, the heart started fluttering,
Like the bride trembling at the slightest noice on the first night.
By (her) shoulder (movement) waves keep forming in her dense tresses,
Like the ever increasing duskiness of the rainy season.
What to talk about the ways of life, some one dies, some one lives,
Like on 'Deewaali', one earthen lamp gets extinguished, other gets lit.
Once the hope was shattered, no joy remained in the heart,
Like the darkness engulfing the house after its sole earthen lamp is snuffed.
O! 'Nushoor', under my chest is it heart or a stringed instrument,
Which gets activated on getting hurt (and) reverberates at the slightest nudge.

'Nushoor' Wahidi.

तिरे ग़म को जाँ की तलाश थी,
तिरे जाँनिसार[1] चले गए।
तिरी राह में जो करते थे सर तलब[2],
सरे-रहगुज़ार[3] चले गए।
तिरी कज़अदाई[4] से हार कर,
शबे-इन्तिज़ार[5] चली गई।
मिरे जब्ते-हाल[6] से रूठ कर,
मिरे ग़मगुसार[7] चले गए।
न सवाले-वस्ल[8] न अर्ज़े-ग़म[9],
न हिकायतें[10] न शिकायतें।
तिरे अहद में दिलेज़ार[11] के,
सभी अख़्तियार[12] चले गए।
ये हमीं थे जिनके लिबास[13] पर,
सरे-रह स्याही[14] लिखी गई।
ये ही दाग़ थे, जिन्हें सजाके हम,
सरे-बज़्मे-यार[15] चले गए।
न रहा जुनूने-रुख़े-वफ़ा[16],
ये रसन[17] ये दार[18], करोगे क्या,
जिन्हें ज़ुर्मे-इश्क़[19] पे नाज़[20] था,
वो गुनाहगार चले गए

'फ़ैज़ अहमद 'फ़ैज़'

1.जान निछावर करनेवाले 2.सरझुकाना 3.खुले आम 4.वादा टालने की आदत 5.प्रतीक्षा की रात 6.हाल छुपाने से 7.दुखबाँटने वाले 8.मिलने का आग्रह 9.दुख का प्रकटिकरण 10.शिकवे 11.कमजोर हदय 12.अधिकार 13.पोशाक 14.कालिख 15.प्रेयसी की महफ़िल 16.वफ़ादारी करने का पागलपन 17.फ़न्दा 18.सूली 19.प्रेम करने का दोष 20.अभिमान

Tire gham ko jaan kee talaash thee,
Tire jaan-nisaar chale gaye.
Teree raah mein jo karte the sar talab,
sare-rah guzaar chale gaye.
Teree kazadaaee se haar kar,
Shabe-intizaar chalee gayee,
Mire jabte-haal se rooth kar,
Mire ghamgusaar chale gaye.
Na sawaale-wasl, na arze-gham,
Na hikaayatein, na shikaayatein.
Tire ahad mein, dilezaar ke,
Sabhee akhtiyaar chale gaye.
Ye humhee the jinke libaas par,
Sare-rah siyahee likhee gayee,
Ye hee daagh the, jinhein sajaake hum,
Sare-bazme-yaar chale gaye.
Na raha junoone-rukhe-wafa,
Ye rasan, ye daar karoge kya,
Jinhe zurme-ishq pe naaz tha,
Wo gunaahgaar chale gaye.

Your sorrow was in search of somebody's life,
(Alas) All those, who were ready to sacrifice Life for you, have gone away.
Those who used to bow their heads on your way,
They have disappeared from the thoroughfare.
Dejected by your habit of breaking promises, The night of waiting has gone away,
Annoyed by concealment of pains on my part, my friends have departed.
Neither the request for union, nor expression of sorrow, nor conversation nor complaints,
All natural rights of the sad heart have vanished in your regime.
It was I alone on whose attire black ink was smeared openly,
And adorned with those black marks I entered (my) beloved's assembly.
That craze for remaining loyal is no more, what will you do with this gibbet, this noose,
Those who were proud at the sin of love, those sinners have (already) gone

Faiz Ahmed 'Faiz'

गर्मी-ए-हसरते-नाकाम[1] से जल जाते हैं,
हम चिराग़ों की तरह शाम से जल जाते हैं।
शमा जिस आग में जलती है नुमाइश के लिए,
हम उसी आग में गुमनाम[2] से जल जाते हैं।
बच निकलते हैं अगर आतिशे-सय्याल[3] से हम,
शोल-ए-आरिज़े-गुलफ़ाम[4] से जल जाते है।
खुदनुमाई[5] तो नहीं शेब-ए-अरबाबे-वफ़ा[6]
जिनको जलना हो वो आराम से जल जाते हैं।
रब्ते-बाहम[7] पे हमें क्या न कहेगें दुश्मन,
आशना[8] अब तेरे पैग़ाम से जल जाते हैं।
जब भी आता है मिरा नाम तिरे नाम के साथ,
जाने क्यों लोग मेरे नाम से जल जाते हैं।

क़तील शिफ़ाई

1.बेकार लालसा की गर्मी 2.बेनाम 3.तरल आग 4.सुन्दरी के गालों की आँच 5. आत्मप्रकाशन 6.प्रेमियों का दृषटीकोण 7.नज़दीकी सम्पर्क 8.दोस्त

Garmeeye-hasrate-naakaam se jal jaate hain,
Hum chiraagon kee tarah shaam se jal jaate hain.
Shama jis aag mein jaltee hai numaaish ke liye,
Hum usee aag mein gumnaam se jal jaate hain.
Bach nikalte hain agar aatishe-sayyaal se hum,
Shol-e-aarize-gulfaam se jal jaate hain.
Khud numaaee tau naheen sheb-e-arbaabe-wafa,
Jin ko jal na ho wo aaraam se jal jaate hain.
Rabte-baaham pe humein kya na kahenge dushman,
Aashna ab tere paighaam se jal jaate hain.
Jab bhee aata hai mera naam tere naam ke saath,
Jaane kyon log mere naam se jal jaate hain.

I get burnt from the heat of unfulfilled desires,
I get lit up in the evening like the earthen lamps.
The candle which burns in the fire for the sake of exhibition,
I get burnt in the same fire silently and unnoticed.
Whenever I am able to escape from the liquid fire,
I get burnt from the flame of the beloved's cheeks.
Showmanship is not befitting to the faithful ones,
Those who have to burn, they burn out quietly.
What all won't the enemies comment on our intimate relationship,
These days (even) friends feel jealous of your message.
whenever my name is linked with your name,
I do not know why people get envious of my name.

Qateel Shifaai

वो दिल आप मिट रहेगें, उठा तेरा ग़म न जिनसे,
वो चिराग़ क्या जलेगें, जिन्हें शब[1] न रास[2] आए।
तेरी बज़्म[3] तक तो आऊँ, जो ये आना रास आए,
ये सुना है जो गए हैं वो बहुत उदास आए।
मुझे मुस्तकि़ल[4] जुदाई में भी एक सुकून[5] सा है,
वो ही मुतमईन[6] नहीं हैं, जो तुम्हारे पास आए।
कभी ऐ 'वसीम' पहुचे जो ग़मों मे मुस्कराने,
उठा शोर मैक़दे[7] से कि वो देवदास आए।

वसीम बरेलवी

1.रात 2.माफ़िक 3.महफ़िल 4.स्थायी 5.शांति,चैन 6.आश्वस्त 7.शराबखाना

Wo dil aap mit rahenge, uthha tera gham na jinse,
Wo chiraagh kya jalenge, jinhe shab na raas aaye.
Teri bazm tak tau aaoon, jo ye aana raas aaye,
Ye suna hai jo gaye hain, wo bahut udaas aaye.
Mujhe mustaqil judaaee mein bhee ek sukoon sa hai,
Wo hee mutmaeen naheen hai, jo tumhaare paas aaye.
Kabhee, aye 'Waseem'! pahunche, jo ghamon mein muskraane,
Uthha shor maiqade se ki, " wo Devdaas aaye".

Those hearts who can not bear the burden of your sorrow, will themselves fade away,
How can those earthen lamps remain lit, who do not relish the night.
I may venture into your assembly, provided it is relishing,
(For) I have heard that those who had visited, had returned in a very sad state.
Even in permanent separation I am almost at peace,
Only those are not contented who dared come any where near you.
Whenever 'Waseem', I approached the bar in order to smile in sorrows,
Rose an uproar from the tavern, "There comes the Devdas"

'Waseem' Bareilvi

दिले-फ़सुर्दा[1] पे सौ बार ताजगी आई,
मगर वो याद कि जा कर न फिर क़भी आई।
चमन में कौन है पुरसाने-हाल[2] शबनम[3] का,
ग़रीब रोई तो गुचों[4] को भी हँसी आई।
ज़माना हँसता है मुझ पर हज़ार बार हँसे,
तुम्हारी आँख में लेकिन ये क्यों नमी आई।
दिये जलाए उमीदों ने दिल के गिर्द बहुत,
किसी तरफ़ से न इस घर मे रौशनी आई।
हजार दीद[5] पे पाबन्दियाँ[6] थी, पर्दे थे,
निगाहे-शौक़[7] मगर उनको देख ही आई।
किसी तरह न मिटा 'अर्श' दाग़े-कुफ़्रे अना[8]
हमारे काम न सज़दे[9] न बन्दगी[10] आई।

अर्श मलसियानी

1.कुम्हलाया हुआ दिल 2.हाल पूछने वाला 3.ओस 4.फूल 5.दर्शन 6.रोक-ठोकें
7.लालची आँख 8.काफ़िर होने की तोहमत 9.सर झुकाना 10.पूजा

Dile-fasurda pe sau baar taajagee aaee,
Magar wo yaad ki jaa kar na phir kabhee aaeee.
Chaman mein kaun hai, pursaane-haal shabnam ka,
Ghareeb roee tau gunchon ko bhee hansee aaee.
Zamaana hansta hai mujh par, hazaar baar hanse,
Tumhaaree aankh mein lekin ye kyon namee aaee.
Diye jalaaye umeedon ne dil ke gird bahut,
Kisee taraf se na is ghar mein raushnee aaee.
Hazaar deed pe paabandeeyaan thee, parde the,
Nigaahe-shauq magar unko dekh hee aaee.
Kisee tarah na mita, 'Arsh' daaghe-kufre-ana,
Humaare kaam na sazde na bandgee aaee.

More then hundred times, freshness did dawn upon the faded heart,
But that memory which once left, never came back.
In the garden who is there to ask about the well-being of the dew,
Even the flowers started laughing when the poor thing wept.
The world laughs at me, let it laugh a thousand times,
But why this moisture has appeared in your eyes?
Hope did kindle many a lamp near the heart,
However, no light came to this house from any direction.
There were thousand screens and restrictions against seeing (her),
Yet (my) greedy eyes did manage to have a look at her.
O! 'Arsh', by no means the stain of infidelity on (my) heart could be erased,
Neither the prostrations nor the worship came to my rescue.

'Arsh' Malsiyaani

सुबह-दम यूँ ही फ़सुर्दा[1] हो गया,
ऐ दिले-नाज़ुक[2] तुझे क्या हो गया।
सीना-ए-बरबत[3] से जो शोला उठा,
ग़मज़दों[4] के दिल का नग़मा हो गया।
शुक्रिया ऐ ग़र्दिशे-जामे-शराब[5],
मैं भरी महफ़िल में तन्हा हो गया।
रात-दिन को था सहर[6] का इन्तिज़ार,
अब ये ग़म है, क्यों सबेरा हो गया।
पूछिये उससे ग़मे-साज़े-ख़ुलूस[7]
चार ही दिन मे जो रुस्वा[8] हो गया।
बुझ गई कुछ इस तरह शमा-ए-'सलाम',
जैसे इक बीमार अच्छा हो गया।

'सलाम' मछलीशहरी

1.उदास 2.नर्म हदय 3.दबा हुआ दिल 4.दुख ग्रस्त लोग 5.दुख की शराब का प्याला 6.सुबह 7.वफ़ादरी का ग़म 8.बदनाम

Subah-dam yoon hee fasurda ho gaya,
Aye dile-naazuk! tujhe kya ho gaya.
Seena-e-barbat se jo shola utha,
Ghamzadon ke dil ka naghma ho gaya.
Shukriya aye ghardishe-jaame-sharaab,
Main bharee mehfil mein tanha ho gaya.
Raat din ko tha sahar ka intizaar,
Ab ye gham hai, kyoon sabera ho gaya.
Poochhiye usse ghame-saaze-khuloos,
Chaar hee din mein jo ruswa ho gaya,
Bujh gayee kuchh is tarah shama-e-'Salaam'
Jaise ik beemaar achchha ho gaya.

Early morning (it) became sad for no reasons,
What has happened to you O, my feeble heart?
The flame emerging out of the breast of the musical instrument,
Became the song of heart of the lovelorn folks,
Many a thanks to you, O incessant rounds of cups of wine,
I have become all alone in the full assembly.
In the night the heart was waiting for the morning,
Now it is sad, why the morning has arrived.
Ask him about the shock of sorrow born out of devotion,
The one who became infamous in no time.
'Salam's' candle got extinguished in such a way,
As (all of a sudden) a sick person has become Ok.

"Salaam' Machhleeshahri

असर उनको जरा नहीं होता
रंज[1] राहत-फ़िज़ा[2] नहीं होता।
बेवफ़ा कहने की शिकायत है,
तो भी वादा वफ़ा नहीं होता।
ज़िक्रे-अग़ियार[3] से हुआ मालूम,
हर्फ़े-नासेह[4] बुरा नहीं होता।
तुम हमारे किसी तरह न हुए,
वर्ना दुनियाँ में क्या नहीं होता।
तुम मेरे पास होते हो गोया।
जब कोई दूसरा नहीं होता।
हाले-दिल यार को लिखूँ क्यूँ कर,
हाथ दिल से जुदा नहीं होता।
क्यूँ सुने अर्ज़े-मुज़्तरिब[5] 'मोमिन',
सनम आखिर ख़ुदा नहीं होता।

मोमिन

1.दुख 2.सुखवर्धक 3.दूसरों के कहने से 4.उपदेशक के शब्द 5.उतावले दिल की प्रार्थना

Asar unko jara naheen hota,
Ranj raahat-fiza naheen hota.
Bewafa kahne kee shikaayat hai,
Tau bhee waada wafa naheen hota.
Zikre-aghiyaar se hua maaloom,
Harfe-naaseh bura naheen hota.
Tum humaare kisee tarah na huye,
Warna duniyaan mein kya naheen hota,
Tum mere paas hote ho goya,
Jab koee doosra naheen hota.
Haale-dil yaar ko likhoon kyoon kar,
Haath dil se juda naheen hota.
Kyoon sune arze-muztarib 'Momin'
Sanam aakhir khuda naheen hota.

There is never any effect on her,
Sorrow is never comforting.
She has a complaint against being called as disloyal,
Yet she doesn't keep any of her promises,
From the talks of others I came to know,
That the words of the preacher were not bad.
In no way you became mine,
Otherwise, what all doesn't happen in the world.
You are with me, whenever no one else is there.
Why for should I write my state of heart to my beloved,
After all hand is no different than the heart.
Why should she listen to the prayer of the dejected heart?
Beloved is no God after all.

'Momin'

यहाँ हर शख़्स[1] हर पल हादिसा[2] होने से डरता है,
खिलौना है जो मिट्टी का, फ़ना[3] होने से डरता है।
मेरे दिल के किसी कोने में, इक मासूम सा बच्चा,
बड़ों की देख कर दुनियाँ, बड़ा होने से डरता है।
न बस में ज़िन्दगी इसके, न इसको मौत पर क़ाबू,
मगर इन्सान फिर भी कब ख़ुदा होने से डरता है।
अजब ये ज़िन्दगी की क़ैद है, दुनिया का हर इन्साँ,
रिहाई[4] माँगता है, और रिहा होने से डरता है।

राजेश रेडडी

1.इन्सान 2.दुर्घटना 3.मरना 4.छुटकारा

Yahaan har shakhs har pal haadisa hone se darta hai,
Khilauna hai jo mittee ka, fana hone se darta hai.
Mere dil ke kisee kone mein ek maasoom sa bachcha,
Badon kee dekh kar duniyaan, bada hone se darta hai.
Na bas mein zindagee iske, na isko maut par qaaboo,
Magar insaan phir bhee kab khuda hone se darta hai.
Ajab ye zindagee kee qaid hai, duniyaan ka har insaan,
Rihaaee maangta hai, aur riha hone se darta hai.

Here, every person at all times is scared of impending mishap,
The one who is made of clay, is scared of merging with the dust.
In some corner of my heart, An innocent child,
After looking at the world of adults, is scared of growing up.
Neither he has any right on life, nor any control on death,
Yet the human being is not even scared, of assuming himself to be the God.
Strange is the prison of life (wherein) every human being of this world,
Has been begging for release from life and is scared of being released.

Rajesh Reddy

न सोच कर कभी अन्ज़ामे-गुम-रही[1] मैनें,
इस एक उम्र में तेरी तलाश की मैनें।
ख़ुशी की धूप मे तल्ख़ी[2] थी इसलिए ऐ दोस्त!
हयात[3] साया-ए-ग़म[4] में गुज़ारदी मैनें।
तमाम रात तेरी आँख का ख़याल बख़ैर,
लबों से जाम लगा कर गुज़ार दी मैनें।
मेरी उदास निगाह ही 'वसीम' काफ़ी थी,
सबूते-ग़म[5] के लिये आँख तर ना की मैनें।

वसीम बरेलवी

1.रास्ता भूलने का नतीजा 2.कड़वाहट 3.जीवन 4.दुख की छाँव 5.ग़म का प्रमाण

Na soch kar kabhee anzaame-gumrahee mainein,
Is ek umr mein teree talaash kee mainein.
Khushee kee dhoop mein talkhee thee isee liye aye dost!
Hayaat saaya-e-gham mein guzaar dee mainein.
Tamaam raat teree aankh ka khyaal bakhair,
Labon se jaam laga kar guzaar dee mainein.
Meree udaas nigaah hee 'Waseem' kaafee thee,
Saboot-e-gham ke liye aankh tar na kee mainein.

Never bothering about the consequence of getting lost on way,
I kept searching for you throughout the life.
There was bitterness in the sunshine of happiness, that is why O, friend!
I spent the entire life under the shade of sorrow.
Immersed in the thought of your eyes,
I spent the entire night with the goblet touching my lips.
My sad eyes were good enough,
I did not wet my eyes to prove my sorrow.

Waseem Bareilvi

गुज़रा हूँ जिस तरफ़ से भी, पत्थर लगे मुझे,
ऐसे भी क्या थे लालो-जवाहर[1] लगे मुझे।
लो हो चुकी शिफ़ा[2], कि मदावाए-दर्दे-दिल[3],
अब तेरी दस्तरस[4] से भी बाहर लगे मुझे।
तरसा दिया है अब्रे-गुरेज़ाँ[5] ने इस क़दर,
बरसे जो बूँद भी, तो समंदर लगे मुझे।
थामे रहोगे जिस्म की दीवार ता-ब-के[6],
यह ज़लज़ला तो रूह के अंदर लगे मुझे।
गर रौशनी यही है तो, ऐ बदनसीब शहर,
अब तीरगी[7] ही तेरा मुक़द्दर लगे मुझे।
मंज़िल कहाँ की ज़ादे-सफ़र[8] को बचाइयो,
अब रहज़नों[9] की नीयते-रहबर[10] लगे मुझे।
वह मुतमइन कि सब की ज़बाँ काट दी गई,
ऐसी ख़मोशियों से मगर डर लगे मुझे।
वह क़हते-हर्फ़े-हक़[11] है कि इस अहद[12] में 'फ़राज़'
ख़ुद-सा गुनाहगार भी पयम्बर लगे मुझे।

अहमद 'फ़राज़'

1.हीरे-जवाहरात 2.ठीक होना 3.दिल के दर्द का इलाज 4.पहुँच 5.जाते बादल 6.कब तक 7.अँधेरा 8.यात्रा का सामान 9.राह में लूटनेवालों 10.राह दिखानेवालों की नियत 11.सच्चाई के शब्द का अकाल 12.युग

Guzra hoon jis taraf se bhee, patthar lage mujhe,
Aise bhee kya the laalo-jawaahar lage mujhe.
Lo ho chukee shifa, ki madaawaaye-darde-dil,
Ab teree dastras se bhee baahar lage mujhe.
Tarsa diya hai abre-gurezaan ne is qadar,
Barse jo boond bhee, tau samandar lage mujhe.
Thaame rahoge jism kee deewaar ta-ba-ke,
Yah zalzala tau rooh ke andar lage mujhe.
Gar raushnee yahee hai tau, aye badnaseeb shahar,
Ab teergee hee tera muqaddar lage mujhe.
Manzil kahaan kee, zaade-safar ko bachaaeeyo,
Ab rahzanon kee neeyate-rahbar lage mujhe.
Wah mutmaeen ki sab kee zabaan kaat dee gayee,
Aisee khamosheeon se magar dar lage mujhe.
Wah qahte-harfe-haq hai, ki is ahad mein 'Faraaz',
Khud-sa gunaahgaar bhee payambar lage mujhe.

From whichever side I passed, I have been hit by stones,
As if I was studded with some sort of diamonds and jewels.
Looks like it is the end of my cure, (so much so) that the treatment of pain of (my) heart,
Now seems beyond the reach of your hands even.
The departing cloud has tantalized me to the extent,
That even one drop of rain appears to me like an ocean.
How long can (I) continue to hold the wall of the body in place,
This earthquake seems to me inside the soul itself.
If this is what you call the light, then, O, unlucky town!
To me it looks that only the darkness is your destiny now.
Forget about the destination, save your travelling-paraphernalia,
The intention of the thugs seems like the intention of the guides to me now.
She is satisfied that everybody's tongue has been chopped off,
But I am feeling scared of such silences.
What kind of famine of true words is this, O, 'Faraaz'!
That in the present era a criminal like myself looks like a prophet to me.

Ahmed 'Faraaz'

माना कि हम पे जौरो-जफ़ा कीजिएगा आप,
लेकिन हमीं न होंगे तो क्या कीजिएगा आप?
हरचन्द ज़ब्त हद से सिवा कीजिएगा आप,
आँसू न थम सकेंगे तो क्या कीजिएगा आप?
तनहाइयाँ तो एक तरफ़, सब के सामने,
पहरों उदास-उदास रहा कीजिएगा आप।
हरचन्द लाइयेगा जबाँ पर न राज़े-इश्क़,
नज़रें पुकार उठेंगी तो क्या कीजिएगा आप?
होना है एक दिन जिन्हें मशहूरे-ख़ासोआम,
किस दिल से वो फ़साने सुना कीजिएगा आप?
छुप छुप के न रो भी सकेंगे बक़द्रे-ज़र्फ़,
घुट-घुट के दिल-ही-दिल में रहा कीजिएगा आप।
आँखों की नींद, दिल की ख़लिश का नहीं इलाज,
बिस्तर से आह करके उठा कीजिएगा आप।
अक्सर तो इन्तहाए-तस्व्वुर में नागहाँ,
आग़ोशे-शौक़ खोल दिया कीजिएगा आप।
छेड़ों पे हमसिनों की तबस्सुम तो क्या मगर
एक फ़र्ज़े-नागवार अदा कीजिएगा आप।
रहता नहीं है जिसमें कि याराए-सब्रो-ज़ब्त,
क्या जाने उस जुनून में क्या कीजिएगा आप?
जब कुछ न बन पड़ेगा मदावा-ए-दर्दे-हिज्र,
रो-रो के मग़फिरत की दुआ कीजिएगा आप।

जिगर मुरादाबादी

Maana ki ham pe jauro-jafa keejiyega aap,
Lekin hameen na honge tau, kya keejiyega aap?
Harchand zabt had se siva keejiyega aap,
Aansoo na tham sakeinge tau kya keejiyega aap?
Tanhaaeeyaan tau ek taraf, sab ke saamne,
Pahron udaas-udaas raha keejiyega aap.
Harchand laaeeyega zabaan par na raaze-ishq,
Nazrein pukaar uthheingee tau kya keejiyega aap?
Hona hai ek din jinhein mashhoore-khaasoaam,
Kis dil se wo fasaane suna keejiyega aap,
Chhup-chhup ke na ro bhee saqeinge baqadre-zarf,
Ghut-ghut ke dil-hee-dil mein raha keejiyega aap,
Aankhon kee neend, dil kee khalish ka naheen ilaaj,
Bistar se aah karke uthha keejiyega aap.
Aksar tau intihaaye-tasawwur mein nagahaan,
Aagoshe-shauq khol diya keejiyega aap?
Chhedhon pe hamsinon kee tabassum tau kya magar,
Ek farze-naagawaar ada keejiyega aap.
Rahta naheen hai jismein ki yaaraaye-sabro-zabt,
Kya jaane us junoon mein kya keejiyega aap?
Jab kuchh na ban padhega madaawaaye-darde-hijr,
Ro-ro ke magphirat kee dua keejiyega aap.

Agreed that you will treat me with tyranny and oppression,
But when I too am no more, then what will you do?
You may exercise utmost control on yourself,
But still the tears would not-stop then what will you do?
Leave aside the solitudes, infront of everyone,
For hours together, you will continue to remain depressed.
You may not bring the secret of love on your tongue, come what may,
But if the eyes cry out, then what will you do?
One day which have to become famous in public,
With what heart will you listen to those stories?
For the sake of profoundity, you will not be able to weep even secretly,
You will have to keep all emotions choked in your heart.
Sleep of the eyes and worry of the heart have no remedy,
You will rise from the bed with a painful sigh.
Often, overpowered by the intense sentiments,
You will inadvertently open your heart's secret.
When teased by friends of equal age, you may not smile openly,
But you will have to act up something of that sort in order to discharge an unpleasant obligation.
Wherein the friendship, patience and tolerance have no place,
God knows, in such a mad state, what will you do?
When no remedy can be found for the pain due separation,
You will cry and cry, and pray for solace.

'Jigar' Muradabadi

मेरी दीवानगी नहीं जाती,
रो रहा हूँ, हंसी नहीं जाती।
तेरे जलवों से आश्कार[1] हूँ मैं,
चाँद की चाँदनी नहीं जाती।
तर्क-ए-मय[2] ही समझ इसे नासेह[3],
इतनी पी है कि पी नहीं जाती।
जब से देखा है उनको बेपर्दा,
नख़वत[4]-ए-आगही[5] नहीं जाती।
शोख़ी-ए-हुस्न-ए-बेइमां[6] की क़सम,
हुस्न की सादगी नहीं जाती।
उनकी दरियादिली[7] को क्या कहिये,
मेरी तिश्ना-लबी[8] नहीं जाती।

शकील बदायूनी

1.प्रकट होना 2.शराब छोड़ना 3.नसीहत करने वाला 4.घमण्ड 5.पूर्व परिचय 6.धर्म भ्रष्ट करने वाली सुन्दरता की अदाएें 7.हृदय की विशालता 8.होंठों की प्यास।

Meree deewaangee naheen jaatee,
Ro raha hoon, hansee naheen jaatee.
Tere jalwon mein aashkaar hoon main,
Chaand kee chaandnee naheen jaatee.
Tark-e-mai hee samajh ise naaseh,
Itnee pee hai ki pee naheen jaatee.
Jab se dekha hai unko beparda,
Nakhwat-e-aagahee naheen jaatee.
Shokhee-e-husn-e-beimaan kee qasam,
Husn kee saadgee naheen jaatee.
Unkee dariyadilee ko kya kahiye,
Meree tishna-labee naheen jaatee.

My insanity does not leave me,
I have been crying (yet) the laughter does not leave me.
I am visible (only) through your splendour,
Moonlight never leaves the moon.
O, preacher! take this as my break up from wine,
Have drunk so much that (I) am unable to drink anymore.
Since the day I have seen her without a veil,
I have not been able to forget the pride on my past relationship(with her).
I swear on the charms of the beauty which destroys one's faith,
That I shall never he able to forget the simplicity of (her) grace.
Why blame her large-heartedness,
This is the thirst of my lips which doesn'ts leave me.

'Shakeel' Badayooni

कैसा दरिया है, कि प्यासा तो न मरने देगा,
अपनी गहराई का अन्दाज़ा[1] न करने देगा।
ख़ाक-ए-पा[2] होके मिलो, जिससे मिलो, फिर देखो,
इस बुलन्दी[2] से तुम्हें कौन उतरने देगा।
प्यार तहज़ीब-ए-तअल्लुक[4] का अजब बन्धन है,
कोई चाहे तो हदें पार न करने देगा।
डूब जाने को जो तक़दीर समझ बैठे हों,
ऐसे लोगों में मुझे कौन उभरने देगा।
दिल को समझाओ कि बेकार परेशां है 'वसीम',
अपनी मनमानी उसे कोई न करने देगा।

वसीम बरेलवी

1.अनुमान 2.चरण रज 3.ऊँचाई 4.सम्बन्धों की संस्कृति

Kaisa dariya hai, ki pyaasa tau na marne dega,
Apnee gahraaee ka andaaza na karne dega.
Khaake-pa hoke milo, jisse milo, phir dekho,
Is bulandee se tumhein kaun utarne dega.
Pyaar tahzeebe-taalluk ka ajab bandhan hai,
Koee chaahe tau hadein paar na karne dega.
Doob jaane ko jo taqdeer samajh baithhe hon,
Aise logon mein mujhe kaun ubharne dega.
Dil ko samjhaao ki bekaar pareshaan hai 'Waseem',
Apni manmaanee use koee na karne dega.

What sort of river is this, that will not let me die of thirst,
(At the same time) Will not allow me to gauge her depth.
Whosover you meet with, meet like (you are) the dust of feet, then watch,
Who will (ever) allow you to get down from these heights.
Love is strange bond of culture of relationships,
Even if someone wishes, it will not allow to cross the limits.
Those who have taken for granted that drowning is their fate,
Amongst such people, who will allow me to surface.
O, 'Waseem' ! counsel your heart, it is unnecessarily excited,
Noone will allow it to act as per its own whims and fancies.

Waseem Bareillvi

है नसीमे-सुबह[1] आवारा उसी के नाम पर,
बू-ए-गुल[2] ठहरी हुई है जिस कली के नाम पर।
कुछ न निकला दिल में दागे़-हसरते-दिल[3] के सिवा।
हाय! क्या-क्या तोहमतें[4] थी आदमी के नाम पर।
फिर रहा हूँ कू-ब-कू[5] ज़ंजीरे-रुस्वाई[6] लिए,
है तमाशा सा तमाशा ज़िन्दगी के नाम पर।
अब ये आलम[7] है कि हर पत्थर से टकराता हूँ सर,
मार डाला एक बुत[8] ने बन्दगी[9] के नाम पर।
कोई पूछे मेरे ग़मरव्वारों[10] से "तुमने क्या किया"?
ख़ैर उसने दुशमनी की दोस्ती के नाम पर।
कुछ इलाज उनका भी सोचा तुमने ऐ चारागरों[11],
वो जो दिल तोड़े गए है, दोस्ती के नाम पर।
कोई पाबन्दिशें[12] हँसने पर न रोना जुर्म है,
इतनी अज़ादी तो है, दीवानगी के नाम पर।
आप ही के नाम से पाई है दिल ने ज़िन्दगी,
ख़त्म होगा अब ये कि़स्सा आप ही के नाम पर।
कारवाने-सुबह[13] यारों कौन सी मंज़िल में है,
मै भटकता फिर रहा हूँ रौशनी के नाम पर।

अख़्तर सईद

1.सुबह की बयार 2.फूल की खुशबू 3.हदय की लालसा का दाग़ 4.लाछँन 5.दरबदर 6.बदनामी की जजींर 7.हालत 8.सुन्दरी 9.पूजा 10.दुख बटाँनेवाले 11.चिक्तिस्कों 12.रोक-ठोकें 13.सुबह का काफि़ला

Hai naseeme-subah aawaara usee ke naam par,
Boo-e-gul thhahree huyee hai jis kalee ke naam par.
Kuchh na nikla dil mein daaghe-hasrate-dil ke siwa,
Haai! kya-kya tohmatein thee aadmee ke naam par.
Phir raha hoon ku-ba-koo zanjeere-ruswaaee liye,
Hai tamaasha sa tamaasha, zindgee ke naam par.
Ab ye aalam hai ki har patthar se takraata hoon sar,
Maar daala ek but ne bandgee ke naam per.
Koyee poochhe mere ghamkhwaaron se"Tumne kya kiya" ?
Khair usne dushmanee kee dostee ke naam par.
Kuch ilaaj unka bhee socha tumne, aye chaaraagaron,
Wo jo dil tode gaye hain, dostee ke naam par.
Koyee paabandishein hansne par na rona jurm hai,
Itnee aazaadee tau hai, deewaangee ke naam par.
Aap hee ke naam se paayee hai dil ne zindgee,
Khatm hoga ab ye qissa aap hee ke naam par.
Kaarwaane-subah yaaron kaun see manzil mein hai,
Main bhatakta phir raha hoon raushnee ke naam par.

This wandering morning breeze is fascinated by the same bud,
For which the fragrance of the flower has been staying put.
Nothing came out of the heart except the scar of desire,
Alas! What all allegations were there on the human being.
(I) Have been wandering all over shackled in infamy,
What sort of a melodrama is this in the garb of life.
This is the state now, that I strike my head against every stone,
A beauteous one has finished me in the name of worship.
Someone should ask my sympathisers "What did you do"?
Agreed, she nursed enmity in the name of friendship.
O, healers! Have you thought of some remedy for those also,
Whose hearts have been broken in the name of friendship.
There are no restrictions on laughs, nor crying is considered a crime,
At least this much freedom is there in the name of insanity.
This heart has found life only because of you,
Ending of this story too will be with your name.
O, friends! At what destination dwells the caravan of morning,
I have been wandering from pillar to post, looking for the light.

Akhtar Saeed

आ कि दिल अब ज़ीस्त[1] से बेजार है तेरे बग़ैर,
हर नफ़स[2] चलती हुई तलवार है तेरे बग़ैर,
ये सुहानी रात और तुझसे जुदाई हाय-हाय,
हर शिकन बिस्तर की नोके-ख़ार[3] है तेरे बग़ैर।
राज़े-उल्फ़त[4] वाए मजबूरी हुआ जाता है फ़ाश[5],
हाले-दिल शर्मिन्द-ए-इज़हार[6] है तेरे बग़ैर।
अब कहाँ वो कैफ़[7] की रातें वो दिलचस्पी के दिन,
ज़िन्दगी एक मुस्तकिल[8] आज़ार[9] है तेरे बग़ैर,
ग़ैर तो हैं ग़ैर, अपने भी पराए हो गये,
सारी दुनियाँ बर-सरे-आज़ार[10] है तेरे बग़ैर।
चश्मे-नरगिस[11] तक ही कुछ महदूद[12] बेताबी[13] नहीं,
गुलसिंता[14] का गुलसिंता बीमार है तेरे बग़ैर।
सुबह के आगोश में नौ-रस[15] शिगूफ़ो[16] की चटक,
लब-ए-अफ़सुर्दा[17] पे कितनी बार[18] है तेरे बग़ैर।
ढूढंता है फिर किसी मौज़ू-ए-रगीं[19] को ख़याल,
फ़िक्रे-'माहिर' तश्न-ए-अशआर[20] है तेरे बग़ैर।

माहिर-उल-क़ादिरी

1.जीवन 2.सांस 3.कांटे की नोक 4.मुहब्बत का रहस्य 5.स्पष्ट 6.हाल कहने पर शर्मिन्दगी 7.आनन्द 8.स्थायी 9.दर्द 10.दुखों से भरी 11.नरगिस की आँख 12.सीमित 13.उतावला पन 14.बाग़ 15.नयारस, ताजा रस 16.कलियाँ 17.उदास होंठ 18.बोझिल 19.रगींन शीर्षक 20.शैंर कहने को प्यासी

Aa ki dil ab zeest se bejaar hai tere baghair,
Har nafas chaltee huyee talwaar hai tere baghair.
Ye suhaanee raat aur tujhse judaaee haai-haai,
Har shikan bistar kee nauke-khaar hai tere baghair.
Raaze-ulfat waaye majbooree huya jaata hai faash,
Haale-dil sharmind-e-izhaar hai tere baghair.
Ab kahaan wo qaif kee raatein, wo dilchaspee ke din,
Zindagee ek mustakil aazaar hai tere baghair.
Ghair tau hain ghair, apne bhee paraaye ho gaye,
Saaree duniyaan bar-sare-aazaar hai tere baghair.
Chashme-nargis tak hee kuch mahdood betaabee naheen,
Gulsitaan ka gulsitaan beemaar hai tere baghair.
Subah ke aagosh mein nau-ras shigoofon kee chatak,
Lab-e-afsurda pe kitnee baar hai tere baghair.
Dhhoondhta hai fir kisee mouzoo-e-rangee ko khyaal,
Fikre-'Maahir' tashn-e-ashaar hai tere baghair.

Come now, for without you the heart is unconcerned with life,
Every breath without you is like a sword in action.
This pleasant night and separation from you, God save me,
Every crease of the bedspread feels like the point of thorn, without you.
Because of helplessness the secret of love is about to get revealed,
For this revelation, the state of heart is shamefaced without you.
Where are those restful nights, those days full of interest, now,
Life is an unending pain without you.
Ok, strangers are strangers, loved ones too have become strangers,
Entire world is full of pains without you.
Desperation is not limited to the eyes of the daffodil alone,
Entire garden is suffering without you.
The irresistible charm of fresh juicy buds in the bosom of dawn,
How heavy it is weighing on the desperate heart without you.
Again the thought is in search of some colourful theme,
Without you, preoccupied with worries, 'Maahir' has been thirsting for new couplets.

Maahir-Ul-Qadri

इस जहां[1] से कब कोई बच कर गया,
जो भी आया, खाके कुछ पत्थर गया।
थी यही कोशिश, मेरी पगड़ी न जाए,
बस इसी कोशिश में मेरा सर गया।
दोस्तों का ख़ौफ़[2] ही काफी है अब,
मेरे दिल से दुश्मनों का डर गया।
हम भी आखिर सबके जैसे हो गए,
रफ़्ता-रफ़्ता[3] अपना वो तेवर[4] गया।
बेच डाला हमने कल अपना ज़मीर[5]
जिन्दगी का आखिरी ज़ेवर[6] गया

राजेश रेडडी

1.संसार 2.डर 3.धीरे-धीरे 4.गुस्सा 5.अन्तः करण 6.आभूषण

Is jahaan se kab koee bach kar gaya,
Jo bhee aaya, khaake kuchh patathar gaya.
Thee yahee koshish, meree pagdee na jaaye,
Bas isee koshish mein mera sar gaya.
Doston ka khauf hee kaafee hai ab,
Mere dil se dushmanon ka dar gaya.
Hum bhee aakhir sabke jaise ho gaye,
Rafta-rafta apna wo tewar gaya.
Bech daala humne kal apna zameer,
Zindagee ka aakheeree zewar gaya.

Who has gone away unscathed from this world,
Whosoever came, went after getting pelted with some stones.
My only endeavour was, to safeguard my turban,
And in this very endeavour my head had to go.
Fear of friends is more than enough now,
Dread of enemies has gone away from my heart.
In the end I too became like everyone else,
By and by all my anger vanished.
I (too) sold my conscience yesterday,
Life's last ornament is no more.

Rajesh Reddy

दौलते-दर्द को दुनियाँ से छुपाकर रखना,
आँख में बूँद न हो, दिल में समंदर रखना।
कल, गए गुज़रे ज़मानों का ख़याल आएगा,
आज इतना भी न रातों को मुनव्वर[1] रखना।
अपनी आशुफ़्ता मिज़ाजी पे हँसी आती है,
दुश्मनी संग से और काँच के पैकर रखना।
आस कब दिल को नहीं थी तेरे आ जाने की,
पर न ऐसी कि कदम घर से न बाहर रखना।
ज़िक्र उसका सही, बज़्म में बैठे हो 'फ़राज़',
दर्द कैसा ही उठे, हाथ न दिल पर रखना।

अहमद फ़राज़

1. रौशन

Daulate-dard ko duniyaan se chhupaakar rakhna,
Aankh mein boond na ho, dil mein samandar rakhna.
Kal, gaye guzre zamaanon ka khyaal aayega,
Aaj itna bhee na raaton ko munawwar rakhna.
Apnee aashufta mizaajee pe hansee aatee hai,
Dushmanee sang se aur kaanch ke paikar rakhna.
Aas kab dil ko naheen thee tere aa jaane kee,
Par na aisee ki qadam ghar se na baahar rakhna.
Zikr uska sahee, bazm mein baithhe ho 'Faraaz'
Dard kaisa hee uthhe, haath na dil par rakhna.

Keep the wealth of pain hidden away from the eyes of the world,
Let there be no drop in the eye, (yet) hold an ocean in the heart.
Tomorrow, (you) will be haunted by the memory of the times gone by,
(Hence) Do not light up present nights so brightly.
I laugh at my self-inflicting nature,
Enmity with the stones and own body of glass,
When didn't the heart have hope of your arrival,
But not to the extent that I (dare not) take even one step out of the house.
Ok, let the talk be about her even, (mind you) you are sitting in the assembly, O 'Faraaz'!
Whatever kind of pain may arise, do not put hand on (your) heart.

Ahmed 'Faraaz'

जलवा-ए-हुस्न-ओ-करम[1] का आसरा[2] करता हूँ मैं,
जो ख़ता मुमकिन है मुझसे बेख़ता करता हूँ मैं।
जब सुबूही[3] ले के दर्द-ए-मरहबा[4] करता हूँ मैं,
जिन्दगी को नीन्द से चौंका दिया करता हूँ मैं।
वो भी क्या दिन थे कि था पीने पिलाने से ही काम,
हाय अब चार आँसूओं पर इकतिफ़ा[5] करता हूँ मैं।
देखने वाले मेरी ख़ामोशी-ए-लब[6] को न देख,
आँखों-आँखों में फ़साना[7] कह दिया करता हूँ मैं।
दिल लरज़ जाता है सुनकर हर सितारे का 'शकील',
चाँद से तनहाईयों[9] में कुछ कहा करता हूँ मैं।

शकील बदायूनी

1.सुन्दरता की कृपा दृष्टि 2.भरोसा 3.प्रातःकाल की शराब 4.दर्द की तारीफ़
5.संतोष 6.होंठों की खामोशी 7.कहानी 8.हिल जाना 9.एकांत।

Jalwa-e-husn-o-karam ka aasra karta hoon main,
Jo khaṭa mumkin hai mujhse bekhata karta hoon main.
Jab suboohee le ke dard-e-marhaba karta hoon main,
Zindgee ko neend se chaunka diya karta hoon main.
Wo bhee kya din the, ki tha peene pilaane se hee kaam,
Haai ab chaar aansuon par iktifa karta hoon main.
Dekhne waale meree khaamoshee-e-lab ko na dekh,
Aankhon-aankhon mein fasaana kah diya karta hoon main.
Dil laraz jaata hai sunkar har sitaare ka 'Shakeel',
Chaand se tanhaaeeon mein kuchh kaha karta hoon main.

I rely on the kind eyes of beauty,
(Hence) Whatever mistakes are possible, I commit them without fail.
After drinking the morning wine, when I start praising the bliss of pain,
I startle the life out of it's slumber.
What (delightful) days were those, when there was no work other than drinking,
Alas! now I become satiated only after shedding four tears.
O, you onlooker! do not look at the silence of my lips,
I recount stories through eye to eye contact.
After listening to that, the heart of every star starts trembling,
What I speak to the moon in solitude.

'Shakeel' Badayooni

मैं आसमां पे बहुत देर रह नहीं सकता,
मगर यह बात ज़मीं से तो कह नहीं सकता।
किसी के चेहरे को कब तक निगाह में रखूँ,
सफ़र में एक ही मंज़र तो रह नहीं सकता।
यह आज़माने की फ़ुर्सत तुझे कभी मिल जाए,
मैं आँखों-आँखों में क्या बात कह नहीं सकता।
सहारा लेना ही पड़ता है मुझको दरिया का,
मै एक क़तरा हूँ, तनहा तो बह नहीं सकता।
लगा के देख ले जो भी हिसाब आता हो,
मुझे घटा के वह गिनती में रह नहीं सकता।
यह चन्द लम्हों[1] की बेइख़्तियारियां[2] है 'वसीम',
गुनह3 से रिश्ता बहुत देर रह नहीं सकता।

वसीम बरेलवी

1.क्षणों 2.क़ाबू न होना 3.पाप

Main aasmaan pe bahut der rah naheen sakta,
Magar ye baat zameen se tau kah naheen sakta.
Kisee ke chehre ko kab tak nigaah mein rakhoon,
Safar mein ek hee manzar tau rah naheen sakta.
Yah aazmaane kee fursat tujhe kabhee mil jaaye,
Main aankhon-aankhon mein kya baat kah naheen sakta.
Sahaara lena hee padhta hai mujhko dariya ka,
Main ek qatra hoon, tanha tau bah naheen sakta.
Laga ke dekh le jo bhee hisaab aata ho,
Mujhe ghatha ke wah gintee mein rah naheen sakta.
Yah chand lamhon kee beikhtiyaariyaan hain 'Waseem',
Gunah se rishta bahut der rah naheen sakta,

I can not stay in the sky for far too long,
But this fact I can not reveal to the earth.
How long can I retain someon's face in my eyes,
Only one particular scene can not continue to prevail through the journey.
May you find some spare moments to test me sometime,
To find out as to what all I am capable of experssing through my eyes.
(I am) Constrained to take the support of the river,
I am a mere droplet, can not flow on my own.
Let her do the accounting through whatever arithmetic she knows,
After subtracting me, she can not remain in the counting.
These uncontrolled acts are but momentary,
The relationship with sin can not last for long.

'Waseem' Bareillvi

हँसने वाले एक काम करें,
चश्मे-गिरियाँ[1] का एहतराम[2] करें,
हम भी करलें जो रौशनी घर में,
फिर अंधेरे कहाँ क़याम[3] करें?
मुझको महरूमि-ऐ-नज़ारा[4] क़बूल[5],
आप जल्वे[6] न अपने आम करें।
एक .गुज़ारिश[7] है, हजरते-नासेह[8],
आप अब कोई और काम करें।
हाथ उठता ही नहीं, दिल से किसी वक़्त 'खुमार',
हम उन्हें किस तरह सलाम करें?

'खुमार बाराबकंवी'

1.रोती हुई आँख 2.आदर 3.ठहराव 4.दर्शनों से महरूम होना 5.मज़ूँर,स्वीकार 6.दर्शन 7.प्रार्थना 8.श्रीमान उपदेशक जी

Hansne waale ek kaam karein,
Chasme-giriyaan kaa eihtraam karein.
Hum bhee karlein jo raushnee ghar mein,
Phir andhere kahaan qayaam karein.
Mujhko mehroomiye-nazaaraa qabool,
Aap jalve na apne aam karein.
Ek ghuzaarish hai, hazrate-naaseh,
Aap ab koee aur kaam karein,
Haath utthta hee naheen dil se kisee waqt 'Khumaar',
Hum unhe kis tarah salaam karein.

O! all you laughing folks, (please) do one thing now,
Start respecting the weeping eyes.
If I too were to brighten my home,
Then where would the darkness rest?
Deprivation of (your) sight is acceptable to me,
Do not expose your charms to public viewing (for my sake).
O! reverend preacher, this is one request to you,
" You take up some other job now ".
The hand never leaves the heart,
How do I salute her?

'Khumaar' Barabankvi

जो चुप रहें तो कसक[1] हो, हँसे तो खूँ टपके,
तेरी नज़र ने दिया ज़ख़्म भी रफ़ू की तरह।
सिखा रहे हैं वो आदाबे-मयकशी[2] हमको,
जो मयकदे[3] में छलकते रहे सुबू[4] की तरह।
सुरागे़ -क़त्ल[5] मिला खुद अदाए-क़ातिल[6] से,
वो रगें-रुख़[7] भी पुकारा मेरे लहू की तरह।
सुकूत[8] पर भी वो शायद बिठाएगें पहरे,
सुकूत भी तो है इक जुर्म[9] गुफ़्तगू[10] की तरह।
तेरे विसाल[11] की खुशबू, तेरे फ़िराक़[12] का रंग,
मेरा वुजूद[13] है इक शहरे-रगों-बू[14] की तरह।
हमें भी देख कि हम आरज़ू[15] के सहरा[16] में,
खिले हुए हैं किसी ज़ख़्मे-आरज़ू की तरह।

शायर लखनवी

1.टीस 2.शराब पीने का करीना 3.मदिरालय 4.शराब का प्याला 5.कत्ल का प्रमाण 6.क़ातिल की अदा 7.सूरत के रंग 8.ख़ामोशी,चुप्पी 9.अपराध 10.बातचीत11.मिलन 12.विरह 13.अस्त्वि 14.रंगीन शहर की ख़ुशबू 15.लालसा 16.रेगिस्तान 18.हसरत भरा घाव

Jo chup rahein tau kasak ho, hanse tau khoon tapke,
Teree nazar ne diya zakhm bhee rafoo kee tarah.
Sikha rahe hain wo aadaabe-maiqashee humko,
Jo maikade mein chhalkte rahe suboo kee tarah.
Suraaghe-qatl mila khud adaaye-qaatil se,
Wo range-rukh bhee pukaara mere lahoo kee tarah.
Sukoot par bhee wo shaayad bithaayenge pahre,
Sukoot bhee tau hai ik jurm, guftgoo kee tarah.
Tere wisaal kee khushboo, tere firaaq ka rang,
Mera wujood hai ik shahre-rango-boo kee tarah.
Humein bhee dekh, ki hum aarzoo ke sahra mein,
Khile huye hain kisi zakhme-aarzoo kee tarah.

It pains if I keep quiet, if I laugh the blood drips,
Thy looks have given me a wound too like the darning.
They are teaching me the etiquettes of drinking,
Those who in the bar kept spilling like the goblet.
The clue to murder was provided by the mannerism of the murderer herself,
That colourful face too called out like my blood.
Perhaps she will put guards on the silence also,
Because silence too is a crime like talking.
The fragrance of your union, the colour of your separation,
My very existence is like a city of colours and scents.
Look at us also, as we, in the desert of desires,
Have been blossoming like a wound of longing.

'Shaayar Lucknavi

उड़ गई यूँ वफ़ा ज़माने से,
कभी गोया किसी में थी ही नहीं।
हम तो दुशमन को दोस्त कर लेते,
पर करें क्या, तेरी ख़ुशी ही नहीं।
हम तेरी आरज़ू[1] पे जीते हैं,
वो नहीं है तो ज़िन्दगी ही नहीं।
दिल-लगी[2], दिल्लगी[3] नहीं नासेह[4],
तेरे दिल को अभी लगी ही नहीं।
लुत्फ़े-मय[5] तुझसे क्या कहूँ ज़ाहिद[6],
हाय कमबख़्त तूने पी ही नहीं।

दाग़ देलहवी

1.इच्छा 2.दिल को लगी चोट 3.मजाक 4.उपदेशक 5.शराब का आनंद 6.पवित्र व्यक्ति

Udh gayee yoon wafa zamaane se,
Kabhee goya kisee mein thee hee naheen.
Hum tau dushman ko dost kar lete,
Par karein kya, teree khushee hee naheen.
Hum teree aarzoo pe jeete hain,
Wo naheen hai tau zindagee hee naheen.
Dil-lagee, dillagee naheen, naaseh,
Tere dil ko abhee lagee hee naheen.
Lutfe-mai tujhse kya kahoon, zaahid,
Haai kambakht toone pee hee naheen.

Loyalty has flown away from this world in such a way,
As if it never dwelt in anyone.
I would have made friend with the enemy,
But what to do, you were not happy (With such an arrangement).
I live only in longing for you,
If that is not there then life does not exist for me.
O, Preacher! falling of heart in love is no joke,
(seems) Your heart has not fallen in love, as yet.
O, holy one! how do I explain to you the bliss of drinking,
Alas! You unfortunate one, you have never drunk.

Daagh Delhivi

सब देखने वाले उन्हे गश[1] खाए हुए हैं
इस पर भी तअज़्ज़ुब[2] है वो शर्माये हुए हैं।
ऐ जाने-जहाँ[3] हमको ज़माने से ग़र्ज़[4] क्या,
जब खोके ज़माने को तुझे पाये हुए हैं।
हैरान हूँ क्यो मुझको दिखाई नही देते,
सुनता हूँ मेरी बज़्म[5] में वो आए हुए हैं।
निस्बत[6] की यह निस्बत है, शरफ़ का यह शरफ़[7] है,
तेरे हैं अगर हम, तिरे ठुकराये हुए हैं।
है देखने वालों को सभँलने का इशारा,
थोड़ी सी निक़ाब आज वो सरकाये हुए हैं।

अर्श मलशियानी

1.चक्कर 2.आश्चर्य 3.संसार की प्रेयसी 4.शिकायत 5.महफ़िल 6.रिश्ता 7.सम्मान

Sab dekhne waale unhein gash khaaye huye hain,
Is par bhee taazzub hai wo sharmaaye huye hain.
Aye jaane-jahaan humko zamaane se gharz kya,
Jab khoke zamaane ko tujhe paaye huye hain.
Hairaan hoon kyon mujhko dikhaaee naheen dete,
Sunta hoon meree bazm mein wo aaye huye hain.
Nisbat kee yeh nisbat hai, sharaf ka yeh sharaf hai,
Tere hain agar hum, tire thhukraaye huye hain.
Hai dekhne waalon ko sambhalne ka ishaara,
Thodee see niqaab aaj wo sarkaaye huye hain.

All those who were looking at her, are in a trance,
Even then, it is quite, strange that she is blushing.
O, loved one of the world! Why should I have
any grudge against the world,
When having lost the world I have found you.
I am puzzled, why she is not visible to me,
I hear that she has arrived in my assembly.
What sort of relation is this, what sort of honour is this,
wherein if I am yours, then I am also the one rejected by you.
There is a word of caution for the onlookers,
(As) Today she has raised her veil a little bit.

Arsh Malsiyaani

कुछ कहे जाता था, ग़र्क़[1] अपने ही अफ़साने[2] में था,
मरते-मरते होश बाक़ी तेरे दीवाने में था।
मुस्कुरा कर झाँकती थी किस अदा से इक परी,
चेहरा-ए-साक़ी[3] का शायद अक्स[4] पैमाने[5] में था।
हाय वो खुद-रफ्तगी[6], उलझे हुए सब सर के बाल,
वो किसी में अब कहाँ, जो तेरे दीवाने में था।
देखता था जिस तरफ़, अपना ही जल्वा[7] था अयाँ[8],
मै न था, वहशी[9] कोई इस आइनाख़ाने[10] में था।
बोरिया था, कुछ शबीना[11] मय थी या टूटे सुबू[12],
और क्या इसके सिवा मस्तों के वीराने में था।
हँसते-हँसते रो दिया करते थे सब बेइख़्तियार[13],
इक नई तरकीब का दर्द अपने अफ़साने[14] में था।
'शाद' कुछ पूछो न मुझसे मेरे दिल के दाग़ को,
टिमटिमाता सा चराग़ इक अपने वीराने में था।

शाद अजीमाबादी

1.ब्यस्त,डूबा हुआ 2.कहानी 3.साक़ी का चेहरा 4.परछाई 5.शराब का प्याला 6.स्वंय को भूलना, 7.खूबसुरती 8.प्रकाशमान 9.पागल 10.काँच का महल 11.रात की बची 12.शराब के प्याले 13.बेकाबू 14.कहानी

Kuchh kahe jaata tha, gharq apne hee afsaane mein tha,
Marte-marte hosh baaqee tere deewaane mein tha.
Muskura kar jhaanktee thee kis ada se ek paree,
Chehra-e-saaqee ka shaayad aks paimaane mein tha.
Haai wo khud-raftgee, uljhe huye sab sar ke baal,
Wo kisee mein ab kahaan, jo tere deewaane mein tha.
Dekhta tha jis taraf, apna hee jalwa tha ayaan,
Main na tha, wahshee koee is aayeenaakhaane mein tha.
Boriya tha, kuchh shabeena mai thee, ya toote suboo,
Aur kya iske siwa maston ke weeraane mein tha.
Hanste-hanste ro diya karte the sab be-ikhtiyaar,
Ik nayee tarkeeb ka dard apne afsaane mein tha.
'Shaad' kuchh poochho na mujh se mere dil ke daagh ko,
Timtimaata sa charaagh ik apne weeraane mein tha.

He was continuously saying something, deeply immersed in his own story,
While dying this much sense was still remaining in your lover.
With what grace a fairy was smiling and peeping,
Perhaps the mirror image of barmaid's face was there in the wine cup.
Alas! that self-forgetfulness (Oblivion), those disheveled hair,
Who has it now, what all was there in your crazy lover.
Whichever side I looked, I found my own beauty,
(Perhaps) It was not me, it was some mad man in the house of mirrors.
There was a jute mat, some leftover wine of the night and some broken goblets,
What else was there in the ruins of us crazy folks.
From laughter, listeners used to burst into uncontrolled crying,
A strange sort of pain was there in my narration.
O, 'Shaad'! Do not ask any thing about the scar of my heart,
It was a dim burning earthen lamp in my ruins.

Shaad Ajeemaa baadee

यही बज़्मे-ऐश[1] होगी यही दौरे-जाम[2] होगा
मगर आज का तसव्वुर[3] यहाँ कल हराम[4] होगा।
मैं कुछ इस तरह जिया हूँ कि यक़ीन हो गया है,
मेरे बाद ज़िन्दगी का बड़ा एहतराम[5] होगा।
मेरी ज़ीस्त[6] एक जनाज़ा[7] है, जो राहे-वक़्त[8] में है,
जो थकेगें दिन के काँधे तो सुपुर्दे-शाम[9] होगा।
यही हादिसाते-ग़म[10] हैं, तो ये डर है जीने वालो,
कोई दिन में ज़िन्दगी का कोई और नाम होगा।
मेरे शेर मेरी साँसें हैं 'वसीम' ज़िन्दगी की।
ये न हों तो सारा क़िस्सा ही मेरा तमाम होगा।

वसीम बरेलवी

1.रगँरेलियों भरी महफ़िल 2.शराब के प्यालों का दौर 3.कल्पना,याद 4.दुखदायी 5.आदर 6.जीवन7.अर्थी 8.समय की राह 9.शाम को समार्पित 10.दुखद दुर्घटनाएँ

Yahee bazme-aish hogee, yahee daure-jaam hoga,
Magar aaj ka tasawwur, yahaan kal haraam hoga.
Main kuchh is tarah jeeya hoon, ki yaqeen ho gaya hai,
Mere baad zindagee ka bada aihtraam hoga.
Meree zeest ek janaaza hai, jo raahe-waqt mein hai,
Jo thakenge din ke kaandhe, tau supurde-shaam hoga.
Yahee haadisaate-gham hai, tau ye dar hai jeene waalon,
Koee din mein zindagee ka koee aur naam hoga.
Mere shair meree saanse hain 'Waseem' zindagee kee,
Ye na hon tau saara qissa hee mera tamaam hoga.

The same gathering of fun and pleasure will be there, same rounds of wine will continue,
But today's memory will prove sinful tomorrow.
I have lived in such a way that I have come to believe,
That after me, life will be held in very high esteem.
My life is a bier, which is on a track of time,
When the shoulders of the day will get tired it will be transferred on to the evening.
If this chain of tragic accidents is life then I am afraid, O, living ones!.
After a few days life will be called by a different name.
O, 'Waseem'! my couplets are the breaths of life,
if these are not there, then my life's story will cease to exist.

Waseem Bareilvi

जो बेक़रार[1] थे हरदम मेरे लहू के लिए,
वो फूल अब भी तरसते हैं रगों-बू[2] के लिए।
चरागे़-राहगुज़र[3] भी न हो तो क्या ग़म है,
तेरा ख़याल ही काफ़ी है जुस्तजू[4] के लिए।
तेरा ख़याल भी दिल को सुकूँ नहीं देता,
कुछ और चाहिए तक़मीले-आरज़ू[6] के लिए
ये क़हक़हे तो मेरी बात का जवाब नहीं,
सलीक़ा[7] चाहिए फूलों को गुफ़्तगूँ[8] के लिए।
ये हमसे पूछ कि कितनी हँसी बहारों का।
हुआ है खून गुलिस्ताँ[9] में रगों-बू के लिए।
'सलीम' इतनी हवादिस[10] के बाद भी दुनियाँ,
तरस रही है मुहब्बत की आबरू[11] के लिए।

सलीम खतौलवी

1.आतुर 2.रंग और खुशबू 3.रास्ते का दिया 4.तलाश 5.शांति 6.चाहत की पराकाष्ठा 7.तरीका 8.बातचीत 9.बाग़ 10.दुर्घटनाएँ 11.इज़्ज़त, आदर

Jo beqaraar the har dam mere lahoo ke liye,
Woh phool ab bhee taraste hain rango-boo ke liye.
Charaaghe-raahguzar bhee na ho tau kya gham hai,
Tera khyaal hee kaafee hai justjoo ke liye.
Tera khyal bhee dil ko sukoon naheen deta,
Kuchh aur chaahiye taqmeele-aarzoo ke liye.
Ye qahqahe tau meree baat ka jawaab naheen,
Saleeqa chaahiye phoolon ko guftgoon ke liye.
Ye humse pooch ki kitnee haseen bahaaron ka,
Hua hai khoon gulistaan mein rango-boo ke liye.
'Saleem' itnee hawaadis ke baad bhee duniyaan,
Taras rahee hai muhabbat kee aabroo ke liye.

Those who were always baying for my blood,
Those flowers still crave for colour and fragrance.
What is there to feel sad about even if there is no road side lamp,
Very memory of yours is good enough for search.
Your thought too doesn't give any solace to (my) heart,
Something else is required for fulfillment of desires.
These guffaws are no answer to my query,
Flowers need to observe etiquettes while talking.
Ask me how many beautiful springs have been,
Sacrificed for providing the colour and fragrance to the garden.
O! 'Saleem', inspite of so many mishaps/tragedies,
This world is still craving for the honour of love.

Saleem Khataulvi

इल्मो-फ़न[1] के दीवाने आशिक़ी से डरते हैं,
ज़िन्दगी के ख़ाईफ़[2] हैं ज़िन्दगी से डरते हैं।
यूँ तो हम ज़माने में कब किसी से डरते हैं,
आदमी के मारे हैं, आदमी से डरते हैं।
जलके आशियाँ[3] अपना ख़ाक हो चुका कब का,
आज तक ये आलम[4] है, रौशनी से डरते हैं।
जब न होश था हमको, दुशमनी से डरते थे,
आया है होश तो हम दोस्ती से डरते हैं।
तौबा और जवानी में 'ख़ुमार' क्या कहना,
लोग आप जैसे ही मुत्तक़ी[5] से डरते हैं।

ख़ुमार बाराबंकवी

1.ज्ञान और कला 2.डरे हुए 3.घोसला 4.हालत 5.तौबा

Ilmo-fan ke deewaane aashiqee se darte hain,
Zindagee ke khaaeef hain, zindagee se darte hain.
Yoon tau hum zamaane mein kab kisee se darte hain,
Aaadmee ke maare hain, aadmee se darte hain.
Jal ke aashiaan apna khaak ho chuka kab ka,
Aaj tak ye aalam hai, raushnee se darte hain,
Jab na hosh tha humko, dushmanee se darte the,
Aayaa hai hosh, tau hum dostee se darte hain.
Tauba! aur zawaanee mein, 'Khumaar' kya kahna,
Log aap jaise he muttaqee se darte hain,

People who are crazy after knowledge and skill are scared of love,
Being wary of life, (they) remain scared of life.
Although I am not afraid of anyone in the world,
(Yet) I am scared of the human beings (as) I have been hurt by them most.
My-nest had been burnt long ago,
Till date such is the state, that I am scared of light.
When! I was immature, I was scared of the enmity,
Having become matured now, I am scared of friendship.
Abstinence! that too in youth, what nonsense O! Khumaar',
Only people like you are scared of temperance.

'Khumaar' Barabankvi

कहने देती नहीं कुछ मुहँ से मुहब्बत तेरी,
लब पे आ जाती है रह-रह के शिकायत तेरी।
अब तेरा ए दिले-बेताब[1] खुदा हाफ़िज़[2] है,
कर चुके हम तो मुहब्बत मे हिफ़ाज़त[3] तेरी।
याद सब है मुझे हिज्र[4] के सदमें[5] ज़ालिम,
भूल जाता हूँ मगर देख के सूरत तेरी।
यार-ओ-ग़मख़्वार[6] मेरे हाल को सब पूछते हैं,
और फिर पूछ के कहते है कि किस्मत[7] तेरी।
कूचाए-यार[8] मे भी जी नही लगता ऐ! 'दाग़',
देखिये जाएगी किस रोज़ ये वहशत[9] मेरी।

दाग़ देलहवी

1.उतावला हदय 2.रक्षक 3.रक्षा 4.विरह 5.दुख 6.दोस्त और दुखबाँटने वाले 7.भाग्य
8.प्रेमिका की गली 9.घबराहट, पागलपन

Kahne detee naheen kuchh muhn se muhabbat teree,
Lab pe aa jaatee hai rah-rah ke shikaayat teree.
Ab tera aye! dile-betaab khuda haafiz hai,
Kar chuke hum tau muhabbat mein hifaazat teree.
Yaad sab hain mujhe hijr ke sadmein zaalim,
Bhool jaata hoon magar dekh ke soorat teree.
Yaaro-ghamkhwaar mere haal ko sab poochhte hain,
Aur phir pooch ke kahte hain ki kismat teree.
Koochaaye-yaar mein bhee jee naheen lagta aye ! 'Daagh'!
Dekhiye jaayegee kis roz ye wahshat meree.

My love for you does not allow me to say anything,
(Yet) Time and again, complaint about you come up to (my) lips.
O, restless heart! now only God is your saviour,
I have, protected you enough in love.
O, cruel one! I remember all traumas of separation,
But I forget (every thing) the moment I look at your face.
Friends and sympathisers all enquire about my state,
And having enquired they say, "your luck (Buddy)".
O, "Daagh". even in the beloved's lane this heart remains restless,
Let us see on which day this madness of mine will depart.

Daagh Delhivi

पयाम आए हैं, उस यारे-बेवफ़ा के मुझे,
जिसे क़रार न आया कहीं भुलाके मुझे।
जुदाइयाँ हों तो ऐसी, कि उम्रभर न मिलें,
फ़रेब दो तो, ज़रा सिलसिले बढ़ाके मुझे।
नशे से कम तो नहीं यादे-यार का आलम,
कि ले उड़ा है कोई दोश[1] पर हवा के मुझे।
मैं ख़ुद को भूल चुका था मगर जहाँ वाले,
उदास छोड़ गए आईना दिखाके मुझे।
तुम्हारे बाम से अब कम नहीं है रफ़अते-दार[2],
जो देखना हो तो देखो नज़र उठाके मुझे।
खिंची हुई है मेरे आँसुओं में एक तस्वीर,
'फ़राज़' देख रहा है वह मुस्कराके मुझे।

अहमद फ़राज़

1.कंधे 2.सूली की ऊँचाई

Payaam aaye hain, us yaare-bewafa ke mujhe,
Jise qaraar na aaya kaheen bhula ke mujhe.
Judaaeeyaan hon tau aisee, ki umr bhar na milein,
Fareb do tau, zara silsile badhha ke mujhe.
Nashe se kam tau naheen, yaade-yaar ka aalam,
Ki le udha hai koee dosh par hawa ke mujhe.
Main khud ko bhool chuka tha magar jahaan waale,
Udaas chhodh gaye aaeena dikhake mujhe.
Tumhaare baam se ab kam naheen hai rafate-daar,
Jo dekhna ho tau dekho nazar uthha ke mujhe.
Khinchee huyee hai mere aansuon mein ek tasweer,
'Faraaz' dekh raha hai wah muskrake mujhe.

Messages have come to me from that unfaithful lover,
Who has not been able to find peace anywhere after forgetting me.
Let there be separations, but such that we never meet again during life-time,
Do ditch me but only after strengthening the relationships a bit more.
Being immersed in beloved's memory is no less than an intoxication,
It is like this that someone has taken me for a flight on the shoulder of the wind.
I had forgotten my own self but these folks of the world,
Have left me desolate after showing the mirror to me.
The height of my gibbet is no less than your roof,
If you wish to see (me), then raise your eyes towards me.
A picture is etched in my tears,
O, 'Faraaz'! she has been looking at me with a smile.

Ahmed 'Faraaz'

तुमने ये क्या सितम किया, ज़ब्त[1] से काम ले लिया,
तर्क-ए-वफ़ा[2] के बाद भी मेरा सलाम ले लिया।
रिन्द-ए-शराबनोश[3] की बेअदबी तो देखिऐ,
नीयत-ए-मयकशी[4] न थी, हाथ में जाम ले लिया।
हाय वो पैकर-ए-हवस[5], आह वो खूगर-ए-क़फ़स[6],
बेच के जिसने आशियाँ[7], हलक़ा-ए-दाम[8] ले लिया।
बादा कुशान-ए-इश्क़[9] को कुछ तो मिला पए-सुकूं,
हुस्न-ए-सहर[10] न ले सके, जलवा-ए-शाम ले लिया।
नामा[11]-ए-शौक़ पढ़ के वो खो गए यक-ब-यक[12] 'शकील',
मुंह से तो कुछ न कह सके, दिल से पयाम[13] ले लिया।

शकील बदायूनी

1.बरदाश्त 2.मौहब्बत की समाप्ति 3.शराब पीने वाला 4.शराब लेने की नियत 5.हवस की मूर्ति 6.कैद खाने का कैदी 7.घोंसला 8.जंजीर की कड़ी 9.मौहब्बत की शराब खींचने वाले 10.सुबह 11.खत, पत्र 12.अचानक 13.संदेश

Tumne ye kya sitam kiya, zabt se kaam le liya,
Tark-e-wafa ke baad bhee mera salaam le liya.
Rind-e-sharaabnosh kee beadabee tau dekhiye,
Neeyat-e-maikashi na thee, haath mein jaam le liya.
Haai wo paiker-e-hawas, aah wo khoogar-e-qafas,
Bech ke jisne aashiyaan, halqa-e-daam le liya.
Baada kushaan-e-ishq ko kuchh tau mila paye-sukoon,
Husn-e-sahar na le sake, jalwa-e-shaam le liya.
Naama-e-shauq padh ke wo kho gaye yak-ba-yak 'Shakeel',
Moohn se tau kuchh na kah sake, dil se payaam le liya.

What injustice you have done, by exercising tolerance,
Even after the break up of love, you have accepted my salute.
Look at the gall of that seasoned drunkard,
(He) Had no urge for drinking, (yet) took the goblet in hand.
Alas! that figure of greed, alas! that imprisoned one,
Who having sold his nest, don the shackles.
The brewer of wine of love ultimately got some solace,
Could not get the beauty of morning, accepted the splendour of the evening (instead).
O,'Shakeel' ! after reading the love letter, all of a sudden she got lost (within herself),
Could not utter anything from mouth, (but) accepted the message through heart.

'Shakeel' Badayooni

क़तरा अब एहतिजाज[1] करे भी तो क्या मिले,
दरिया जो लग रहे थे, समन्दर से जा मिले।
हर शख़्स दौड़ता है यहाँ भीड़ की तरफ़,
फिर यह भी चाहता है, उसे रास्ता मिले।
इस आरज़ू ने और तमाशा बना दिया,
जो भी मिले हमारी तरफ़ देखता मिले।
दुनियाँ को दूसरों की नज़र से न देखिए,
चेहरे न पढ़ सके, तो किताबों में क्या मिले।
रिश्तों को बार-बार समझने की आरज़ू,
कहती है फिर मिले तो कोई बेवफ़ा मिले।
इस दौर-ए-मुनिसफ़ी[2] में ज़रूरी नहीं 'वसीम',
जिस शख़्स की ख़ता[3] हो उसी को सज़ा मिले।

वसीम बरेलवी

1.विरोध 2.न्याय का युग 3.त्रुटि, अपराध

Qatra ab aihtijaaj kare bhee tau kya mile,
Dariya jo lag rahe the, samandar se ja mile.
Har shakhs daudhta hai yahaan bheedh kee taraf,
Phir ye bhee chaahta hai, use raasta mile.
Is aarzoo ne aur tamaasha bana diya,
Jo bhee mile hamaaree taraf dekhta mile.
Duniyaan ko doosron kee nazar se na dekhiye,
Chehre na padh sake, tau kitaabon mein kya mile,
Rishton ko baar-baar samajhne kee aarzoo,
Kahtee hai phir mile tau koee bewafa mile.
Is daure-munsifee mein zarooree naheen 'Waseem',
Jis shakhs kee khata ho usee ko saza mile.

Even if a droplet raises an objection, what use it will be of,
Those who were appearing like river, went and merged with the ocean.
Every person over here, runs towards the crowd,
And also aspires to find the (right) path.
This fad has made me more of a spectacle,
That whoever passes by, should be looking at me.
Do not look at the world through other people's eyes,
If you could not read faces, what do you expect to find in the books.
The desire to understand the relationships constantly,
Tells that should someone meet again, that one should be disloyal (too).
During this era of justice, O ,' Waseem' ! it is not mandatory,
That the punishment will be dished out only to the one who is guilty.

'Waseem' Bareillvi

जाने कितनी उड़ान बाकी है,
इस परिन्दे में जान बाक़ी है।
जितनी बटँनी थी बँट चुकी ये ज़मीन,
अब तो बस आसमान बाक़ी है।
अब वो दुनियाँ अजीब[1] लगती है,
जिसमे अम्नो–अमान[1] बाक़ी है।
इम्तेहान से गुज़र के क्या देखा,
इक नया इम्तेहान बाक़ी है।
सर क़लम[2] होगें कल यहाँ उनके,
जिनके मुँह मे ज़ुबान बाक़ी है।

राजेश रेडडी

1.सुख–शाँति 2.काटना

Jaane kitnee udhaan baaqee hai,
Is parinde mein jaan baaqee hai.
Jitnee batnee thee bant chukee ye zameen,
Ab tau bas aasmaan baaqee hai.
Ab wo duniyaan ajeeb lagtee hai,
Jisme amno-amaan baaqee hai.
Imtehaan se guzar ke kya dekha,
Ek naya imtehaan baaqee hai.
Sar qalam honge kal yahaan unke,
Jinke muhn mein zubaan baaqee hai.

God knows, how much flight is left,
There is still some life remaining in this bird.
Whatever could be divided of this earth, has been divided,
Now, only the sky is left.
These days, that world looks strange (to me),
In which some rest and peace is (still) remaining,
After getting through the ordeal, I found,
That a new ordeal was waiting (for me),
Tomorrow all those will be beheaded here,
In whose mouths, tongues are (still) remaining.

Rajesh Reddy

उफ़ ये मस्ती, ये ख़ुमार-आलूदा[1] आँखें, ये शबाब,
आप अपने साथ इक मयख़ाना लेकर आए हैं।
हाय सावन की हवा, अब्रे-सियाह[2] का झूमना,
जैसे बादल दावते-ख़ुमनामा[3] लेकर आए हैं।
जी वतन में भी नही लगता हमारा ऐ 'शफ़ीक़',
जब से यादे-कूचा[4] ए-जानाना लेकर आए हैं।

'शफ़ीक़ जौनपुरी'

1.नशे में डूबी हुई आँखें 2.काले बादल 3.शराब के मटकों की तरफ से निमंत्रण 4.प्रेमिका की गली की याद

Uf ye mastee, ye khumaar-aalooda aankhein, ye shabaab,
Aap apne saath ik maikhaana lekar aaye hain.
Haai saawan kee hawa, abre-siyaah ka jhoomna,
Jaise baadal daawate-khumnaama lekar aaye hain,
Jee watan mein bhee naheen lagta humaara aye 'Shafeeq',
Jab se yaade-koochaaye-jaanaana lekar aaye hain.

My God, this rapture, these drunken eyes, this youth,
You have brought the whole tavern with you.
Oh! wet wind, the swaying of dark clouds,
As if the clouds have come with an invitation from the pitchers of wine.
O! 'Shafeeq'! my heart has stopped relishing the motherland even,
Ever since I have brought the memory of beloved's lane.

'Shafeeq' Jaunpuri

नीची नज़र से मुझको न देख,
घड़ लेगें अफ़साने[1] लोग।
क्या सुनते नासेह[2] की बात,
हम ठहरे दीवाने लोग।
देख के मुझको गुमसुम हैं,
आए थे समझाने लोग।
दीवाना कहते हैं 'अमीर',
खूब मुझे पहचाने लोग।

आग़ा अमीर क़ज़लबाश

1.कहानियाँ 2.उपदेशक

Neechee nazar se mujhko na dekh,
Ghad lenge afsaane log.
Kya sunte naaseh kee baat,
Hum thhahre deewaane log.
dekh ke mujhko gumsum hain.
Aaye the samjhaane log.
Deewaana kahte hain 'Ameer',
Khoob mujhe pehchaane log.

Don't look at me with stealthy eyes,
People will spin yarns out of it.
Why would we have paid any heed to the preacher's prattle,
We are mad fellows, after all.
On seeing me (they) are dumbfound,
(The) People who had come to counsel me.
O, 'Ameer'! they call me 'crazy',
How well people have understood me,

Aaghaa Ameer Qazalbaash

दोस्त बन कर भी नहीं साथ निभानेवाला,
वही अंदाज़ है ज़ालिम का ज़मानेवाला।
अब उसे लोग समझते हैं गिरफ़्तार मेरा,
सख़्त नादिम[1] है मुझे दाम[2] में लानेवाला।
सुब्ह-दम छोड़ गया निकहते-गुल की सूरत[3],
रात को गुंच-ए-दिल[4] में सिमट आनेवाला।
क्या कहें, कितने मरासिम[5] थे हमारे उससे,
वह जो एक शख़्स है मुँह फेर के जानेवाला।
तेरे होते हुए आ जाती थी सारी दुनिया,
आज तन्हा हूँ तो, कोई नहीं आनेवाला।
मुंतजिर किसका हूँ टूटी हुई दहलीज़ पे मैं,
कौन आएगा यहाँ, कौन है आनेवाला।
क्या ख़बर थी, जो मेरी जाँ में घुला है इतना,
है वही मुझको सरे-दार[6] भी लानेवाला।
मैंने देखा हे बहारों में चमन को जलते,
है कोई ख़्वाब की ताबीर[7] बतानेवाला?
तुम तकल्लुफ़ को इख़लास[8] समझते हो 'फ़राज़',
दोस्त होता नहीं हर हाथ मिलानेवाला

अहमद फ़राज़

1.शर्मिंदा 2.जाल 3.फूल की खुशबू की तरह 4.दिल की कली 5.सम्बन्ध 6.सूली पर 7.स्वप्न का अर्थ 8.प्रेम

Dost bankar bhee naheen saath nibhaane waala,
Wahee andaaz hai zaalim ka zamaane waala.
Ab use log samajhte hain giraftaar mera,
Sakht naadim hai mujhe daam mein laanewaala.
Subah-dam chhodh gaya nikhate-gul kee soorat,
Raat ko gunch-e-dil mein simat aanewaala.
Kya kahein, kitne maraasim the hamaare us se,
Wah jo ek shakhs hai moohn pher ke jaanewaala.
Tere hote huye aa jaatee thee saaree duniya,
Aaj tanha hoon tau, koee naheen aanewaala.
Muntzir kiska hoon tootee huyee dahleez pe main,
Kaun aayega yahaan, kaun hai aanewaala.
Kya khabar thee, jo meree jaan mein ghula hai itna,
Hai wahee mujhko sare-daar bhee laanewaala.
Maine dekha hai bahaaron ko chaman mein jalte,
Hai koee khawwaab kee taabeer bataanewaala.
Tum takalluf ko bhee ikhlaas samajhte ho 'Faraaz',
Dost hota naheen har haath milaanewaala.

Even after becoming a friend, she is not going to remain by my side,
Her attitude too is cruel like that of this world.
Now people think that she is my prisoner,
She who has lured me into the net is highly embarassed.
By morning she left me like the fragrance of flower,
She who in the night used to snuggle in the bud of (my) heart.
How to say, what varied relations I had with her,
She who had turned her face and walked away.
With you by my side, entire world used to visit me,
Today I am alone, nobody is likely to come.
Why I am in waiting at somebody's broken threshold,
Who will come here, who is expected to come.
I had no idea, that the one who was so much blended with my soul,
Was the one, who brought me to the gallows.
I have seen the springs burning in the garden,
Is there someone who can tell me the meaning of this dream.
O, 'Faraaz' ! you claim even formality to be love,
Not everybody who shakes hands with you, is your friend.

Ahmed 'Faraaz'

नज़र से क़ैद-ए-तअयुन[1] उठाई जाती है,
तजल्ली-ए-रूख़-ए-जाना[2] दिखाई जाती है।
जब उनको होसला-ए-दिल पे एतबार नहीं,
तो फिर नज़र से नज़र क्यों मिलाई जाती है?
खुम-ओ-सुबु[3] की ज़रूरत के हम नहीं क़ायल,
शराब मस्त नज़र से पिलाई जाती है।
सितम नावाज़ि-ए-पीहम[4] है इश्क़ की फ़ितरत[5],
फ़िज़ूल हुस्न पे तोहमत[6] लगाई जाती है।
भुला दिया था ग़म-ए-रोज़गार ने जिसको,
वो दास्ताँ मुझे फिर याद आई जाती है।
'शकील' दूरी-ए-मंज़िल से नाउम्मीद न हो,
अब आई जाती है मंज़िल अब आई जाती है।

शकील बदायूनी

1.विशेष पाबन्दी 2.महबूब के चेहरे की रौनक 3.शराब का मटका व प्याला 4.बार-बार का सितम 5.प्रकृति 6.इल्ज़ाम

Nazar se qaid-e-tayun uthhaaee jaatee hai,
Tajalleeye-rukh-e-jaana dikhaaee jaatee hai.
Jab unko hoslaa-ye-dil pe aitbaar naheen,
Tau phir nazar se nazar kyon milaaee jaatee hai?
Khum-o-subu kee zaroorat ke ham naheen qaayal,
Sharaab mast nazar se pilaaee jaatee hai.
Sitam-naawaazi-ye-peeham hai isq kee fitrat,
Fizool husn pe tohmat lagaaee jaatee hai.
Bhula diya tha gham-e-rozgaar ne jisko,
Wo daastaan mujhe phir yaad aaee jaatee hai.
'Shakeel' dooree-e-manzil se naaummeed na ho,
Ab aaee jaatee hai manzil ab aaee jaatee hai

· That special restriction on the eyes is being removed,
Splendour of the beloved's face is (now) being shown.
When she doesn't have faith in the courage of her heart,
Then why this exchanging of looks (every now then)?
I am not convinced about the need for the goblet and the pitcher,
The wine is offered through the dreamy eyes.
Repeatedly asking for injustice is the very nature of love,
Quite unnecessarily the beauty is blammed (all the times).
Which the worldly woes had made me forget,
The same story has started haunting me again.
O, 'Shakeel' ! do not get disheartened by the (great) distance to the destination,
It is about to come, the destination is just about to come.

Shakeel Badayooni

तुम्हारी राह में मिटटी के घर नहीं आते,
इसीलिए तो तुम्हें हम नज़र नहीं आते।
मुहब्बतों के दिनों की यही इक ख़राबी है,
यह रूठ जायें तो फिर लौट कर नहीं आते।
जिन्हें सलीक़ा[1] है तहज़ीब-ए-ग़म[2] समझने का,
उन्हीं के रोने में आंसू नज़र नहीं आते।
ख़ुशी की आँख में आँसू की भी जगह रखना,
बुरे ज़माने कभी पूछ कर नहीं आते।
बिसातें इश्क़[3] पे बढ़ना किसे नहीं आता,
मगर हर एक को बचने के घर नहीं आते।
'वसीम', ज़हन[4] बनाते हैं, तो वही अख़बार,
जो लेके एक भी अच्छी ख़बर नहीं आते।

वसीम बरेलवी

1.ढंग 2.दुख की संस्कृति 3.प्रेम की बाज़ी 4.मानसिकता

Tumhaaree raah mein miththee ke ghar naheen aate,
Iseeliye tau tumhein hum nazar naheen aate.
Muhabbaton ke dinon kee yahee ik kharaabee hai,
Ye roothh jaayein tau phir laut kar naheen aate.
Jinhein saleeqa hai tahzeebe-gham samjhne ka,
Unheen ke rone mein aansoo nazar naheen aate.
Khushee kee aankh mein aansoo kee bhee jagah rakhna
Bure zamaane kabhee poochh kar naheen aate.
Bisaate isq pe badhna kise naheen aata,
Magar har ek ko bachne ke ghar naheen aate.
'Waseem', zahan banaate hain, tau wahee akhbaar,
Jo leke ek bhee achchhee khabar naheen aate.

On your way, you do not come across the mud-houses,
That is why you do not (ever) see me.
The only bad thing about the days of love is this,
Once they get annoyed, they never return again.
Those who know the art of understanding the culture of grief,
Tears are never visible when they are crying,
In (your) happy eye, do keep some place for the tears too.
(For) Bad times never announce their arrival.
(After all) Who does not know how to advance in the game of love,
But not everybody knows the safeguards.
O, 'Waseem' ! mental attitude is formed only by those newspapers,
Which never bring single good news.

'Wassem' Bareillvi

ये उदास-उदास ठंडक, जो असीर[1] है पवन में,
कहीं बिजलियाँ न भर दे किसी गोश-ए-चमन[2] में।
ये अजीब फ़स्ले-गुल[3] है किसी भी गुल की रगंत,
न जँची मिरी नज़र में, न रची तिरे बदन में।
मै तुलू-ए-सुब्हे-नौ[4] से अभी मुतमईन[5] नहीं हूँ,
तिरा हुस्न भी तो होता किसी ख़ुशनुमा[6] किरन में।
सरे-बाम[7] भी पुकारा, लबे-दार[8] भी सदा दी,
मै कहाँ-कहाँ न पहुँचा तेरी दीद[9] की लगन में।
मिरी मुफ़लिसी[10] से बचकर कहीं और जानेवाले,
ये सुकून[11] ना मिल सकेगा तुझे रेशमी कफ़न में।
मैं लिये-लिये फिरा हूँ ग़मे-ज़िन्दगी[12] का लाशा[13],
कभी अपनी ख़लवतों[14] में, कभी तेरी अंजुमन[15] में।
तिरे ग़म में बह गया है मिरा एक-एक आसूँ,
नही अब कोई सितारा जो चमक सके गगन में।
मैं 'क़तील' वो मुसाफ़िर हूँ जहाने-बेबसी[16] में,
जो भटक के रह गया हो किसी अजनबी वतन में।

क़तील शिफ़ाई

1.बन्दी 2.बाग का कोना 3.फूलों की फ़सल 4.नई सुबह 5.आश्वस्त 6.मुस्कराती हुई 7.छत पर से 8.सूली पर से 9.दर्शन 10.गरीबी 11.चैन 12.दुखग्रस्त जीवन 13.लाश 14.तन्हाईयाँ 15.महफ़िल 16.मजबूरियों भरा संसार

Ye udaas-udaas thhandak jo aseer hai pawan mein,
Kaheen bijliyaan na bharde kisee gosh-e-chaman mein.
Ye ajeeb fasle-gul hai, ki kisee bhee gul kee rangat,
Na janchee miree nazar mein, na rachee tire badan mein.
Main tuloo-e-subahe-nau se abhee mutmaeen naheen hoon,
Tira husn bhee tau hota kisee khushnuma kiran mein.
Sare-baam bhee pukaara, labe-daar bhee sada dee,
Main kahaan-kahaan na pahuncha teree deed kee lagan mein.
Miree muflisee se bach kar, kaheen aur jaane waale,
Ye sukoon na mil sakega tujhe reshmee qafan mein.
Main liye-liye phira hoon ghame-zindgee ka laasha,
Kabhi apnee khalwaton mein, kabhee teree anjuman mein.
Tire gham mein bah gaya hai, mira ek-ek aansoon,
Naheen ab koee sitaara jo chamak sake gagan mein.
Main 'Qateel', wo musaafir hoon jahaane-bebasee mein,
Jo bhatak ke rah gaya ho kisee ajnabee watan mein.

This Sad-sad coldness which is imprisoned in the breeze,
(I am afraid) It may fill some part of the garden with lightnings.
This is a strange season of flowers, wherein the colour of no flower,
Is pleasing to my eyes, nor it is blending with your body.
I am not satisfied with the charm of the new morning as yet,
Your beauty too should have been there in some smiling ray.
Called you from rooftop also, hailed you from gallows too,
Where All didn't I reach in my quest for having a look at you.
O, the one! Avoiding my poverty and going elsewhere,
You will not be able to find such a solace in a silken shroud.
Burdened with the dead Body of sorrowful life, I have wandered,
Sometimes in my own loneliness, sometimes in your assembly.
Every single tear of mine has flowed in your sorrow,
There is no star left, which can now shine in the sky.
O, 'Qateel'! I am that traveller in this world,
Who after having lost the way, has got stuck in some strange country.

Qateel Shifaai

अजब अपना हाल होता, जो विसाले-यार[1] होता,
कभी जान सदके होती, कभी दिल निसार[2] होता।
जो तुम्हारी तरह तुमसे कोई झूठे वादे करता,
तुम्ही मुंसिफ़ी[3] से कह दो, तुम्हे एतबार होता?
ये मज़ा था दिल-लगी का कि बराबर आग लगती,
न तुझे क़रार[4] होता, न मुझे क़रार होता।
तेरे वादे पे सितमगर[5] अभी और सब्र करते,
अगर अपनी ज़िन्दगी का हमें एतबार होता।
ये वो दर्दे-दिल नहीं है, कि जो हो चारासाज़[6] कोई,
अगर एक बार मिटता तो हज़ार बार होता।

दाग़ देहलवी

1.प्रेयसी से मिलन 2.बलिहारी 3.सच्चाई, इमानदारी 4.चैन, शांति 5.अत्याचारी 6.इलाज करनेवाला

Ajab apna ħaal hota, jo wisaale-yaar hota,
Kabhee jaan sadke hoti, kabhee dil nisaar hota.
Jo tumhaaree tarah tumse koee jhoonthhe waade karta,
Tumhee munsifee se kahdo, tumhe aitbaar hota?
Ye maza tha dil-lagee ka ki baraabar aag lagtee,
Na tujhe qaraar hota, na mujhe qaraar hota.
Tere waade pe sitamgar abhee aur sabr karte,
Agar apnee zindagee ka humein aitbaar hota.
Ye wo darde-dil naheen hai, jo ho chaaraasaaz koee,
Agar ek baar mithta tau hazaar baar hota.

Strange would have been my state, had there been a 'union' with the beloved,
Sometime the soul sometime the heart would have made the offering.
If some one were to make false promises to you like you do,
You only tell (me) in all fairness, "would you have believed"?
Would have been fun in love, if there was equal fire on both sides,
No peace for you, no rest for me either.
O, Cruel one! I would have waited on your promise yet longer,
If I had been sure of continuance of my life.
This is not that 'pain of heart', for which there is some healer,
If cured once, it would have recurred thousand times.

Daagh Dehlivi

तिरी महफ़िल में लोगों के चेहरे ये क्यूँ,
मेरे उठने से पहले उतरने लगे।
क्या ये अपने किये पे पशेमाँ[1] हुए,
या मेरी बेगुनाही[2] से डरने लगे।
मेरी नाकामियाँ[3] एक अलग चीज़ हैं,
इश्क़ का मुझपे ये भी तो अहसान है।
ये क्या कम है किसी ख़ाना-बर्बाद[4] की,
ज़िन्दगी तेरे ग़म मे गुज़रने लगे।
अब मुहब्बत के अज़ांम[5] को सोचना,
मेरे टूटे हुए दिल की तौहीन[6] है।
ये तुम ही हो कि बरबाद करके मुझे,
आज दुनियाँ की नज़रों से डरने लगे।
एक शायर ने दिल में जलाया जिन्हें,
अब वो मासूम ग़म के दिये बुझ चले।
आपके ज़िक्र का एक ज़रिया तो था,
हाय! ये क्या हुआ ज़ख़्म भरने लगे।
खत्म है जिन्दगी का सफ़र ऐ 'वसीम'
आ गई मेरी मंज़िल करीब आ गई।
दिल ठहरने लगा, सांस रुकने लगी,
चलते-चलते मेरे पाँव भरने लगे।

वसीम बरेलवी

1.शर्मिंदा 2.निर्दोषिता 3.असफलताएँ 4.नष्ट-भ्रष्ट 5.अंत 6.अनादर

Tiree mehfil mein logo ke chehre ye kyoon,
Mere uthhne se pahle utarne lage.
Kya ye apne kiye pe pashemaan huye,
Ya meree begunaahee se darne lage.
Meree naaqaamiyaan ek alag cheez hain,
Ishq ka mujh pe ye bhee tau aihsaan hai.
Ye kya kam hai kisee khaana-barbaad kee,
Zindagee tere gham mein guzarne lage.
Ab muhabbat ke anzaam ko sochna,
Mere toote huye dil kee tauheen hai.
Ye tum hee ho, ki barbaad karke mujhe,
Aaaj duniyaan kee nazron se darne lage.
Aik shaayar ne dil mein jalaaya jinhein,
Ab wo maasoom gham ke diye bujh chale.
Aap ke zikr ka ek zariya tau tha,
Haai! ye kya hua zakhm bharne lage.
Khatm hai zindagee ka safar aye! 'Waseem',
Aagayee meree manzil qareeb aagayee,
Dil thhaharne laga, saans rukne lagee,
Chalte-chalte mere paaon bharne lage.

In your assembly, why the faces of people have started looking crestfallen,
Even before my (impending) ouster?
Are they feeling ashamed of their own doings,
Or they are becoming scared of my innocence?
My failures are a different thing, the love sure has done me this favour,
Is it any less that the life of a desolate one is being spent in your sorrow.
At this stage, to think about the consequence of love, will tantamount to an insult to my broken heart,
This is you alone who after destroying me, have started getting scared of the eyes of the world.
These lamps of innocent sadness, kindled by a poet in his heart,
Now have started getting extinguished.
Your reference was a big solace, alas! What has happened?
the wounds have started getting healed up.
O! 'Waseem' the journey of life is about to end, my destination has been drawing nearer.
The heart has started stopping, the breath is running out,
By the constant walking my feet are getting heavier and heavier.

Waseem Bareilvi

मेरे फ़क़ीरे-दिल की जिसे बददुआ[1] मिले,
शहरे-तरब[2] में रह के भी वो ग़मज़दा[3] मिले।
अवराके-याददाश्त[4] को पलट कर तो देखिए,
शायद किसी वर्क़ पे मिरा तज़किरा[6] मिले।
वो दर्द हो कि अश्क, मसर्रत[7] हो या अलम[8],
मुझको तो राहे-इश्क़ में सब बेवफ़ा मिले।
तुम ख़्वाब मे भी आओ अगर भूलकर कभी,
बीमारे-इंतिज़ार तुम्हें जागता मिले।
यूँ मुझको तेरे ग़म ने गिरफ़्तार कर लिया,
जैसे बगैर जुर्म किसी को सज़ा मिले।
दिल मे अगर चराग़े-तजस्सुस[9] हो ज़ो-फ़गन[10],
तारीक[11] बुतकदे[12] में भी तुझको ख़ुदा मिले।
ए नाक़दाने-वक़्त[13] जरा गौर से पढ़ो,
शायद कलामे-कैफ़[14] मे कुछ फलसफा[15] मिले।

कैफ़ अहमद सिद्दिकी

1.श्राप 2.खुश शहर 3.शोक-व्यस्त 4.यादों के प्रष्ठ 5.पन्ना,प्रष्ठ 6.ज़िक्र 7.खुशी 8.दुख 9.तलाश करने के लिए चिराग़ 10.रोशनी डालने वाला 11.अंधेरे 12.मन्दिर 13.आजकल के आलोचक 14.कैफ़ की शायरी 15.दार्शनिकता

Mere faqeere-dil kee jise bad-dua mile,
Shahre-tarab mein rah ke bhee wo ghamzada mile.
Awraaqe-yaaddaasht ko palat kar tau dekhiye,
Shaayad kisee warq pe mira tazkira mile.
Wo dard ho ki ashk, masarrat ho ya alam,
Mujhko tau raahe-ishq mein sab bewafa mile .
Tum khwwaab mein bhee aao agar bhool kar kabhee,
Beemaare-intizaar tumhe jaagta mile.
Yoon mujhko tere gham ne giraftaar kar liya,
Jaise bagair zurm kisee ko saza mile.
Dil mein agar charaaghe-tajassus ho jo-fagan,
Taareek butkade mein bhee tujhko khuda mile.
Aye naaqadaane-waqt jara gaur se padho,
Shaayad kalaame-kaif mein kuchh phalsapha mile.

If some were to receive the curse from this beggarly heart of mine,
He/she shall remain desolate even in the city of joy.
Do (please) turn over the pages of memory,
Perhaps on some leaf you may find my reference.
Be it pain or tear, be it happiness or sorrow,
During the course of love, all of them proved disloyal to me.
Even by mistake if you were to visit (me) in dream,
You would find the 'sick-in-waiting' wide awake.
Your sorrow has entrapped me in such a way,
Like some one getting sentenced for no fault of his.
If you have the 'Search lamp' burning in the heart,
You will find the God even in the dark temple.
O, ye modern 'day's critics! do read carefully,
Perhaps you may find some philosophy in Kaif 's poetry.

Kaif Ahmed Siddeeqee

होती है तेरे नाम से वहशत[1] कभी-कभी,
बरहम[2] होती है यूँ भी तबियत कभी-कभी।
है दिल के नसीब ये तौफ़ीक़े[3] इज़तिराब[4],
मिलती है ज़िन्दगी में ये राहत कभी-कभी,
जोशे जुनूं में दर्द की तुगयानियों[5] के साथ,
अश्कों में ढल गई तेरी सूरत कभी-कभी।
तेरे क़रीब रह के भी दिल मुतमईन[6] ना था,
गुज़री है मुझ पे ये भी क़यामत[7] कभी-कभी।
कुछ अपना होश था ना तुम्हारा ख़याल था,
यूँ भी गुज़र गई शबे-फ़ुरक़त[8] कभी-कभी।
ऐ दोस्त हमने तर्के-मुहब्बत[9] के बावजूद,
महसूस की है तेरी ज़रूरत कभी-कभी।

नासिर काज़मी

1.घबराहट 2.अस्त-व्यस्त 3.सामर्थ्य 4.बेचैनी 5.तूफानों 6.संतुष्ट 7.प्रलय 8.विरह की रात 9.प्रेम का टूटना

Hotee hai tere naam se wahshat kabhee-kabhee,
Barham hotee hai yoon bhee tabiyat kabhee-kabhee.
Hai dil ke naseeb ye taufeeqe iztiraab,
Miltee hai zindagee mein ye raahat kabhee-kabhee.
Joshe junoon mein dard kee tugyaaniyon ke saath,
Ashkon mein dhal gayee teree soorat kabhee-kabhee.
Tere qareeb rahke bhee dil mutmaeen na tha,
Guzree hai mujhpe ye bhee qayaamat kabhee-kabhee.
Kuchh apna hosh tha na tumhaara khyaal tha,
Yoon bhee guzar gayee shabe-furqat kabhee-kabhee.
Aye dost humne tarke-muhabbat ke baawajood,
Mahsoos kee hai teree zaroorat kabhee-kabhee.

At times I feel uneasy by the mention of your name,
For no reasons at times I get the feeling of nervousness.
Along with the anxiety the heart has been blessed with the tolerance,
In life, only at times this sort of solace is available.
In the mad enthusiasm, along with the storms of pain,
Your face too has merged with tears at times.
Even while staying close to you, the heart was not satisfied,
Such a hell has broken down on me at times.
Neither I was aware of myself, nor your thought was in mind,
At times, in such a way the night of separation was spent.
O, friend! despite the break up I have felt your need at times.

Naasir Kaazmi

वारफ़्तगी[1] में दिल का चलन इंतहा का था,
अब बुत-परस्त है, जो न क़ायल ख़ुदा का था।
मुझको ख़ुद अपने आप से शर्मिंदगी हुई,
वह इस तरह कि, तुझपे भरोसा बला का था।
वार इस क़दर शदीद कि, दुश्मन ही कर सके,
चेहरा मगर ज़रूर किसी आशना का था।
अब यह कि, अपनी किश्ते-तमन्ना[2] को रोइए,
अब उससे क्या गिला कि, वह बादल हवा का था।
तूने बिछड़के अपने सिर इल्ज़ाम ले लिया,
वर्ना 'फ़राज़' का तो यह रोना सदा का था।

अहमद फ़राज़

1.आशिक़ी 2.प्रेम की खेती की बर्बादी

Waaraftgee mein dil ka chalan intaha ka tha,
Ab but-parast hai, jo na qaayal khuda ka tha.
Mujhko khud apne aap se sharmindgee huyee,
Wah is tarah ki, tujhpe bharosa bala ka tha.
Waar is qadar shadeed ki, dushman hee kar sake,
Chehra magar zaroor kisee aashna ka tha.
Ab yah ki, apnee kishte-tamanna ko roeeye,
Ab usse kya gila ki wah baadal hawa ka tha.
Toone bichhadhke apne sir ilzaam le liya,
Warna, 'Faraaz' ka tau yah rona sada ka tha.

During courtship the behaviour of the heart was at exreme,
One who never believed in God, now is an idolater.
I felt ashamed of myself,
That was for the reason, that I had blind faith in you.
Attack so severe, that only an enemy could carry out,
But the face, for sure was that of a friend.
Now the state is such, that cry on the destruction of your yield of love,
What to complain about her, (for) she was a cloud of wind.
Having separated from me, you have taken the blame on your head,
Otherwise, this weeping has been 'Faraaz's' ageold past-time.

Ahmed 'Faraaz'

बस इन्तिज़ार था, एहसास-ए-इन्तिज़ार[1] न था,
वो दिन भी क्या थे, कि जब खुद पे इख़्तियार न था।
किसी भी चश्म-ए-करम[2] का उम्मीदवार न था,
मैं तश्नालब[3] था मगर मयकदे[4] पे बार[5] न था।
किस आसरे पे तिरे ग़म से अहद[6] कर लेता,
हयात भी वो मिली, जिसका एतबार[7] न था।
अजीब लोग थे, क़ब्रों पे जान देते थे,
सड़क की लाश का कोई भी दावेदार न था।
'वसीम' धूप से बचने भी हम कहाँ आए,
इक ऐसे पेड़ के नीचे, जो सायादार न था।

वसीम बरेलवी

1.प्रतीक्षा का आभास 2.दयावान दृष्टि 3.प्यासा 4.मदिरालय 5.बोझ 6.क़रार 7.विश्वास

Bas intizaar tha aihsaase-intizaar na tha,
Wo din bhee kya the, ki jab khud pe ikhtiyaar na tha.
Kisee bhee chashme-karam ka ummeedwaar na tha,
Main tashnaalab tha magar maikade pe baar na tha.
Kis aasre pe tire gham se ahad kar leta,
Hayaat bhee wo milee, jiska aitbaar na tha.
Ajeeb log the, qabron pe jaan dete the,
Sadhak kee laash ka koee bhee daawedaar na tha.
'Waseem' dhoop se bachne bhee ham kahaan aaye,
Ik aise pedh ke neeche, jo saayaadaar na tha.

Only waiting was there, any feeling about the waiting was not there,
What sort of days were those, wherein there was no control on self.
(I) Was no aspirant for any benevolent eye,
I was thirsty but was not a burden on the tavern.
On what basis could I have given a promise to your sorrow,
Even the life which I had received, was not reliable (itself).
Strange were the people, ready to die on graves,
There was no claimant for the dead body lying on the road.
O, 'Waseem' ! in order to safeguard myself against the sunlight, where had I arrived,
Under such a tree which was shadeless.

Waseem Bareillvi

जहाँ-जहाँ मुझे सहरा[1] दिखाई देता है,
मेरी तरह से अकेला दिखाई देता है।
ये एक अब्र[2] का टुकड़ा कहाँ-कहाँ बरसे,
तमाम दश्त[3] ही प्यासा दिखाई देता है।
ये किस मुक़ाम[4] पे लाई है जुस्तजू[5] तेरी,
जहाँ से अर्शे[6] भी नीचा दिखाई देता है।
ये भीगी पलकें किसी की ये अश्क-बार[7] आँखें,
पसे-गुबार[8] भी क्या-क्या दिखाई देता है।

शाकेब जलाली

1.रेगिस्तान 2.बादल 3.रेगिस्तान, जगँल 4.जगह 5.तलाश 6.आसमान 7.आसूँओं से भरी 8.गुबार के नीचे

Jahaan- jahaan mujhe sahra dikhaaee deta hai,
Meree tarah se akela dikhaaee deta hai.
Ye ek abr ka thukda kahaan-kahaan barse,
Tamaam dasht hee pyaasa dikhaaee deta hai.
Ye kis muqaam pe laayee hai justjoo teree,
Jahaan se arsh bhee neecha dikhaaee deta hai.
Ye bheegee palkein, kisi kee ye ashkbaar aankhein,
Pase-gubaar bhee kya-kya dikhaaee deta hai.

Wherever I see the desert,
It looks as lonesome as myself.
Whereall, this solitary piece of cloud can cause rain,
The entire desert/forest seems parched.
Search for you has brought me to such a place,
From where even the sky is appearing low.
These wet eyelids, these tearful eyes of some one,
What all is visible behind the veil of dust-cloud.

'Shaakeb Jalaali'

यूँ ही बेसबब[1] न फिरा करो, कोई शाम घर भी रहा करो,
वो ग़ज़ल की सच्ची किताब है, उसे चुपके-चुपके पढ़ा करो।
मुझे इश्तिहार[2] सी लगती हैं ये मोहब्बतों की कहानियाँ,
जो कहा नहीं वो सुना करो, जो सुना नहीं वो कहा करो।
ये ख़िज़ा[3] की ज़र्द[4] सी शाल में, जो उदास पेड़ के पास है,
ये तुम्हारे घर की बहार है, इसे आसूँओं से हरा करो।
अभी राह में कई मोड़ हैं, कोई आएगा कोई जाएगा।
तुम्हे जिसने दिल से भुला दिया, उसे भूलने की दुआ करो।
कोई हाथ भी ना मिलाएगा, जो गले मिलोगे तपाक[5] से,
ये नये मिज़ाज[6] का शहर है, जरा फ़ासले से मिला करो।
नहीं बेहिजाब[7] वो चांद सा, कि नज़र का कोई असर न हो,
उसे इतनी गर्मिए-शौक़[8] से बड़ी देर तक न तका करो।

बशीर बद्र

1.बिना कारण 2.विज्ञापन 3.पतझड़ 4.पीली 5.उत्सुकता 6.प्रकृती, आदत 7.बेशर्म 8.बेताबी

Yoon hee besabab na phira karo, Koee shaam ghar bhee raha karo,
Wo ghazal kee sachchee kitaab hai, use chupke-chupke padkha karo.
Mujhe ishtihaar see lagtee hain, ye mohabbaton kee kahaaniyaan,
Jo kaha naheen wo suna karo, jo suna naheen wo kaha karo.
Ye khizaan kee zard see shaal mein jo udaas pedh ke paas hai,
Ye tumhaare ghar kee bahaar hai, ise aasuon se hara karo.
Abhee raah mein kaee modh hain, koee aayega, koee jaayega,
Tumhein jisne dil se bhula diya, use bhoolne kee dua karo.
Koee haath bhee na milaayega, jo gale miloge tapaak se,
Ye naye mizaaj ka shahar hai yahaan faasle se mila karo.
Naheen behijaab wo chaand sa ki nazar ka koee asar ho,
Use itnee garmiye-shauq se badhee der tak na taka karo.

Do not keep wandering aimlessly, some evening stay at home too,
He is true book of poems, read him on the quiet.
These stories of love appear to me similar to posters,
You must listen to what has not been said (and) say what you have not heard.
The one in a yellowish shawl of autumn, standing sad near the tree,
Is (in fact) the spring of your home, make it green with your tears.
On the track there are still some turns, someone will come, someone will go,
You should pray to forget the one who has removed you from his heart.
Nobody will even shake hands if you show keenness to embrace,
This is a city of new trend, (here) you should meet keeping a little distance.
She is not shameles like the moon which remains unaffected by the stares,
You should not stare at her for long with lustful eyes.

Bashir Badr

पत्थर सुलग रहे थे, कोई नक़्शे-पा[1] ना था,
हम जिस तरफ़ चले थे, उधर रास्ता न था।
परछाईयों के शहर की तन्हाईयाँ ना पूछ,
अपना शरीके़-ग़म[2], कोई अपने सिवा ना था।
पत्तों के टूटने की सदा घुट के रह गई,
जँगल में दूर-दूर हवा का पता ना था।
'राशिद' किसे सुनाते गली में तेरी ग़ज़ल,
उसके मकाँ का कोई दरीचाँ[3] खुला ना था।

मुमताज 'राशिद'

1.क़दम का निशान 2.दुख बटाँने वाला 3.खिड़की

Patthar sulag rahe the, koee naqshe-pa na tha,
Hum jis taraf chale the, udhar raasta na tha.
Parchhaaeeon ke shahar kee tanhaaeeyaan na pooch,
Apna shareeqe-gham, koee apne siwa na tha.
Patton ke tootne kee sada ghuth ke rah gaee,
Jangal mein door-door hawa ka pata na tha.
'Raashid' kise sunaate galee mein teree ghazal,
Uske makaan ka koee dareecha khula na tha.

Stone were somouldering, there was no footprint in sight,
The direction, which I had taken, had no track on it.
Do not ask (me) about the loneliness of the town of shadows,
Except for ownself there was no one to share my sorrow.
The crackling sound of broken leaves remained choked,
There was no trace of wind for miles in the forest.
O, 'Raashid'! in the lane for whom would I have recited your poem,
Not a single window of her house was open.

Mumtaaj 'Raashid'

निगाहे-शौक़[1] भर ना जाए कहीं,
तू भी दिल से उतर ना जाए कहीं।
आज देखा है तुझको देर के बाद,
आज का दिन गुज़र ना जाए कहीं।
सामना कर उदास लोगों से,
हुस्न तेरा बिखर ना जाए कहीं।
आरज़ू है कि तू यहाँ आए,
और फिर उम्र मर न जाए कहीं।
आओ, कुछ देर रो भी लें 'नासिर'
फिर ये दरिया[2] उतर ना जाए कहीं।

नासीर काज़मी

1.नज़र का उतावलापन 2.नदी

Nigaahe-shauq bhar na jaaye kaheen,
Too bhee dil se utar na jaaye kaheen.
Aaj dekha hai tujhko der ke baad,
Aaj ka din guzar na jaayee kaheen.
Saamna kar udaas logon se,
Husn tera bikhar na jaaye kaheen.
Aarzoo hai ki too yahaan aaye,
Aur phir umr bhar na jaaye kaheen.
Aao, kuchh der ro bhee lein 'Naasir',
Phir ye dariya utar na jaaye kaheen.

The Zeal in the eyes may not get saturated too,
May the heart not get fed up of you too.
Today I have seen you after ages,
This day may not come to an end.
After seeing the sad people,
May your beauty not get scattered.
There is this desire, that you should come here,
(And) Not to go somewhere else throughout the life.
Come let us cry a bit more O, 'Naasir',
Ere this river start receding.

'Naasir Kaazmi'

जब किसी से कोई गिला[1] रखना,
सामने अपने आईना रखना।
यूँ उजालों से वास्ता[2] रखना,
शम्मा के पास ही हवा रखना।
घर की तामीर[3] चाहे जैसी हो,
इसमे रोने की कुछ जगह रखना।
मस्जिदें ग़ैर-नमाजियों[4] के लिए।
अपने घर में कहीं खुदा रखना।
मिलना-जुलना जहाँ ज़रूरी हो,
मिलने जुलने का हौंसला रखना।

निदा फ़ाजली

1.शिकायत,गर्ज 2.मतलब 3.बनावट 4.नमाज़ ना पढ़ने वाले

Jab kisee se koee gila rakhna,
Saamne apne aayeena rakhna.
Yoon ujaalon se waasta rakhna,
Shamma ke paas hee hawa rakhna.
Ghar kee taameer chaahe jaisee ho,
Ismein rone kee kuchh jagah rakhna.
Masjidein ghair namaajion ke liye ,
Apne ghar mein kaheen khuda rakhna.
Milna julna jahaan zarooree ho,
Milne-julne ka haunsla rakhna.

While nurturing a grudge against someone,
Keep a mirror infront of yourself.
Maintain such a relationship with the lights,
That the wind prevails close to the candle.
Whatever may be the construction of the house,
Do keep some room in if for crying.
Let the mosques be for those who don't offer prayers,
Do install the God somewhere in your dwelling.
Whenever it is necessary to meet each other,
Some courage must be reserved for such meets.

Nida Fazli

कुछ तो नक़ूशे-इश्क़े-जुनूं-खे़ज[1] छोड़िए,
शबनम की आरजू है तो शोले निचोड़िए।
सदमा हो शाख को ना हो पत्ता कोई उदास,
इस हुस्ने-एहतियात से फूलों को तोड़िए।
ऊँचे मकां बना तो लिए हैं हुज़ूर।
अब आँधियों का रूख़ भी किसी तरह मोड़िए।
मल्लाह मोम के हैं, कड़ी धूप का सफ़र,
किश्ती को नाखुदा[2] के सहारे न छोड़िए।
शाइस्तगी[3] लफ़्ज़-ओ-बयां भूल जाइए,
संगे-ज़बां[4] से शीशाए-पिनदार[5] तोड़िए।
इस दौरे-बेचराग़ में कुछ और एहतियात,
जलते हुए चराग़ को तनहा ना छोड़िए।
किसको है आज .फुर्सते-चारागरी[6],
अपने सर को आप ही पत्थर से तोड़िए।

मुशीर झिन्जानवी

1.इश्क़ की दीवानगी के चिन्ह 2.मल्लाह 3.शिष्टाचार 4.पत्थर की .ज़ुबान 5.शीशे का अहंकार 6.उपचार करने की .फुर्सत

Kuchh tau naqooshe-ishqe-junoon-khej chhodhiye,
Shabnam kee aarzoo hai tau shole nichodhiye.
Sadma ho shaakh ko na ho patta koee udaas,
Is husne-aihtiyaat se phoolon ko todhiye,
Oonche makaan bana tau liye hain huzoor,
Ab aandhiyon ka rukh bhee kisee tarah modhiye.
Mallaah mom ke hain, kadhee dhoop ka safar,
Kishtee ko naakhuda ke sahaare na chhodhiye.
Shaaistgee lafz-o-bayaan bhool jaaiye,
Sange-zabaan se sheeshaaye-pindaar todhiye.
Is daure-becharaagh mein kuchh aur aihtiyaat,
Jalte huye charaagh ko tanha na chhodiye.
Kisko hai aaj fursate-chaaraagaree,
Ab apne sar ko aap hee patthar se todhiye.

Leave (behind) at least some signs of the madness of love,
Should you have a desire for the dew, then squeeze the flames (first).
Neither the branch should get into a trauma nor any leaf should become sad,
With such a graceful care flowers be plucked.
Your highness! now that you have erected high-rise buildings,
Somehow you ought to change the direction of hurricanes too.
The boatmen are made of wax, voyage is under scorching sun,
Do not leave the boat in the hands of the boatman.
Forget about the courtesy and sweet talk,
Break the high-headedness of the mirror by the tongue of stone.
As an added precaution in this dark era,
Don't leave the burning earthen lamp alone.
These days, who has the time for healing,
Now break own head by yourself with the stone.

Musheer Jhinjaanvi

कुछ तो मजबूरियाँ रही होगीं,
यूँ कोई बेवफ़ा नही होता।
जी बहुत चाहता है, सच बोलें,
क्या करें हौसला[1] नहीं होता।
रात का इन्तिज़ार कौन करे,
आजकल दिन में क्या नहीं होता?

बशीर बद्र

1.हिम्मत

Kuchh tau majbooriyaan rahee hongee,
Yoon koee bewafa naheen hota.
Jee bahut chaahta hai sach bolein,
Kya Karein hausla naheen hota.
Raat ka intizaar kaun kare,
Aajkal din mein kya naheen hota.

There sure must have been some compulsions,
No one becomes disloyal for no rhyme or reason,
The heart yearns to speak the truth,
But can't for want of courage.
Who has the patience to wait for the nightfall,
What all doesn't happen during the broad daylight these days?

Bashir Badr

कोई आहट ना सदा[1] है मुझमें,
जाने क्या टूट गया है मुझमें।
आईना मुझको दिखाने वाले,
तेरा पैकर[2] भी छुपा है मुझमें।
आसरा देके मेरे अश्क[3] न छीन,
यही ले दे के बचा है मुझमें ।
कौन मिट्टी का ख़रीदार यहाँ,
उसने क्या देख लिया है मुझमें।

मुमताज राशिद

1.आवाज 2.चेहरा 3.आँसू

Koyee aahat na sada hai mujhmein,
Jaane kya toot gaya hai mujhmein.
Aayeena mujh ko dikhaane waale,
Tera paikar bhee chhupa hai mujhmein.
Aasara deke, mere ashk na chheen,
Yahee le deke bacha hai mujh mein
Kaun mittee ka khareedaar yahaan,
Usne kya dekh liya hai mujhmein.

There is no resonance, no voice in me,
Don't know what has snapped inside me.
You, who is showing the mirror to me,
Your face is also hidden within me.
By giving hope, don't snatch my tears (from me),
This is all I am left with after all the give and take.
Who is this buyer of dust here,
What has she seen in me?

Mumtaaj Raashid

अब तो इन्सान को इन्सान बनाया जाए,
या कोई और ही भगवान बनाया जाए।
शरीके़-जुर्म[1] यहाँ हर किसी का चेहरा है
किसका इसाँफ़[2] यहाँ किससे कराया जाए।
रहनुमा[3] खुद को सभी पाक-साफ़[4] कहते हैं।
आईना किसको यहाँ कैसे दिखाया जाए।
लोग छिप-छिप के यहाँ रोज़ बिका करते हैं,
शर्त है मोल[5] को चुपके से बताया जाए।

'नामवर'

1.अपराध में शामिल 2.न्याय 3.पथप्रदर्शक 4.पवित्र 5.कीमत

Ab tau insaan ko insaan banaaya jaaye,
Ya koyee aur hee bhagwaan banaaya jaaye.
Shareeqe-jurm yahaan har kisee ka chehra hai,
Kiska insaaf yahaan kis se karaaya jaaye.
Rahnuma khud ko sabhee paak-saaf kahte hain,
Aayeena kisko yahaan kaise dikhaaya jaaye.
Log chhip-chhip ke yahaan roz bika karte hain,
Shart hai mol ko chupke se bataaya jaaye.

It is time now; that human being be converted into a real human being,
Else, let us create a different God.
Every face here, is involved in some crime,
Who is worth delivering justice to whom.
All the leaders proclaim themselves above board and pious,
How the mirror be shown to whom here.
People clandestinely sell themselves daily here,
The condition is that the price be told under the rose.

'Naamwar'

हादसों की ज़द[1] पे हैं, तो मुस्कुराना छोड़ दें,
ज़लज़लों के ख़ौफ़ से क्या घर बनाना छोड़ दें।
तुमने मेरे घर न आने की क़सम खाई तो है,
आंसुओं से भी कहो आँखों में आना छोड़ दें।
प्यार के दुश्मन कभी तू प्यार से कहके तो देख,
एक तेरा दर ही क्या हम तो ज़माना छोड़ दें।
घोसले वीरान हैं, अब वो परिन्दे ही कहाँ,
इक बसेरे के लिए जो आबोदाना[2] छोड़ दें।

वसीम बरेलवी

1.निशाना 2.दाना-पानी

Haadson kee zad pe hain, tau muskuraana chhodh dein,
Zalzalon ke khauf se kya ghar banaana chhodh dein.
Tumne mere ghar na aane kee qasam khaaee tau hai,
Aansuon se bhee kaho aankhon mein aana chhodh dein.
Pyaar ke dushman kabhee too pyaar se kahke tau dekh,
Ek tera dar hee kya hum tau zamaana chodh dein.
Ghosle weeraan hain, ab wo parinde hee kahaan,
Ek basere ke liye jo aabodaana chhodh dein.

If (I am) in the gunsight of the mishaps, does it mean that I should give up smiling,
Should (we) stop building houses out of the fear of earthquakes.
(Agreed) You have sworn never to visit my home, but,
Then tell the tears also, not to come into the eyes.
O, enemy of love ! just ordain me with love and see,
What to talk of your door, I will even leave this world (for good).
Nests are deserted, where are those birds now,
Who for a perch would give up water and grains.

Waseem Bareillvi

तू पास भी हो तो, दिल बेक़रार अपना है,
कि हमको तेरा नहीं, इंतज़ार अपना हैं।
मिले कोई भी, तेरा ज़िक्र छेड़ देते हैं,
कि जैसे सारा जहाँ राज़दार अपना है।
वह दूर हो तो ब-जा तर्के-दोस्ती[1] का ख़याल,
वह सामने हो तो कब इख़्तियार अपना है।
ज़माने भर के दुखों को लगा लिया दिल से,
इस आसरे पे कि, एक ग़मगुसार अपना है।
बला से जाँ का ज़ियाँ[2] हो इस एतमाद[3] की खैर,
वफ़ा करे न करे, फिर भी यार अपना है।
'फ़राज़' राहते-जाँ[4] भी वही है, क्या कीजे,
वह जिसके हाथ से सीना फ़िगार[5] अपना है।

अहमद फ़राज़

1.दोस्ती का त्याग 2.जान की हानि 3.विश्वास 4.सुखदायी 5.ज़ख़्मी

Too paas bhee ho tau, dil beqaraar apna hai,
Ki hamko tera naheen, intzaar apna hai.
Mile koee bhee, tera zikr chhedh dete hain,
Ki jaise saara jahaan raazdaar apna hai.
Wah door ho tau ba-ja tarke-dostee ka khyaal,
Wah saamne ho tau kab ikhtiyaar apna hai.
Zamaane bhar ke dukhon ko laga liya dil se,
Is aasre pe ki, ek ghamgusaar apna hai.
Bala se jaan ka ziyaan ho, is eitmaad kee khair,
Wafa kare na kare, phir bhee yaar apna hai.
'Faraaz' raahate-jaan bhee wahee hai, kya keeje,
Wah jiske haath se seena figaar apna hai.

Even when you are next to me, my heart remains restless,
As if it is not for you but myself that I have been waiting for.
Whomsoever I happen to meet, I start talking about you,
As if the entire world is my trustee.
When she is away, then the thought of breaking relationship sounds logical,
But when she is right infront, then where do I have the control.
(I) Have embraced all worldly woes to my heart,
On the premise that there (sure) is someone to share my grief.
To hell with it if the life is lost, long live this confidence,
Loyalty or no loyalty, she is still my beloved.
O, 'Faraaz' ! what can you do, she alone is the solace of your life,
The one who has inflicted wounds on your heart.

Ahmed 'Faraaz'

ये दौरे-नामुरादी[1], हाए यह महसूस होता है,
मैं अपनी क़ब्र पर ख़ुद पढ़ रहा हूँ फ़ातेहा[2] जैसे।
हम अपने दिल की बर्बादी का फ़ैसला सुन के यूँ चुप हैं,
किसी दुश्मन पे गुज़रा हो यह सारा वाक़या[3] जैसे।
ये कैसी रहगुज़र[4] है, रौशनी तलवों में चुभती है,
किसी ने तोड़ कर बिखरा दिया हो आईना जैसे।
मुसाफ़िर चलते-चलते थक गए, मंज़िल नहीं मिलती,
क़दम के साथ बढ़ता जा रहा हो फ़ासला जैसे।
ज़माना हो गया 'कैसर' मगर महसूस होता है,
अभी गुज़रा हो दिल के टूटने का हादसा[5] जैसा।

कैसरूल जाफ़री

1.विफलता का समय/दौर 2.मृतक की शांति के लिए प्रार्थना 3.प्रसंग 4.राह, रास्ता 5.दुर्घटना

Ye daure -naamuraadee, haai ye mahsoos hota hai,
Main apnee qabr par khud padh raha hoon faateha jaise.
Hum apne dil kee barbaadee ka faisla sun ke yoon chup hain,
Kisee dushman pe guzra ho yah saara waaqya jaise.
Ye kaisee rahguzar hai, raushnee talwon mein chubhtee hai,
Kisee ne todh kar bikhra diya ho aayeena jaise.
Musaafir chalte-chalte thak gaye, manzil naheen miltee,
Qadam ke saath badhta jaa raha ho faasla jaise.
Zamaana ho gaya 'Qaisar' magar mahsoos hota hai,
Abhee guzra ho dil ke tootne ka haadsa jaise.

Alas! during this period of failures I suffer from this feeling,
As if I have been reading a requiem over my own grave.
Having heard the verdict for destruction of my heart, I am dumb struck,
As if the entire tragedy had befallen on an enemy.
What sort of track is this, the light has been pricking the soles,
As if some one has broken a mirror and scattered enroute.
The travellers have become tired of trekking, haven't found the destination,
Seems as if the distance is getting increased with each step.
O,'Qaiser'! it has been ages but I feel,
As if the mishap involving destruction of my heart has just happened

Qaisrul Jaafree

खुदा हमको ऐसी ख़ुदाई[1] न दे,
कि अपने सिवा कुछ दिखाई न दे।
ख़तावार[2] समझेगी दुनियाँ तुझे,
अब इतनी ज़ियादा सफ़ाई न दे।
हँसो आज इतना कि इस शोर में,
सदा[3] के सिवा कुछ सुनाई न दे।
अभी तो बदन मे लहू है बहुत,
क़लम छीन ले रौशनाई न दे।
ख़ुदा ऐसे अहसास[4] का नाम है,
रहे सामने और दिखाई न दे।

बशीर बद्र

1.अहंकार 2.दोषी 3.आवाज 4.अनुभव

Khuda humko aisee khudaaee na de,
Ki apne siva kuchh dikhaaee na de.
Khataawaar samjhegee duniyaan tujhe,
Ab itnee ziaada safaaee na de.
Hanson aaj itna ki is shor mein,
Sada ke siva kuchh sunaaee na de.
Abhee tau badan mein lahoo hai bahoot,
Qalam chheen le raushnaaee na de.
Khuda aise aihsaas ka naam hai,
Rahe saamne aur dikhaaee na de.

May God bless me not with such a Godliness,
Wherein I can not see anything except myself.
This world will consider you guilty,
Now, do not give so much justification.
Today (you) must laugh so much in this commotion,
That nothing should be heard except (your) voice.
Lot of blood is there in my body as yet,
Snatch the pen and do not give (me) any ink.
God is the name of such realisation,
(Which) Remains in front (of you), yet invisible.

'Bashir Badr'

ऐसे घर में बस रहा हूँ, देख ले बेशक कोई,
जिसके दरवाजे की क़िस्मत मे नहीं दस्तक[1] कोई।
यूँ तो होने को सभी कुछ है मिरे दिल में मगर,
इस दुकां में आज तक आया नही ग्राहक कोई।
मिल गया आँखों को फ़र्शे-राह बनने का सिला[2],
आंसुओं की दे गया सौगात में दीमक कोई।
बाग़ मे कल रात फूलों की हवेली लुट गई,
चश्मे-शबनम[3] से चुरा कर ले गया ठंडक कोई।
एक भी ख़्वाहिश[4] के हाथों में ना मेहंदी लग सकी,
मेरे जज़्बों मे ना दूल्हा बन सका अब तक कोई।
मेरी बस्ती के घरों का पूछते हो हाल क्या,
आंगनों मे आज कल बजती नही ढोलक कोई।
वो भी था 'साजिद' मिरे जज़्बों की चोरी मे शरीक[5],
उसकी जानिब[6] क्यों नहीं उठती निगाहे-शक[7] कोई।

इक़बाल साजिद

1.खटखटाहट 2.नतीजा 3.ओस की आँख 4.इच्छा, कामना, लालसा 5.शामिल 6.तरफ़, ओर 7.संदेह की नज़र

Aise ghar mein bas raha hoon, dekhle beshak koee,
Jiske darwaaze kee qismat mein naheen dastak koee.
Yoon tau hone ko sabhee kuchh hai mere dil mein magar,
Is dukaan mein aaj tak aaya nahee graahak koee.
Mil gaya aankhon ko farshe-raah banne ka sila,
Aaansuon kee de gaya saugaat mein deemak koee.
Baagh mein kal raat phoolon kee havelee lut gayee,
Chashme-shabnam se chura kar le gaya thhandhak koee.
Ek bhee khwwaahish ke haathon mein na mehendi lag sakee,
Mere jazbon mein na doolha ban saka ab tak koee.
Meree bastee ke gharon ka poochhte ho haal kya,
Aangnon mein aajkal bajtee naheen dholak koee.
Wo bhee tha 'Saajid' mire jazbon kee choree mein shareek,
Uskee jaanib kyon naheen uthhtee nigaahe-shak koee.

Everyone is welcome to have a look (for) I have been dwelling in such a house,
Which has been destined to receive no knock.
Even though there is every thing in my heart,
Yet till date this shop has not been visited by any buyer,
(My) Eyes have received the payoff for the waiting,
Some one has presented (them) with the termite of tears.
Yesterday night in the garden the mansion of flowers was looted,
Someone stole the coolness from the eyes of dew.
No henna could ever be applied on the palms of any of (my) desire.
Till now not even a single sentiment of mine has been able to become a bridegroom.
Why do you ask about the plight of my colony,
In the courtyards no drums are played these days.
O! 'Saajid', she too was a party to the theft of my emotions,
Why no doubting eyes are being raised towards her?

' Iqbaal Saajid '

तमाम उम्र न जुड़ने का ग़म उठाते हैं,
वो एतबार[1] के रिश्ते जो टूट जाते हैं।
तुम अपने चेहरे का हम से हिसाब ले लेना,
ये आइने तो कोई दिन में टूट जाते हैं।
जो एक प्यास को पानी न दे सका फिर भी,
उसी को लोग समन्दर बताये जाते हैं।
'वसीम' रश्क[2] से देखूँ न क्यूँ परिन्दों को,
ये शाम होते, घरों को तो लौट आते हैं।

वसीम बरेलवी

1.विश्वास 2.ईर्ष्या

Tamaam umr na judhne ka gham uthhaate hain,
Wo aitbaar ke rishte jo toot jaate hain.
Tum apne chehre ka ham se hisaab le lena,
Ye aaeene tau koee din mein toot jaate hain.
Jo ek pyaas ko paanee na de saka phir bhee,
Usee ko log samandar bataaye jaate hain.
'Waseem' rashk se dekhoon na kyon parindon ko,
Ye shaam hote, gharon ko tau laut aate hain.

Throughout the life they suffer from the sorrow of not being able to tie up (again),
Those relationships of faith which get broken once.
You (should) take the account of your features from me,
These mirrors get broken in a few days.
The one who could not give water to a single thirst,
The same one is being hailed by the people as the ocean.
O, 'Wassem' ! why should I not look at the birds with envy.
(After all) With the onset of evening at least they return to their (respective) homes.

Wassem Bareilvi

अबके हम बिछड़े तो शायद कभी ख़्वाबों में मिलें,
जिस तरह सूखे हुए फूल किताबों में मिलें।
ढूँढ़ उजड़े हुए लोगों में वफ़ा के मोती,
ये ख़ज़ाने तुझे मुमकिन है खराबों में मिलें।
ग़मे-दुनियां भी ग़मे-यार में शामिल कर लो,
नश्शा बढ़ता है शराबें जो शराबों में मिलें।
तू खुदा है, न मेरा इश्क़ फ़रिश्तों जैसा,
दोनों इंसाँ हैं तो क्यों इतने हिजाबों[1] में मिलें।
आज हम दार[2] पे खींचे गए जिन बातों पर,
क्या अजब कल वो ज़माने को निसाबों[3] में मिलें।
अब न वह मैं हूँ, न वह तू है, न वह माज़ी है 'फ़राज़',
जैसे दो शख़्स तमन्ना के सराबों[4] में मिलें।

अहमद फ़राज़

1.शर्म 2.सूली 3.पाठ्क्रमों 4.मृग-मरीचिकाओं

Abke ham bichhdhe tau shaayad kabhee khawwaabon mein milein,
Jis tarah sookhe huye phool kitaabon mein milein.
Dhoondh ujdhe huye logon mein wafa ke motee,
Ye khazaane tujhe mumkin hai kharaabon mein milein.
Ghame-duniya bhee ghame-yaar mein shaamil kar lo,
Nashsha badhta hai sharaabein jo sharaabon mein milein.
Too khuda hai, na mera ishq farishton jaisa,
Dono insaan hain tau kyon itne hijaabon mein milein.
Aaj ham daar pe kheenche gaye jin baaton par,
Kya ajab kal wo zamaane ko nisaabon mein milein.
Ab na wah main hoon, na wah too hai, na wah maazee hai 'Faraaz',
Jaise do shakhs tamanna ke saraabon mein milein.

If we part this time, then perhaps we may meet in dreams sometime,
Like the dried flowers found inside the (old) books.
Look for pearls of loyalty in the desolate folks,
Perhaps you may find these treasures in the ruins.
Do include the worldy woes in the sorrow for lover,
Intoxication increases when diffeerent wines are mixed together.
Neither you are God, nor my love is akin to being angelic,
If both are homo sapiens, then why should we feel ashamed while meeting.
Acts, for which I have been brought on to the gibbet today,
No wonder if tomorrow the world finds the same acts in the text-books/curriculum.
Now, I am not the same, you are not the same, so is not the past, O 'Faraaz' !
It is like meeting of two people in mirages of desires.

Ahmed 'Faraaz'

दोस्ती जब किसी से की जाए,
दुश्मनों की भी राय ली जाए।
मौत का ज़हर है फ़िज़ाओं[1] में,
अब कहाँ जाके साँस ली जाए।
बस इसी सोच में हूँ डूबा हुआ,
ये नदी कैसे पार की जाए।
मेरे माज़ी[2] के ज़ख़्म भरने लगे,
आज फिर कोई भूल की जाए,
बोतलें खोल के तो पी बरसों,
आज दिल खोल कर भी पी जाए।

राहत इन्दौरी

1.वातावरण 2.भूतकाल

Dostee jab kisee se kee jaaye,
Dushmanon kee bhee raai lee jaaye.
Maut ka zahar hai fizaaon mein,
Ab kahaan jaa ke saans lee jaaye.
Bas isee soch mein hoon dooba hua,
Ye nadee kaise paar kee jaaye.
Mere maazee ke zakhm bharne lage,
Aaj phir koyee bhool kee jaaye.
Botlein khol ke tau pee barson,
Aaj dil khol kar bhee pee jaaye.

While befriending someone,
Even the enemies' opinion be sought.
The deathly poison lingers in the environment,
Where does one go to take a breath now?
I am deeply submerged in this thought,
As to how this river be crossed.
Wounds of my past have started healing,
Today again, let me commit a mistake.
We have opened the bottles and drank enough for years,
Today, let us open ourselves and drink to our hearts' content.

Raahat Indoree

शोला हूँ भड़कने की गुज़ारिश[1] नहीं करता,
सच मुँह से निकल जाता है, कोशिश नहीं करता।
माथे के पसीने से महक आए न जिसकी,
वो ख़ून मेरे जिस्म में गर्दिश[2] नहीं करता।
गिरती हुई दीवार का हमदर्द[3] हूँ लेकिन,
चढ़ते हुए सूरज की परस्तिश[4] नहीं करता।
हम दर्दि-ए-अहबाब[5] से डरता हूँ 'मुज़फ़्फ़र'
मैं ज़ख़्म तो रखता हूँ नुमाइश नहीं करता।

मुज़फ़्फ़र वारसी

1.प्रार्थना 2.हरकत,चक्कर 3.दुख बाँटने वाला 4.पूजा 5.दोस्तों की सहानुभूती

Shola hoon, bhadhakne kee guzaarish naheen karta,
Sach muhn se nikal jaata hai, koshish naheen karta.
Maathe ke paseene se mahak aaye na jiskee,
Wo khoon mere jism mein gardish naheen karta.
Girtee huyee deewaar ka humdard hoon lekin,
Chadhte huye sooraj kee parastish naheen karta.
Hum dardi-e-aihbaab se darta hoon 'Muzaffar',
Main zakhm tau rakhta hoon, numaaish naheen karta.

I am a flame (I) do not seek permission to flare-up,
Truth comes out of the mouth by itself, I don't try',
The scent of which doesn't emanate from the sweat of the forhead,
Such a blood doesn't circulate in my body.
I am a sympathiser of the crumbling wall but,
I don't worship the rising sun.
I am afraid of the sympathies of friends. O, 'Muzaffar'!
I do house wounds, but do not hold exibition.

'Muzaffar Waarsi'

बरसों तपिशे-ग़म[1] में ये एहसास[2] जले है।
तब जाके कहीं शेर के साँचें में ढले है।
कुछ ऐसे तेरी बज़्म[3] में बैठा हूँ अकेला,
जिस तरह सरे-राह[4] कोई शम्मा जले है,
इस मंज़िले-दुश्वार[5] से हँस-हँस के गुजर जा,
पगले कहीं रोने से शबे-हिज्र[6] ढले है।
अल्लाह किसी शख़्स[7] को रुस्वा[8] न करे यूँ,
मुझसे मेरा साया[9] भी तो अब बच के चले है।
इस दिल को घरोंदा सा बना रखा है उन्ने,
आबाद करे है, कभी बरबाद करे है।

इशरत

1.दुख की आग 2.महसूसियत 3.महफ़िल 4.खुले आम 5.कठिन मुक़ाम 6.विरह की रात 7.आदमी,इन्सान 8.बदनाम 9.परछाई

Barson tapishe-gham main ye aihsaas jale hai,
Tab jaake kaheen shair ke saanche mein dhhale hai.
Kuchh aise teree bazm mein baitha hoon akela,
Jis tarah sare-raah koyee shamma jale hai.
Is manzile-dushwaar se hans-hans ke guzar ja,
Pagle kaheen rone se shabe-hijr dhhale hai.
Allaah kisee shakhs ko ruswa na kare yoon,
Mujhse mera saya bhee tau ab bach ke chale hai.
Is dil ko gharonda sa bana rakhkha hai unne,
Aabaad kare hai, kabhee barbaad kare hai.

For ages the thought smoulders in the fire of sorrows,
Only then it gets moulded in the form of a couplet.
I am sitting in your assembly all alone like,
A candle is burning on the thoroughfare.
Laugh off through this tedious trek,
O, mad man! The night of severance does not get over by crying.
May God not cause infamy to any one in such a way,
Today even my own shadow shirks my company.
She has converted this heart into a mud house,
Constructing at times, destroying at times.

Ishrat

कोई फूल धूप की पत्तियों में हरे रिबन से बँधा हुआ,
वो ग़ज़ल का लहजा नया-नया, ना कहा हुआ ना सुना हुआ।
मुझे हादसों[1] ने सजा-सजा के बहुत हसीन बना दिया,
मेरा दिल भी जैसे दुल्हन का हाथ हो, महन्दियों से रचा हुआ।
मेरे साथ जुगनू है हमसफ़र, मगर इस शरर[2] की बिसात क्या,
ये चिराग़ कोई चिराग़ है, ना जला हुआ, ना बुझा हुआ।
वो ही शहर है, वो ही रास्ते, वो ही घर है और वो ही लान भी,
मगर उस दरीचे[3] से पूछना, "वो दरख़्त[4] अनार का क्या हुआ"?
जिसे ले गई है अभी हवा, वो वरक़[5] था दिल की किताब का,
कही आँसूओं से लिखा हुआ, कहीं आँसूओं से मिटा हुआ।
वही ख़त कि जिसमें, जगह-जगह दो महकते होटों के चान्द थे,
किसी भूली बिसरी सी ताक़ पर तहे-गर्द[6] होगा दबा हुआ।
वो थका हुआ मेरी बाहों में जरा सो गया था, तो क्या हुआ?
अभी मैने देखा है चाँद भी किसी शाखे़-गुल[7] पे झुका हुआ।
कई मील रेत को काट कर, कोई मौज[8] फूल खिला गई,
कोई पेड़ प्यास से मर रहा है, नदी के पास खड़ा हुआ।

बशीर बद्र

1.दुर्घटनाएँ 2.चिंगारी 3.खिड़की 4.पेड़ 5.प्रष्ठ 6.धूल के नीचे 7. फूलों की डाल 8.लहर

Koee phool dhoop kee pattion mein hare riban se bandha hua,
Wo ghazal ka lahja naya-naya, na kaha hua na suna hua.
Mujhe haadson ne saja-saja ke bahut haseen bana diya,
Mera dil bhee jaise dulkhan ka kaath ho, mehndiyon se racha hua.
Mere saath jugnoo hai humsafar, magar is sharar kee bisaat kya,
Ye chiraagh koee chiraagh hai, na jala hua na bujha hua.
Wo hee shahar hai, wo hee raaste, who hee ghar hai, aur wo hee laan hai,
Magar us dareeche se poochhna, "wo darakhat anaar ka kya hua?"
Jise le gayee hai abhee hawa, wo waraq tha dil kee kitaab ka,
Kaheen aansuon se likha hua, kaheen aasuon se mita hua.
Wahee khat ki jispe, jagah-jagah do mahakte hothhon ke chaand the,
Kisi bhoolee bisree see taaq par tahe-gard hoga daba hua.
Wo thaka hua meree baahon mein jara so gaya tha, tau kya hua,
Abhee mainein dekha hai chaand bhee kisee shaakhe-gul pe jhuka hua.
Kaee meel ret ko kaat kar, koee mauj phool khila, gayee,
Koee pedh pyaas se mar raha hai, nadee ke pass khada hua.

Some flower tied up with a green ribbon amongst the leaves of sunshine,
That new tone of poem, neither spoken nor heard of.
Mishaps have repetitively adorned me, making me very attractive,
My heart too is like the hand of a bride, all decked up in Henna.
Firefly is with me as a co-traveller, but what is the worth of this spark,
What sort of lamp is this, neither lit nor extinguished.
This is the same city, the same tracks, the same house and the same lawn too,
But ask that window, "what happened to that pomegranate tree"?
The one which has just been blown away by the wind, was a leaf of heart.
Written by tears at places, smudged by tears at places.
The letter on watch at many places were planted moons of two fragrant lips,
(The very same letter) Must be lying under the dust on some forgotten ledge.
Due tiredness if she fell asleep in my arms for a while, so what, then?
Just now I have seen the moon too stooped over some branch of flowers.
After cutting the sand for quite a few miles, some wave has set the flowers on bloom,
(This side) Some tree standing near the river, has been dying of thirst.

Bashir Badr

ये मेरा ज़र्फ़[1] भी शायद किसी नज़र में रहे,
कि सारे ख़्वाब बिखर कर भी चश्म-ए-तर[2] में रहे।
न मेरा ग़म कोई समझा, न मैंने समझाया,
वो अश्क हूँ जो किसी चश्म-ए-मोअतबर[3] में रहे।
ये आरज़ू ही तबाही का पेशलफ़्ज़[4] बनी,
किसी नज़र में रहें और कोई नज़र में रहे।
'वसीम' कैसे मिरी मन्ज़िलें क़रीब आतीं,
तमाम उम्र इरादे मिरे सफ़र में रहे।

वसीम बरेलवी

1.क्षमता 2.भीगी हुई आँख 3.विश्वसनीय आँख 4.भूमिका

Ye mera zarf bhee shaayad kisee nazar mein rahe,
Ki saare khawwab bikhar kar bhee chashme-tar mein rahe.
Na mera gham koee samjha, na maine samjhaaya,
Wo ashk hoon jo kisi chashme-moatbar mein rahe.
Ye aarzoo hee tabaahee ka peshlafz banee,
Kisee nazar mein rahein aur koee nazar mein rahe.
'Waseem' kaise miree manzilein qareeb aateen,
Tamaam umr iraade mire safar mein rahe.

Perhaps this fortitude of mine may also dwell in some eye,
(For) All my dreams even after getting shattered, remained in moist eyes.
Nobody unerstood my grief, nor I ever explained,
I am that teardrop that dwells in a reliable eye.
This yearning alone became the foreword of (my) destruction,
To remain in someone's eyes and someone to remain in my eyes.
O, 'Waseem'! how my destinations could have come near me,
Throughout the life all my resolves remained in transit.

Waseem Bareilvi

सिलसिला और भी कुछ ग़म का बढ़ाया जाए,
इस बियाबां[1] को समन्दर से मिलाया जाए,
जिस में हम लोग चराग़ों की तरह जलते हैं,
आओ वो शहर ज़माने को दिखाया जाए।
अपने क़ब्ज़े में तो ज़ख़्मों की बड़ी दौलत है,
क्यों न फिर वक़्त का सब कर्ज़ चुकाया जाए।
दिल मे इस क़द्र तिरे दर्द को रख लेता हूँ,
जैसे घर में किसी मुजरिम[2] को छुपाया जाए।
मुझसे खुद अपना पता पूछ रहा था इक दिन
हाए! वो शख़्स[3] भुलाए ना भुलाया जाए।
मैं कोई राज़ की तहरीर[4] नही हूँ 'जामी',
बंद कमरे मे जिसे लाके जलाया जाए।

ख़ुरशीद अहमद जामी

1.वीराना जंगल 2.अपराधी 3.इन्सान,आदमी 4.लिखावट

Silsila aur bhee kuchh gham ka badhaaya jaaye,
Is biyaabaan ko samandar se milaaya jaaye.
Jis mein hum log charaaghon kee tarah jalte hain,
Aao wo shahar zamaane ko dikhaaya jaaye.
Apne qabze mein tau zakhmon kee badhee daulat hai,
Kyon na phir waqt ka sab qarz chukaaya jaaye.
Dil mein is qadr tire dard ko rakh leta hoon,
Jaise ghar mein kisi mujrim ko chhupaaya jaaye.
Mujhse khud apna pata poochh raha tha ik din,
Haaye! wo shaksh bhulaaye na bhulaaya jaaye.
Main koee raaz kee tahreer naheen hoon 'Jaamee',
Band kamre mein jise laake jalaaya jaaye.

Let us increase the intensity of sorrow some more,
Let us introduce this deserted-forest to the ocean.
Come, let us show to the world that city,
In which we people burn like the earthen-lamps.
Under our control we do have a huge asset of wounds,
Then why not repay the entire debt of time.
I stash your sorrow in my heart in such a way,
Like hiding a criminal in the house,
One day (some one) was asking his own address from me,
Alas! inspite of best efforts I am unable to forget that person.
O! 'Jaamee', I am no document of some secrecy,
Which is to be burnt in a closed room.

Khursheed Ahmad 'Jaamee'

मेरे दुख की कोई दवा न करो,
मुझको मुझसे अभी जुदा[1] न करो।
नाखुदा[2] को खुदा कहा है तो फिर,
डूब जाओ, खुदा-खुदा ना करो।
ये सिखाया है दोस्ती ने हमें,
दोस्त बनकर कभी वफ़ा न करो।

इश्क़ है इश्क़ ये मज़ाक़ नहीं,
चन्द लम्हों[3] में फ़ैसला न करो।
आशिक़ी हो कि बन्दगी[4] 'फ़ाकिर'
बेदिली[5] से तो इब्तिदा[6] न करो।

सुदर्शन फ़ाकिर

1.अलग 2.मल्लाह 3.पलों 4.पूजा 5.अनिच्छा से 6.शुरूआत

Mere dukh kee koyee dawa na karo,
Mujhko mujhse abhee juda na karo.
Naakhuda ko khuda kaha hai tau phir,
Doob jaao, khuda-khuda na karo.
Ye sikhaaya hai dostee ne humein,
Dost ban kar kabhee wafa na karo.
Ishq hai ishq ye mazaaq naheen,
Chand lamhon mein faisla na karo.
Aashiqee ho ki bandgee 'Faakir',
Bedilee se tau ibtida na karo.

Do not give any medicine to heal my pain,
Do not separate me from myself as yet.
Since (you) have proclaimed the boatman as God, then,
Get drowned, "Don't cry O, God! O, God!"
Friendship has taught me this,
After becoming friend, never exercise loyalty.
Love is love, it is no joke,
Don't take decision in few seconds.
Be it love or worship, O 'Faakir'!
At least don't begin without putting your heart into it.

Sudarshan 'Faakir'

दुआ करो कि ये पौधा सदा हरा ही लगे,
उदासियों में भी चेहरा खिला-खिला ही लगे।
वो ज़ाफ़रानी[1] पुलोवर[2] उसी का हिस्सा है,
कोई जो दूसरा पहने तो दूसरा ही लगे।
अजीब शख़्स है, नाराज़ होके हसँता है,
मैं चाहता हूँ, खफ़ा[3] हो तो वो खफ़ा ही लगे।
हज़ारों भेस में फिरते हैं रोज़ राम-ओ-रहीम,
कोई ज़रूरी नहीं है, भला भला ही लगे।

बशीर बद्र

1.पीला या केसरी रंग 2.स्वेटर 3.नाराज़

Dua karo ki ye paudha sada hara hee lage,
Udaasiyon mein bhee chehra khila-khila hee lage.
Wo zaafraani pulover usee ka hissa hai,
Koee jo doosra pahne tau doosra hee laga.
Ajeeb shakhs hai, naaraaz hoke hansta hai.
Main chaahta hoon, khafa ho tau wo khafa hee lage.
Hazaaron bhes mein phirte hain roz Raam-O-Raheem,
Koee zarooree naheen hai, bhala bhala hee lage.

(Let us) Pray that this plant may look green for ever,
May (her) face remain beaming with happinesss even among sorrows.
That saffron coloured pullover is a part of her alone,
If someone else were to put it on, that someone would look different.
(She) Is a strange person, laughs on getting angry,
I want that she should look angry when angry.
Everyday Raamaas and Raheems roam in thousand disguise,
It is not mandatory that a good soul should appear good only.

Bashir Badr

अब ख़ुशी है, न कोई दर्द रुलाने वाला,
हमने अपना लिया हर रंग, ज़माने वाला।
उसको रुख़सत[1] तो किया था मुझे मालूम न था,
सारा घर ले गया, घर छोड़ के जाने वाला।
इक मुसाफ़िर[2] के सफ़र जैसी है सबकी दुनियाँ,
कोई जल्दी में, कोई देर से जानेवाला।
एक बेचेहरा[3] सी उम्मीद है, चेहरा-चेहरा,
जिस तरफ़ देखिये आने को है, आने वाला।

निदा फ़ाज़ली

1.विदा 2.यात्री 3.बिना चेहरे की

Ab khushee hai, na koyee dard rulaane waala,
Humne apna liya har rang, zamaane waala.
Usko rukhsat tau kiya tha mujhe maaloom na tha,
Saara ghar le gaya, ghar chhodh ke jaane waala.
Ik musaafir ke safar jaisee hai sabkee duniyaan,
Koyee jaldee mein, koyee der se jaane waala.
Ek be-chehra see ummeed hai, chehra-chehra,
Jis taraf dekhiye aane ko hai, aane waala.

Now, neither happiness is there nor any pain to make me cry,
(After) I have adopted every colour of this world.
While giving her farewell, it had not occured to me,
That the one leaving the house would carry away the entire life of the house hold.
(Over here) Everyone's world is like the journey of a traveller,
Some in quick time, others a little later will depart.
A faceless hope prevails on every face,
Whichever direction you look into, someone is about to arrive.

Nida Fazli

ग़म रात-दिन रहे तो ख़ुशी भी कभी रही,
इक बेवफ़ा से अपनी बड़ी दोस्ती रही।
उनसे मिलन की शाम घडी दो घड़ी रही,
और फिर जो रात आई तो बरसों खड़ी रही।
शामे-विसाल[1] दर्द ने जाते हुए कहा,
"कल फिर मिलेंगें दोस्त, अगर ज़िन्दगी रही"।
बस्ती उजड़ गई भी तो कीकर हरे रहे,
दर बंद हो गए भी तो खिड़की खुली रही।
'अख़तर' अगरचे चारों तरफ तेज धूप थी,
दिल पर ख़्याले-यार[2] की शबनम[3] पड़ी रही।

सईद अहमद अख़्तर

1.मिलन की शाम 2.प्रेयसी की याद 3.ओस

Gham raat-din rahe tau khushee bhee kabhee rahee,
Ik bewafa se apnee badhee dostee rahee.
Unse milan kee shaam ghadhee do ghadhee rahee,
Aur phir jo raat aayee tau barson khadhee rahee.
Shaame-wisaal dard ne jaate huye kaha,
"Kal phir milenge dost, agar zindagee rahee",
Bastee ujadh gayee bhee tau keekar hare rahe,
Dar band ho gaye bhee tau khidhkee khulee rahee.
'Akhtar' agarche chaaron taraph tej dhoop thee,
Dil par khyaale-yaar kee shabnam padhee rahee.

If the sorrows stayed day in and day out, then joy too stayed at times,
I had a long lasting friendship with a disloyal one.
The night of union with her lasted for a minute or two,
After that when the night came, it stood standstill for years.
On the evening of union, while departing, the pain said,
"O, Friend! life willing, we will meet again tomorrow."
Even after the destruction of settlement, the thorny trees remained green,
Window remained open even after the closure of doors.
O, 'Akhtar! even though there was intense sunlight all around,
The heart remained covered with the dew of beloved's thought.

Saeed Ahmed Akhtar

हिज्र की शब नाला-ए-दिल[1] वो सदा देने लगे,
सुननेवाले रात कटने की दुआ देने लगे।
किस नज़र से आपने देखा दिले-मजरुह[2] को,
ज़ख़्म जो कुछ भर चले थे फिर हवा देने लगे।
जुज़[3] ज़मीने-कूए-जाना[4] कुछ नहीं पेशे-निगाह[5],
जिसका दरवाज़ा नज़र आया, सदा देने लगे।
बाग़बां ने आग दी जब आशियाने[6] को मेरे,
जिनपे तकिया[7] था वही पत्ते हवा देने लगे।
मुटठियों में ख़ाक लेकर दोस्त आए वक्ते-दफ़्न[8],
ज़िन्दगी भर की मुहब्बत का सिला देने लगे।
आईना हो जाए मेरा इश्क़ उनके हुस्न का,
क्या मज़ा हो दर्द अगर ख़ुद ही दवा देने लगे।

साक़िब लखनवी

1.दिल का रूदन 2.घायल दिल 3.सिवाय,अतिरिक्त 4.प्रेमिका की गली की ज़मीन 5.आँख के सामने 6.घोसला 7.सहारा,बुनियाद 8.दफ़न के समय

Hijr kee shab naalaa-e-dil wo sada dene lage,
Sun-ne waale raat katne kee dua dene lage.
Kis nazar se aapne dekha dile-majrooh ko,
Zakhm jo kuchh bhar chale the phir hawaa dene lage.
Juz zameene-kooe-jaana kuchh naheen peshe-nigaah,
Jiska darwaaza nazar aaya, sada dene lage.
Baaghwaan ne aag dee jab aashiyaane ko mere,
Jin pe takiya tha wahee patte hawa dene lage.
Muththhiyon mein khaak lekar dost aaye waqte-dafn,
Zindagee bhar kee muhabbat ka sila dene lage.
Aaeena ho jaaye mera ishq unke husn ka,
Kya maza ho dard agar khud hee dawa dene lage.

During the night of separation, the weeping heart emitted such (soulful) cries,
That the listeners started praying for the night to pass.
With what eyes did you look at the wounded heart,
The half-healed wounds started getting fresh again.
Apart from the land of beloved's lane, nothing else was in sight,
Who so ever's door became visible, (I) started giving a call,
When the gardener set my nest on fire,
The leaves, on which it was founded, started fannig the fire.
With dust in their fists, came the friends at the burial,
(And) Started giving the reward for the life long friendship.
Let my love become the mirror for her beauty,
What fun, if the pain itself starts giving medicine.

Saaqib Lucknavi

कभी तो आसमाँ से चाँद उतरे, जाम हो जाए
तुम्हारे नाम की एक खूबसूरत शाम हो जाए।
समन्दर के सफ़र में इस तरह आवाज दे हमको,
हवाएँ तेज़ हों और कश्तियों में शाम हो जाए।
मैं खुद भी एहतियातन[1] उस तरफ से कम गुजरता हूँ,
कोई मासूम क्यों मेरे लिए बदनाम हो जाए।
उजाले अपनी यादों के हमारे साथ रहने दो,
ना जाने किस गली में ज़िन्दगी की शाम हो जाए।

बशीर बद्र

1. सावधानीवश

Kabhee tau aasmaan se chaand utre, jaam ho jaaye,
Tumhaare naam kee ek khoobsoorat shaam ho jaaye.
Samandar ke safar mein is tarah aawaaz de humko,
Hawaaein tez hon aur Kashtiyon mein shaam ho jaaye.
Main khud bhee aihtiyaatan us taraf se kam guzarta hoon,
Koee maasoom kyon mere liye badnaam ho jaaye
Ujaale apnee yaadon ke humaare saath rahne do,
Na jaane kis galee mein zindgee kee shaam ho jaaye.

Someday let the moon come-down and transform into a drink,
Let there be a beautiful evening dedicated to you.
During the seafaring, call me in such a way,
That the winds may speed up and the evening dawns on the boats.
As a precaution I myself rarely pass through that side,
Why should an innocent become infamous because of me.
Let the glows of your memories stay with me,
One never knows in which lane the life may reach its evening.

Bashir Badr

वो नामुराद[1] हूँ मैं जहाने-ख़राब[2] में,
जिसने किया शबाब[3] का मातम शबाब में।
ऐ शैख हमसे बादा-कशाने-शिकस्ता-दिल[4],
पीते है आँसुओं को मिलाकर शराब में।
महसूस हो भी जाए तो होता नही बयां,
नाजुक सा फ़र्क है जो गुनाहो-सवाब[5] में।
महशर[6] मे आप वाकई होगें, तो रोजे-हश्र[7],
तबदील क्यो न होगा शबे-माहताब[8] में
रहमत ने मेरा जज़्बा-ए-इख़्लास[9] देखकर,
सारे गुनाह कर दिए शामिल सवाब में।
ऐ 'शाद' जिन्दगी में जिन्हें कोई ग़म नहीं,
वो भी तो खुश नहीं है जहाने-खराब[10] में।

नरेश कुमार शाद

1.भाग्यहीन 2.ख़राब संसार 3.ज़वानी 4.टूटे हुए दिल वाले शराबी 5.पाप-पुन्य
6.जवाब देही का दिन 7.प्रलय के दिन 8.चांदनी रात 9.निष्कपट भाव

Wo naamuraad hoon mein jahaane-kharaab mein,
Jisne kiya shabaab ka maatam shabaab mein.
Aye, sheikh! humse baadaa-kashaane-shikastaa-dil,
Peete hain aansuon ko mila kar sharaab mein.
Mahsoos ho bhee jaaye tau hota naheen bayaan,
Naajuk sa fark hai jo gunaaho-sawaab mein.
Mahshar mein aap waaqaee honge, tau roze-hashr,
Tabdeel kyon na hoga shabe-maahtaab mein.
Rahmat ne mera jazbaa-e-ikhlaas dekh kar,
Saare gunaah kar diye shaamil sawaab mein.
Aye, 'Shaad'! zindagee mein jinhein koee gham naheen,
Wo bhee tau khush naheen hain jahaane-kharaab mein.

I am that unlucky one in this bad world,
Who had to mourn (own) youth in the prime of life.
O, old wise man! broken hearted drunkard like us,
Drink wine by mixing (our) tears in it.
One may be able to feel it yet it is not possible to explain,
The subtle difference between the sin and the virtue.
You too in real will be present on the judgement day,
Wouldn't it get converted into a full moon night.
The divine favour, after taking my selfless attitude into account,
Has included all (my) sins in virtues.
O, 'Shaad' ! people who do not have any sorrows in the life,
They too are not happy in this woeful world.

Naresh Kumar 'Shaad'

मैं सोचता हूँ, कहीं साथ छूट जायेगा,
ये तेरा ग़म भी कहाँ तक मुझे निभायेगा।
कली की तरह खिलो, खिलते ही बिखर जाओ,
ये शर्त है, तो भला कौन मुस्करायेगा।
शराब-ख़ाने[1] के बाहर का हाल मत पूछो,
तुम्हारे हाथ से पैमाना छूट जायेगा।
हमारे शैरों में इक दौर[2] सांस लेता है,
'वसीम' कैसे ज़माना हमें भुलायेगा।

वसीम बरेलवी

1. मधुशाला 2. युग

Main sochta hoon, kaheen saath chhooth jaayega,
Ye tera gham bhee kahaan tak mujhe nibhaayega.
Kalee kee tarah khilo, khilte hee bikhar jaao,
Ye shart hai tau bhala kaun muskaraayega.
Sharaab-khaane ke baahar ka haal mat poochho,
Tumhaare haath se paimaana chhoth jaayega.
Hamaare shairon mein ik daur saans leta hai,
'Waseem' kaise zamaana hamein bhulaayega.

I contemplate that somewhere our companionship will terminate,
Even your sorrow, how long will it be able to cope up with me.
Bloom like a bud, and immediatly after blooming get scattered,
If this is the binding, well, then who will (ever) smile.
Do not ask about the state of affairs prevailing outside the tavern,
The cup of wine will slip from you hands.
An era breathes within my couplets,
O, 'Waseem', how this world will ever be able to forget me.

Waseem Bareilvi

इस अंधेरे के सुनसान जंगल में हम,
डगमगाते रहे मुस्कराते रहे।
रौशनी की तरह लड़खड़ाते रहे,
पर क़दम अपने आगे बढ़ाते रहे।
अजनबी शहर में अजनबी रास्ते,
मेरी तन्हाई पर मुस्कराते रहे।
मैं बहुत देर तक यूँ ही चलता रहा,
तुम बहुत देर तक याद आते रहे।
कल कुछ ऐसा हुआ मैं बहुत थक गया,
इसलिए सुन के भी अनसुनी कर गया।
कितनी यादों के भटके हुए कारवाँ,
दिल के ज़ख़्मों के दर खटखटाते रहे।
ज़हर मिलता रहा ज़हर पीते रहे।
रोज मरते रहे रोज जीते रहे।
ज़िन्दगी भी हमें आज़माती रही।
और हम भी उसे आज़माते रहे।
ज़ख़्म जब भी कोई ज़हनो-दिल[1] पर लगा,
ज़िन्दगी की तरफ इक दरीचा[2] खुला।
हम भी गोया[3] किसी साज के तार हैं,
चोट खाते रहे गुनगुनाते रहे।

मासूम रज़ा राही

1.दिमाग़ और दिल 2.खिड़की 3.शायद

Is andhere ke sunsaan jungle mein hum,
Dagmagaate rahe, muskraate rahe,
Raushnee kee tarah ladhkhadhaate rahe,
Par qadam apne aage badhaate rahe.
Ajnabee shahar mein ajnabee raaste,
Meree tanhaaee par muskraate rahe.
Main bahut der tak yoon hee chalta raha,
Tum bahut der tak yaad aate rahe.
Kal kuchh aisa huya, main bahut thak gaya,
Is liye sun ke bhee ansunee kar gaya.
Kitnee yaadon ke bhatke huye kaarwaan,
Dil ke zakhmon ke dar khatkhataate rahe.
Zahar milta raha, zahar peete rahe,
Roz marte rahe, roz jeete rahe.
Zindagee bhee humhein aazmaatee rahee,
Aur hum bhee use aazmaate rahe.
Zakhm jab bhee koee zahan-o-dil pe laga,
Zindagee kee taraf ik dareecha khula,
Hum bhee goya kisee saaz ke taar hain,
Chot khaate rahe, gungunaate rahe.

In this deserted jungle of darkness,
I kept on staggering yet smiling.
Like the flickering light I kept on faltering
Yet kept going ahead.
In the strange city, the strange paths,
Kept smiling at my lonliness.
I kept walking this way for quite sometime,
You kept coming to my mind for quite sometime.
Yesterday a strange thing happened, I got very tired,
And perhaps that's why, I did hear yet ignored.
The sound of strayed caravans of memories,
Which kept knocking at the doors of my heart's wounds.
Kept getting poison, kept on drinking it,
Kept dying every day, kept on living every day.
Life. kept testing me,
I too. kept testing her.
Whenever any wound struck my mind and heart,
It was like opening of a window towards the life itself.
As if I was the string of a musical instrument,
Kept getting hurt and kept on humming.

Maasoom Raza 'Rahi'

किसी से मेरी मंजिल का पता पाया नहीं जाता,
जहाँ मै हूँ फ़रिशतों से वहाँ जाया नहीं जाता।
मेरे टूटे हुए पाए-तलब[1] का मुझपे एहसाँ है,
तुम्हारे दर से उठकर अब कहीं जाया नहीं जाता।
चमन तुमसे इबारत्त[2] है बहारें तुमसे ज़िन्दा हैं,
तुम्हारे सामने फूलों से मुस्कराया नहीं जाता।
हर एक दाग़े-तमन्ना[3] को कलेजे से लगाता हूँ,
कि घर आई हुई दौलत को ठुकराया नहीं जाता।
मुहब्बत के लिए कुछ खास दिल मख़सूस[4] होते हैं।
ये वो नग़मा है जो हर साज़ पे गाया नहीं जाता।

मख़मूर देहलवी

1.इच्छा रूपी पांव 2.तुम ही उपवन हो 3.इच्छा का दाग़ 4.चुने हुए

Kisee se meree manzil ka pata paaya naheen jaata,
Jahaan mein hoon, farishton se wahaan jaaya naheen jaata.
Mere toote huye paa-e-talab ka mujhpe aihsaan hai,
Tumhaare dar se uthhkar ab kaheen jaaya naheen jaata.
Chaman tumse ibaarat hai, bahaarein tumse zinda hain,
Tumhaare saamne phoolon se murjhaaya naheen jaata.
Har ek daaghe-tamanna ko kaleje se lagaata hoon,
Ki ghar aayee huee daulat ko thhukraaya naheen jaata.
Muhabbat ke liye kuchh khaas dil makhsoos hote hain,
Ye wo naghma hai jo har saaz pe gaaya naheen jaata.

Nobody has been able to locate my destination,
Where I am, the angels are unable to reach there.
This broken foot of desire has done me a favour,
I am unable to get up and leave from your door steps now.
The garden exists because of you, the spring is alive because of you,
The flowers dare not fade in front of you.
I nurture every unfulfilled wish close to my heart,
Because one does not turn away the wealth coming home.
For love, some special hearts are earmarked,
This is that song which is not sung on every instrument.

'Makhmoor' Dehlvi

हज़ार गर्दिशे-शाम-ओ-सहर[1] से गुज़रें हैं
वो क़ाफ़िले जो तेरी रह-गुज़र से गुज़रे हैं।
अभी हवस को मयस्सर[2] नहीं दिलों का गुदाज़[3],
अभी ये लोग मुक़ामे-नज़र[4] से गुज़रें है।
हर एक नक़्श[5] पे था तेरे नक़्शे-पा[6] का गुमान[7]
क़दम-क़दम पे तेरी रह-गुज़र से गुज़रे हैं।
न जाने कौन सी मंज़िल पे जा के रूक जाएँ,
नज़र के क़ाफ़िले दिवार-ओ-दर[8] से गुज़रें हैं।
कुछ और फैल गईं दर्द की कठिन राहें,
ग़मे-फ़िराक़[9] के मारे जिधर से गुजरे हैं।
जहाँ सरूर[10] मयस्सर था जाम-ओ-मय[11] के बग़ैर,
वो मयकदे[12] भी हमारी नजर से गुज़रें है।

सूफ़ी ग़ुलाम मुस्तफ़ा तबस्सुम

1.काल चक्र 2.प्राप्त था नसीब 3.कोमलता 4.दृष्टि स्तर 5. निशान 6.पैर का निशान 7.भ्रम 8.दीवार और दरवाज़ा 9.विरह से दुखी 10.नशा 11.शराब और शराब का प्याला 12.शराबखाने

Hazaar gardishe-shaam-o-sahar se guzre hain,
Wo qaafile jo teree rahguzar se guzre hain.
Abhee hawas ko maissar naheen dilon ka gudaaz,
Abhee ye log muqaame-nazar se guzre hain.
Har ek naqsh pe tha tere naqshe-pa ka gumaan,
Qadam-qadam pe teree rahguzar se guzre hain.
Na jaane kaun see manzil pe jaake ruk jaayein,
Nazar ke qaafile diwaar-o-dar se guzre hain.
Kuchh aur phail gayeen dard kee kathhin raahein,
Ghame-firaaq ke maare jidhar se guzre hain.
Jahaan saroor maissar tha jaam-o-mai ke baghair,
Wo maikade bhee humaaree nazar se guzre hain.

They have travelled through a thousand time-frames of evening and morning,
The caravans which have passed through your street.
The lust is yet to achieve the sensitivity of hearts,
These people have passed through the peripheri only.
At every step there was the false sense of your foot-print,
Each step has taken me through your street.
God knows at which destination these may get settled,
The caravans of (my) eyes have (just) passed through some walls and doors.
The difficult tracks of pain have stretched further,
Whenever the separation-stricken folks have treaded on them.
Where intoxication could be achieved without a cup of wine,
Those taverns too have passed through my eyes.

Soofee Ghulaam Mustafa 'Tabassum'

अपने होठों, पर सजाना चाहता हूँ,
आ तुझे मैं गुनगुनाना चाहता हूँ।
कोई आँसू तेरे दामन पर गिरा कर,
बूंद को मोती बनाना चाहता हूँ।
थक गया मैं करते-करते याद तुझको,
अब तुझे मैं याद आना चाहता हूँ।
छा रहा है सारी बस्ती में अंधेरा,
रौशनी हो, घर जलाना चाहता हूँ।
आखिरी हिचकी तेरे जानूँ[1] पे आए,
मौत भी मैं शायराना चाहता हूँ।

क़तील शिफ़ाई

1. जाँघ

Apne honthon par sajaana chaahta hoon,
Aa tujhe main gungunaana chaahta hoon.
Koyee aansoo tere daaman par gira kar,
Boond ko motee banaana chaahta hoon.
Thak gaya main karte-karte yaad tujhko,
Ab tujhe main yaad aana chaahta hoon.
Chha raha hai saaree bastee mein andhera,
Raushnee ho, ghar jalaana chaahta hoon,
Aakhiree hichkee tere jaanoon pe aaye,
Maut bhee main shaairaana chhahta hoon.

(I) Want to adorn you on my lips,
Come, I wish to hum you.
After dropping one tear on your hem,
I wish to convert a drop into a pearl,
I have become tired of remembering you nonstop,
Now, I want myself to be remembered by you.
Darkness is descending over the entire town,
For brightness, I wish to burn (my own) house.
Let the last hiccup come (to me) in your lap,
I want the death, too, to be poetic.

'Qateel Shifaai'

आदमी, आदमी को क्या देगा,
जो भी देगा वही खुदा देगा
मेरा क़ातिल ही मेरा मुँसिफ़[1] है,
क्या मेरे हक़[2] में फैसला देगा।
ज़िन्दगी को क़रीब से देखो,
इसका चेहरा, तुम्हें रुला देगा।
हमसे पूछो न दोस्ती का सिला[3],
दुश्मनों का भी दिल हिला देगा।
इश्क़ का ज़हर पी लिया 'फ़ाकिर'
अब मसीहा[4] भी क्या दवा देगा।

सुदर्शन फ़ाकिर

1.न्यायाधीश 2.पक्ष 3.परिणाम 4.चिकित्सक

Aadmee, aadmee ko kya dega,
Jo bhee dega, wahee khuda dega.
Mera qaatil hee mera munsif hai,
Kya mere haq mein faisla dega.
Zindagee ko qareeb se dekho,
Iska chehra tumhein rula dega.
Humse poochho na dostee ka sila,
Dushmanon ka bhee dil hila dega.
Ishq ka zahar pee liya 'Faakir',
Ab maseeha bhee kya dawa dega.

What can a human being give to another human being,
What ever is to be given, will be given by the God.
My killer herself is my judge,
Will she pronounce the judgement in my favour?
Watch the life from close quarters,
It's face will make you cry.
Don't ask me the reward of friendship,
The revelation will jolt even the enemies' heart to the core.
O, 'Faakir'! I have drunk the poison of love,
Now, what medicine the doctor can give?

'Sudarshan Faakir'

इक मुअम्मा[1] है समझने का न समझाने का,
ज़िन्दगी काहे को ख़्वाब है दीवाने का।
ज़िन्दगी भी तो पशेमां[2] है यहाँ लाके मुझे,
ढूढंती है कोई हीला[3] मेरे मर जाने का।
तूने देखा है कभी घर को बदलते हुए रंग,
आओ देखो ना तमाशा मेरे ग़मखाने[4] का।
अब इसे दार[5] पे ले जाके सुला दे साक़ी।
यूँ बहकना नहीं अच्छा तेरे दीवाने का।
दिल से पहुँचीं तो हैं आँखों में लहू की बूदें,
सिलसिला शीशे से मिलता तो है पैमाने का
हर नफ़स[7] उम्रे-गुज़श्ता[8] की है मय्यत[9] 'फ़ानी'
ज़िन्दगी नाम है मर-मर के जिये जाने का।

फ़ानी बदायूनी

1.पहेली 2.शर्मिन्दा 3.बहाना 4.दुखी घर 5.सूली 6.बोतल 7.सांस 8.बीती हुई उम्र 9.अर्थी

Ek muamma hai samjhne ka na samjhaane ka
Zindagee kaahe ko khwaab hai deewaane ka,
Zindagee bhee tau pashemaan hai yahaan laake mujhe,
Dhhoondhtee hai koee heela mere mar jaane ka
Toone dekha hai kabhee ghar ko badalte huye rang,
Aao, dekho na tamaasha mere ghamkhaane ka.
Ab ise daar pe le jaake sula de saaqee,
Yoon bahakna naheen achchha tere deewaane ka.
Dil se pahooncheen tau hain aankhon mein lahoo kee boonde,
Silsila sheeshe se milta tau hai paimaane ka.
Har nafas umre-guzashta kee hai mayyat 'Faanee',
Zindagee naam hai mar-mar ke jeeye jaane ka.

It is like a riddle, not to be understood, not to be explained,
Life is like a madman's dream.
Life too is shamefaced after bringing me here,
(And) Has been trying to find some excuse for my death.
Have you ever seen a house changing colours,
Come, why not have a look at my sad abode.
Barmaid!, now take him to the gallows and make him sleep,
This sort of craziness is not good on part of your lover.
From the heart, the blood drops have managed to reach the eyes,
There sure is a connection between the bottle and the goblet.
Every breath is the dead body of the age gone by O, 'Faani'!
Life is the name of resurrection after repeated deaths.

'Faani' Badayooni

है जुस्तजू कि ख़ूब से है खूबतर[1] कहाँ,
अब ठहरती है देखिए जाकर नज़र कहाँ।
यारब इस इख़्लात[2] का अजा़म हो बख़ैर[3],
था उसको हमसे रब्त[4] मगर इस क़दर कहाँ।
इक उम्र चाहिए कि गवारा हो नीशे-उम्र[5],
रखी है आज लज़्ज़ते-जख़्मे-जिगर[6] कहाँ।
हम जिसपे मर रहे हैं वो है बात ही कुछ और,
आलम[7] मे तुझसे लाख सही, तू मगर कहाँ।
'हाली'-निशाते-नग़्मा-ओ-मय[8] ढूंढते हो अब,
आए हो वक्ते-सुबह रहे रातभर कहाँ।

हाली

1.श्रेष्ठ 2.मेलमिलाप 3.शुभ 4.सम्बन्ध 5.उम्र रूपी डंक 6.हदय के घाव का सुखद स्वाद 7.संसार 8.शराब और संगीत का आन्नद

Hai justjoo ki khoob se hai khoobtar kahaan,
Ab thhahartee hai dekhiye jaakar nazar kahaan.
Yaarab is ikhilaat ka anzaam ho bakhair,
Tha usko humse rabt, magar is qadar kahaan.
Ek umr chaahiye ki gawaara ho neeshe-umr,
Rakhee hai aaj lazzate-zakhme-jigar kahaan,
Hum jispe mar rahe hain wo hai baat hee kuchh aur,
Aalam mein tujhse laakh sahee, too magar kahaan.
'Haalee' nishaate-naghma-o-mai dhhoondhte ho ab,
Aaye ho waqte-subah, rahe raat bhar kahaan.

Search is on for locating the one better than the best,
Let us see where the eyes reach and get settled.
O, God! let the end result of our frequent meetings better be good.
She was close to me earlier also but not this much.
It requires ages to get used to the sting of life,
These days who has the gumption to relish the sweet pain of the heart's wound.
I have been dying for someone, who has something unique about her,
There may be a million like you in this world, but not you.
O, 'Haali' ! looking for the bliss of song and wine, now?
You have come at the wee hours, where were you all night?

'Haali'

क्या दुख है समन्दर को बता भी नहीं सकता,
आँसू की तरह आँख तक आ भी नहीं सकता।
तू छोड़ रहा है, तो ख़ता इसमें तिरी क्या,
हर शख़्स मिरा साथ निभा भी नहीं सकता।
प्यासे रहे जाते हैं, ज़माने के सवालात,
किसके लिए ज़िन्दा हूँ, बता भी नहीं सकता।
घर ढूंढ रहे हैं मिरा रातों के पुजारी,
मैं हूँ कि चराग़ों को बुझा भी नहीं सकता।
वैसे तो इक आँसू ही बहाकर मुझे ले जाये,
ऐसे कोई तूफ़ान हिला भी नहीं सकता।

वसीम बरेलवी

Kya dukh hai samandar ko bata bhee naheen sakta,
Aansoo kee tarah aankh tak aa bhee naheen sakta.
Too chhodh raha hai, tau khata ismein tiree kya,
Har shakhs mira saath nibha bhee naheen sakta.
Pyaase rahe jaate hain, zamaane ke sawaalaat,
Kiske liye zinda hoon, bata bhee naheen sakta.
Ghar dhoondh rahe hai mira raaton ke pujaaree,
Main hoon ki charaagon ko bujha bhee naheen sakta.
Waise tau ak aansoo hee bahakar mujhe lejaaye,
Aise koee toofaan hila bhee naheen sakta.

What is (my) agony, can not even tell it to the ocean,
(I) can not even come up to the eye like a tear.
You are leaving me, then what is your fault in doing so,
Not everybody can keep pace with me.
All queries of the world, remain unquenched,
For whom I am living, can not reveal even this much.
Worshippers of the darkness have been searching for my house,
(Look at me) I can't even extinguish the earthen lamps.
That way even a teardrop may sweep me away,
This way even a cyclone can not budge me.

'Waseem' Bareilvi

कुछ तुझको खबर है हम क्या-क्या, ऐ शोरिशे-दौराँ[1] भूल गये,
वो .ज़ुल्फ़े-परीशां भूल गये वो दीदा-ए-गिरियां[2] भूल गये।
ऐ शौके़-नज़ारा क्या कहिए, नज़रो में कोई सूरत ही नहीं,
ऐ जौके़-तसव्वुर[3] क्या कीजे, हम सूरते-जानां भूल गये।
अब गुल से नजर मिलती ही नहीं, अब दिल की कली खिलती ही नहीं,
ऐ फ़स्ले-बहारां रुख़सत[4] हो, हम लुत्फ़े बहांरा[5] भूल गये।
सबका तो मुदावा[6] कर डाला, अपना ही मुदावा कर न सके।
सबके तो गिरेबां सी डाले, अपना ही गिरेबां भूल गये।
ये अपनी वफ़ा का आलम है, अब उनकी जफ़ा[7] को क्या कहिये,
इक नशतरे-ज़हर-आगी[8] रखकर नज़दीके-रगे-जां[9] भूल गये।

मजाज़ लख़नवी

1.ससाँर के शोर, हंगामे 2.सजल नेत्र 3.ख़याल का शौक़ 4.विदा
5.बहारों का आनन्द 6.इलाज 7.जुल्म 8.ज़हर बुझी छुरी 9.सांस की नली के निकट

Kuchh tujhko khabar hai hum kya-kya, aye shorishe-dauraan bhool gaye,
Wo zulfe-pareeshaan bhool gaye, wo deeda-e-giriyaan bhool gaye.
Aye shauqe-nazaara kya kahiye, nazaron mein koee soorat hee naheen,
Aye jouqe-tasawwur kya keeje, hum soorate-jaana bhool gaye.
Ab gul se nazar miltee hee naheen, ab dil kee kalee khiltee hee naheen,
Aye fasle-bahaaran rukhsat ho, hum lutfe-bahaaraan bhool gaye.
Sabka tau mudaawa kar daala, apna hee mudaawa kar na sake,
Sab ke tau girebaan see daale, apna hee girebaan bhool gaye.
Ye apnee wafa ka aalam hai, ab unkee jafa ko kya kahiye,
Ek nashtare-zahar-aangeeh rakh kar nazdeeke-rage-jaan bhool gaye.

Do you have any idea, what all shingigs of this world I have forgotten,
(I) Have forgotten those perplexed tresses, those tearful eyes.
What to talk about the craze for her sight, there is not even one figure in my eyes these days,
About remembering someone in inagination, I have even forgotten the contours of my beloved.
Now the gaze doesnot fall on the flower, nor does the bud of heart bloom,
O, spring season! go away, I have forgotten the bliss of spring.
I have found the cure for everyone else, couldn't cure only myself,
Have sewen eyeryone's collar, forgotten only own collar.
This is the state of my faithfulness, what to talk about her cruelty,
That (I) knowingly kept a poisoned knife close to (my) jugular vein and forgot.

'Majaaz' Luckhnavi

इन्तिहाए-ग़म[1] में मुझको मुस्कराना आ गया,
हाथ इख़्फ़ाऐ-मुहब्बत[2] का बहाना आ गया।
इस तरफ इक आशियाने[3] की हक़ीक़त[4] खुल गई,
उस तरफ उस शोख़[5] को बिजली गिराना आ गया।
रो दिये वो खुद भी मेरे गिरिया-ए-पैहम[6] पे आज,
अब हक़ीक़त में मुझे आँसू बहाना आ गया।
मेरी ख़ाके-दिल[7] भी आख़िर उनके काम आ ही गई,
कुछ नहीं तो उनको दामन ही बचाना आ गया।
वो ख़राशे-दिल[8] जो 'जज़्बी' मेरी हमराज़ थी,
आज उसे भी ज़ख़्म बन कर मुस्कराना आ गया।

जज़्बी

1.दुख की पराकाष्ठा 2.मुहब्बत छिपाने का बहाना 3.घोसला 4.असलियत 5.चंचल,सुन्दरी 6.लगातर रुदन 7.दिल की राख़ 8.दिल की फाँस

Intihaaye-gham mein mujhko muskaraana aa gaya,
Haath ikhfaaye-muhabbat ka bahaana aa gaya.
Is taraf ik aashiyaane kee haqeeqat khul gayee,
Us taraf us shokh ko bijlee giraana aagaya.
Ro diye wo khud bhee mere giriyaa-e-paiham pe aaj,
Ab haqeeqat mein mujhe aansoo bahaana aagaya
Meree khaake-di bhee aakhir unke kaam aa hee gayee,
Kuch naheen tau unko daaman hee bachaana aagaya.
Wo kharaashe-dil jo 'Jazbi'! meree humraaz thee,
Aaaj use bhee zakhm ban kar muskaraana aagaya.

In the ultimate sorrow I have learnt to smile,
(This way) I have acquired an excuse to hide my love.
This side, the reality of a nest has been revealed,
That side, that beautiful coquette has learnt how to drop lightnings.
She herself cried today on my continuous wailing,
In reality now only have I learnt to shed tears.
At last the ashes of my heart proved to be of some use to her,
If nothing else, then at least she has learnt to safeguard her hem.
O, 'Jazbee' ! that hidden thorn in my heart, which used to share my secret,
Today that too has learnt to smile by becoming an open wound.

'Jazbi'

किसी कली ने भी देखा न आँख भरके मुझे,
गुज़र गई जरसे-गुल[1] उदास करके मुझे।
मैं सो रहा था किसी याद के शबिस्ताँ[2] में,
जगा के छोड़ गए क़ाफ़िले सहर के मुझे।
मैं तेरे दर्द की तुग़ियानियों[3] में डूब गया,
पुकारते रहे तारे उभर-उभर के मुझे।
तेरे फ़िराक़ की रातें कभी न भूलेंगीं,
मज़े मिले इन्हीं रातों में उम्र भर के मुझे।
जरा सी देर ठहरने दे ऐ ग़मे-दुनियाँ,
बुला रहा है कोई बाम[4] से उतर के मुझे।
फिर आज आई थी इक मौजे-हवा-ए-तरब[5]
सुना गई है फ़साने इधर-उधर के मुझे।

नसीर काज़मी

1.फूलों के खिलने की अवाज़ 2.सोने का कमरा 3.बाढ़ों 4.छत या कोठा 5.हर्ष की लहर

Kisee kalee ne bhee dekha na aankh bhar ke mujhe,
Guzar gayee jarse-gul udaas kar ke mujhe.
Main so raha tha kisee yaad ke shabistaan mein,
Jaga ke chodh gaye qaafile sahar ke mujhe.
Main tere dard ki tughiyaanion me doob gaya,
Pukaarte rahe taare ubhar-ubhar ke mujhe.
Tere firaaq kee raatein kabhee na bhooleingee,
Maze mile inheen raaton mein umr bhar ke mujhe.
Jaraa see der thhaharne de aye ghame-duniyaan,
Bula raha hai koee baam se utar ke mujhe.
Phir aaj aayee thee ik mauje-hawa-e-tarab,
Suna gayee hai fasaane idhar-udhar ke mujhe.

No bud ever saw me with wistful eyes,
The rustle of blossoming flower made me sad and passed.
I had been deep in slumber in the fold of some memory,
The morning caravans woke me up and left.
I got drowned in the flood of your sorrow,
The stars kept me calling from the heights.
I will never forget the nights of separation from you,
These very nights had given me the best times of life.
Let me stay for some more time, O woeful world!
Having descended from the roof, someone has been calling for me.
Today again a wave of ecstasy in the form of a breeze had come this side,
And had recounted tales of varied places (related to me)

'Naseer kazmi'

हरचन्द[1] के अब तुमसे मुलाक़ात ना होगी,
पर दिल से भुलाने की तुम्हें बात ना होगी।
तुम मद्दे-मुक़ाबिल[2] हो मगर जान हो मेरी,
मैं चाल चलूँगा तो तुम्हें मात[3] ना होगी।
आँखों में घटाएँ तो उतर सकती हैं लेकिन,
इस अब्र[4] से जाना कभी बरसात ना होगी।
तुम जिस दिन मुझसे मिलके ना घर लौट के जाओ,
क्या ऐसी कोई शाम, कोई रात ना होगी?

फ़रहत शहज़ाद

1.माना 2.प्रतिद्वन्दी 3.शिकस्त 4.बादल

Harchand ke ab tumse mulaaqaat na hogee,
Par dil se bhulaane kee tumhe baat na hogee.
Tum madde-muqaabil ho, magar jaan ho meree,
Main chaal chaloonga tau tumhe maat na hogee.
Aankhon mein ghataayein tau utar saktee hain lekin,
Is abr se jaana kabhee barsaat na hogee.
Tum jis din mujhse milke na ghar laut ke jaao,
Kya aisee koee shaam, koee raat na hogee?

I know there is now no possibility of our meeting again,
However, there will not be any talk about forgetting you from heart.
Even though an opponent, you are my life,
Whatever move I make, will not culminate in your defeat.
It is possible that my eyes may get overcast,
But from these clouds there will never be any rain.
Will such An evening, such a night never be there for me,
In which you come to meet me never to return home.

Farhat Shahzaad

ख़ुश्क है आँखें पलक भी नम नहीं,
अब कोई आँसू शरीके-ग़म[1] नहीं।
जिसको लोग आपस में मिलकर बाँट लें,
ज़िन्दगी ऐसा तो तेरा ग़म नहीं।
ठोकरों से क्यूँ सकूने-दिल[2] नहीं,
ज़िन्दगी एक राह है मंज़िल नहीं।
और तदबीरें[3] मेरी नाकाम कर,
मै अभी तक़दीर[4] का क़ायल[5] नहीं।
छोड दो तुम भी मुझे सबकी तरह,
रास्तों मेरी कोई मंज़िल नहीं।
अपने माज़ी[6] को न दोहराओ 'वसीम',
सबके सीने में तुम्हारा दिल नहीं।

'वसीम बरेलवी'

1.दुख मे शामिल 2.दिल की शांति 3.कोशिशें 5.मानने वाला 6.भूतकाल

khushk hain aankhen palak bhee nam naheen,
Ab koee aansoo shareeke-gham naheen.
Jisko log aapas mein milkar baant lein,
Zindagee aisa tau tera gham naheen.
Thokron se kyun sakoone-dil naheen,
Zindagee ek raah hai manzil naheen.
Aur tadbeerein meree naakaam kar,
Main abhee taqdeer ka qaayal naheen,
Chhod do tum bhee mujhe sab kee tarah,
Raaston meree koee manzil naheen.
Apne maazee ko na dohraao 'Waseem',
Sabke seene mein tumhaara dil naheen.

Eyes are dry, eyelids too are devoid of dampness,
These days no tear is there to share the sorrow.
That which may be shared by people among themselves,
O! life, such is not your sorrow.
Foil more of my endeavours,
I am not a fatalist as yet,
You too must desert me like all others,
O! tracks, I have no destination.
'Waseem',! Do not repeat your past,
All others do not have a heart like yours.

'Waseem' Bareilvi

आशियाने[1] की बात करते हो,
दिल जलाने की बात करते हो।
सारी दुनियाँ के रजों-ग़म[2] दे कर,
मुस्कुराने की बात करते हो।
ज़िक्र मेरा सुना तो चिड़ के कहा,
"किस दीवाने की बात करते हो"!
हादिसा[3] था गुज़र गया होगा,
किसके चाहने की बात करते हो।
हमको अपनी ख़बर नही यारों,
तुम ज़माने की बात करते हो।

जावेद क़ुरैशी

1.घोसले 2.दर्द-दुख 3.दुर्घटना

Aashiyaane kee baat karte ho,
Dil jalaane kee baat karte ho.
Saaree duniyaan ke ranjo-gham de kar,
Muskuraane kee baat karte ho.
Zikr mera suna tau chidh ke kaha,
"Kis deewaane kee baat karte ho".
Haadisa tha guzar gaya hoga,
kiske chaahne kee baat karte ho.
Humko apnee khabar naheen yaaron,
Tum zamaane kee baat karte ho.

Your talking about the nest,
Is tantamount to burning of (my) heart.
After giving me gamut of worldly-woes,
You expect me to smile.
On hearing about my reference she got ragged and said,
" Why talk about the crazy man".
It was a mishap, must have passed,
Why talk about someone I had wanted once.
Friends! I do not have any news of myself,
(And) You are talking about the world.

'Jaaved ' Quraishi

मोहब्बत करने वाले कम ना होगें,
तेरी महफ़िल[1] में लेकिन हम न होगें।
ज़माने भर के ग़म या इक तेरा ग़म,
ये ग़म होगा तो कितने ग़म ना होगें।
दिलों की उलझने बढती रहेगीं,
अगर कुछ मशगले[2] बाहम[3] ना होगें।
अगर तू इत्तिफ़ाकन[4] मिल भी जाए,
तेरी .फुर्कत[5] के सदमे[6] कम न होगें।

हफ़ीज़ होशियारपुरी

1.सभा 2.पुराने प्रश्न 3.हल 4.अचानक 5.विद्रोह 6.झटके, दुख

Mohabbat-karne waale kam na honge,
Teree mahfil mein lekin hum na honge.
Zamaane bhar ke gham ya ek tera gham,
Ye gham hoga tau kitne gham na honge.
Dilon kee uljhanein badhhtee rahengee,
Agar kuchh mashghale baaham na honge,
Agar too ittifaakan mil bhee jaaye,
Teree furkat ke sadme kam na honge.

Number of people loving (You) will never decrease,
(However) I shall no more be there in your assembly.
Entire range of worldly woes vis-a-vis the sorrow on account of you,
If I have your sorrow, many other sorrows won't matter (to me).
Peplexities of heart will go on increasing,
If certain critical past issues are not resolved.
Even if by chance you happen to meet (me),
The traumas caused by separation from you will not decrease.

'Hafeez Hoshiyaarpuri'

तुम, और फ़रेब[1] खाओ बयाने-रक़ीब[2] से,
तुमसे तो कम गिला[3] है, ज़ियादा नसीब[4] से।
गोया तुम्हारी याद ही मेरा इलाज है,
रहता है पहरो ज़िक्र तुम्हारा तबील[5] से।
बर्बाद दिल का आखिरी सरमाया[6] थी उमीद,
वो भी तो तुमने छीन लिया मुझ ग़रीब से ।
धुधँला चली निगाह, दमे-बापसी[7] है अब,
आ पास आके देख लूँ तुझको क़रीब से।

'आग़ा हश्र'

1.धोका 2.शत्रु के बयान से 3.शिकायत 4.भाग्य 5.एकाँत 6.धन, पूँजी 7.लौटने का समय

Tum, aur fareb khaao bayaane-raqeeb se,
Tumse tau kam gila hai, ziaada naseeb se.
Goya tumhaaree yaad hee mera ilaaj hai,
Rahta hai pahron zikr tumhaara tabeel se.
Barbaad dil ka aakhiree sarmaaya thee umeed,
Wo bhee tau tumne chheen liya mujh ghareeb se.
Dhundhla-chalee nigaah, dame-baapasee hai ab,
Aa pass aa ke dekh-loon tujhko qareeb se.

You (of all people) getting swayed by the statement of rival,
I have less complaint against you, more against (my) own luck.
Looks as if your memory alone is my remedy,
(I) keep talking for hours about you with the solitude,
Hope was the last asset of the ravaged heart,
That too has been snatched away by you from poor me.
The eyes have started getting blurred, it is time to return,
Come near, let me see you from close quarters.

Agha Hashr

उसे समझने का कोई तो रास्ता निकले,
मैं चाहता भी यही था वह बेवफ़ा निकले।
किताबेमाज़ी[1] के औराक़[2] उलटके देख ज़रा,
न जाने कौन सा सफ़हा[3] मुड़ा हुआ निकले।
मैं तुझसे मिलता हूँ, तफ़सील[4] में नहीं जाता,
मेरी तरफ़ से तेरे दिल में जाने क्या निकले।
जो देखने में बहुत ही क़रीब लगता है,
उसी के बारे में सोचो तो फ़ासला निकले।
तमाम शहर की आँखों में सुर्ख़ शोले हैं,
'वसीम', घर से अब ऐसे में कोई क्या निकले।

वसीम बरेलवी

1.अतीत की किताब 2.पन्ने 3.पृष्ठ 4.विवरण (गहराई, विस्तार)

Use samajhne ka koee tau raasta nikle,
Main chaahta bhee yahee tha wah bewafa nikle.
Kitaabe-maazee ke auraaq ulat ke dekh zara,
Na jaane kaun sa safha muda hua nikle.
Main tujhse milta hoon, tafseel mein naheen jaata,
Meree taraf se tere dil mein jaane kya nikle.
Jo dekhne mein bahut hee qareeb lagta hai,
Usee ke baare mein socho tau faasla nikle.
Tamaam shahar kee aankhon mein surkh sholay hain,
'Waseem', ghar se ab aise mein koee kya nikle.

There ought to be some way to understand her true self,
I myself had wanted that she should turn out to be a disloyal one.
Turn the pages of the book of memories and see,
You may find an odd page folded somewhere in it.
I do meet you, (but) do not go into details,
God knows, what may be there in your heart for me.
From out side, one who appears to be very close,
When think about the same one, then you will come to know the real distance.
There are red flames in the eyes of entire town,
'Waseem' ! under these cirumstances, what is the idea of stepping out of the house

Waseem Bareilvi

दिन भर जितना चाहे घूमो, लेकिन इतना ध्यान रहे,
उसकी गली में मुड़ जाते हैं सारे रस्ते शाम के बाद।
यादों का लोबान[1] जलेगा दर्द की रूहें[2] नाचेगीं,
मन की हवेली में जागेगें सोने वाले शाम के बाद।
बचपन में जब जाग उठती थी, चाँद को छूने की ख़्वाहिश,[3]
माँ कहती थी, "ज़िद नहीं करते अच्छे बच्चे शाम के बाद"।
हिज्र[4] की इन लम्बी रातों में जश्ने-चरागाँ[5] क्या मागें,
दिल ख़ुद ही जलने लगता है, धीरे-धीरे शाम के बाद!

आग़ा सरोश

1.कपूर 2.आत्माऐं 3.इच्छा 4.वियोग 5.रौशनी का त्योहार

Din bhar jitna chaahe ghoomo, lekin itna dhyan rahe,
Uskee galee mein mudh jaate hein saare raste shaam ke baad,
Yaadon ka lobaan jalega, dard kee roohein naachengee,
Man kee havelee mein jaagenge, sone waale shaam ke baad.
Bachpan mein jab jaag uthhtee thee, chhand ko chhoone kee khwaahish,
Maan kahtee thee, " Zid naheen karte achchhe bachche shaam ke baad".
Hijr kee in lambee raaton mein, jashne charaaghaan kya maangein,
Dil khud hee jalne lagta hai, dheere-dheere shaam ke baad.

Throughout the day you may roam around to your heart's content, but keep this in mind,
That all paths turn towards her lane, after the onset of evening.
Camphor of memories will start burning, souls of pain will start dancing,
All sleeping ones will wake up into consciousness, after the onset of evening.
During childhood whenever arose the desire to touch the moon,
Mother used to say, "Good children don't act stubborn after the onset of evening."
During the long nights of separation, what is the use of asking for the festival of lights,
The heart isself starts burning gradually after the onset of evening.

Aagha 'Sarosh'

कोई तितली हमारे पास आती भी तो क्या आती,
सजाए उम्र भर काग़ज़ के फूल और पत्तियाँ हमने।
यूँ ही घुट-घुट के मर जाना हमें मँज़ूर था लेकिन,
किसी कमजर्फ़[1] पर ज़ाहिर[2] न की मजबूरियाँ हमने।
हम उस महफ़िल में बस इक बार सच बोले थे ऐ, 'वल्ली'!
ज़ुबाँ पर उम्र भर महसूस की चिगाँरियाँ हमने।

वल्ली आसी

1.छिछोरा 2.प्रकट करना

Koee Titlee humaare paas aatee bhee tau kya aatee,
Sajaaye umr bhar kaaghaz ke phool aur pattiyaan humne.
Yoon hee ghut-ghut ke mar jana humein manzoor tha lekin,
Kisi kamzarf par zaahir na kee majbooriyaan humne.
Hum us mehfil mein bus ek baar sach bole the aye, 'Walli'!
Zubaan par umr bhar mahsoos kee chingaariyaan humne.

Why any butterfly should have come any where near me,
(After all) I had lived with paper flowers and paper leaves throughout the life.
Dying of choked emotions was acceptable to me but,
I did not let my helplessness be known to any shallow person.
O, 'Walli'! I had spoken the truth in that assembly, only once,
(since then), Throughout the life I have been feeling the sparks on my tongue.

'Walli' Aasi

यूँ देखिए तो, आँधी में बस इक शजर[1] गया,
लेकिन न जाने कितने परिन्दों का घर गया।
मैं ही सबब[2] था इस बार भी अपनी शिकस्त[3] का,
इल्ज़ाम अबकी बार भी क़िस्मत के सर गया।
जैसे गलत पते पर चला आए कोई शख़्स[4],
सुख ऐसे मेरे दर पे रुका और गुज़र गया।

राजेश रेडडी

1.पेड़ 2.कारण 3.हार 4.इन्सान

Yoon dekhiye tau, aandhee mein bas ek shajar gaya,
Lekin na jaane kitne parindon ka ghar gaya.
Main hee sabab tha is baar bhee apnee shikast ka,
Ilzaam abkee baar bhee qismat ke sar gaya.
Jaise galat pate par chala aaye koee shakhs,
Sukh aise mere dar pe ruka aur guzar gaya.

Though, apparently only one tree was uprooted during the gale,
Yet none knew how many birds had lost their nests.
This time also I was the cause of my own defeat,
The blame went to the luck, this time too.
Like a person arriving at a wrong address,
Same way, the happiness stopped at my doorstep and went away.

Rajesh Reddy

ये करिश्मा[1] बता हुआ कैसे,
तू किसी का सगा हुआ कैसे।
सारी बस्ती तो जल के ख़ाक हुई,
ये बता तेरा घर बचा कैसे।

इतना मजबूर भी नहीं था तू,
फिर बता बावफ़ा[2] हुआ कैसे।
क़त्ल का जिसके सर पे था इल्ज़ाम
मुझको सब पता है वो छुटा कैसे।
तू तो यों भी अनाँ[3] से रौशन था,
आज लौटा बुझा-बुझा कैसे।

दिक्षित इन्दौरी

1.जादू 2.वफ़ादार 3.अँहकार

Ye karishma bata hua kaise,
Too kisee ka saga hua kaise.
Saari bastee tau jal ke khaak huee,
Ye bata tera ghar bacha kaise.
Itna majboor bhee naheen tha too,
Phir bata baawafa hua kaise.
Qatl ka jiske sar pe tha ilzaam,
Mujhko sab pata hai woh chhuthha kaise.
Too tau yon bhee anaan se raushan tha,
Aaj lauta bujha-bujha kaise.

Tell me how this miracle took place,
How you became kin of someone.
Entire town has been burnt into ashes,
Tell me, how come your house has remained intact.
You were never so helpless,
Then tell me how come you became loyal.
The person who was an alleged killer.
How he got released, I know all about it.
Throughout you had remained in the halo of your ego,
How come today you have returned all snuffed out.

Dikshit 'Indori'

मेरी आँखों को यह सब कौन बताने देगा,
ख़्वाब जिसके हैं वही नींद न आने देगा।
उसने यूँ बाँध लिया खुद को नये रिश्तों में,
जैसे मुझपर कोई इल्ज़ाम[1] न आने देगा।
सब अंधेरे से कोई वादा[2] किये बैठे हैं,
कौन ऐसे में मुझे शमअ[3] जलाने देगा
भीगती झील, कमल, बाग़ महक, सन्नाटा,
यह मेरा गांव, मुझे शहर न जाने देगा।
वह भी आँखों में कई ख़्वाब लिये बैठा है,
यह तसव्वुर[4] ही कभी नींद न आने देगा।
कल की बातें न करो, मुझ से कोई अहद न लो,
वक़्त बदलेगा तो कुछ याद न आने देगा।
अब तो हालात से समझौता ही कर लीजे 'वसीम'
कौन माज़ी[5] की तरफ़ लौट के जाने देगा।

वसीम बरेलवी

1.आरोप 2.वचन 3.मोमबत्ती 4.कल्पना 5.अतीत

Meree aankhon ko yah sab kaun bataane dega,
Khwwaab jiske hain wahee neend na aane dega.
Usne yoon baandh liya khud ko naye rishton mein,
Jaise mujh par koee ilzaam na aane dega.
Sab andhere se koee waada kiye baithe hain,
Kaun aise mein mujhe shama jalaane dega.
Bheegtee jheel, kamal, baagh, mahak, sannaata,
Yah mera gaaon, mujhe shahar na jaane dega.
Wah bhee aankhon mein koee khwwaab liye baitha hai,
Yah tasawwur hee kabhee neend na aane dega.
Kal kee baatein na karo, mujhse koee ahad na lo,
Waqt badlega tau kuchh yaad na aane dega.
Ab tau haalaat se samjhauta hee kar leeje 'Waseem',
Kaun maazee kee taraf laut ke jaane dega.

Who will allow my eyes to tell all this,
The one about whom I dream, she herself will not allow the sleep to come (near me),
She has tied herself with new relationships in such a way,
As if she will not let any blame come on to me.
Everybody has been sitting (here), having made some promise to the darkness,
Under such circumstances who will allow me to light the candle.
The drenched lake, the lotus, the garden, the fragrance, the solitude,
This village of mine will (never) allow me to depart for the town.
She too has been waiting with some dreams in eyes,
This very thought will never allow any sleep come to me.
Do not talk about tomorrow, do not ask me to make any promise,
When the time will change, it will not allow you to remember any thing.
O, 'Waseem', now you too must compromise with your present lot,
Who will let you return towards the old times.

'Waseem' Bareilvi

प्यार करने की, ये इस दिल को सज़ा दी जाए,
उसकी तस्वीर सरे-आम[1] लगा दी जाए।
ख़त में इस बार उसे भेजिये सूखा पत्ता,
और उस पत्ते पे इक आँख बना दी जाए।
इतनी पी जाए कि मिट जाए मैं और तू की तमीज़,
यानी ये होश की दीवार गिरा दी जाए।
आज हर शय[2] का असर लगता है उलटा यारों
आज 'शहज़ाद' को जीने की दुआ दी जाए।

फ़रहत शहज़ाद

1.खुले आम 2.चीज, वस्तु

Pyaar karne kee, ye is dil ko saza dee jaaye,
Uskee tasweer sare-aam laga dee jaaye.
Khat mein is baar use bhejiye sookha patta,
Aur us patte pe ek aankh bana dee jaaye.
Itnee pee jaaye ki mit jaaye mein aur too kee tameez,
Yaanee ye hosh kee deewaar gira dee jaaye.
Aaj har shai ka asar lagta hai ulta yaaron,
Aaj 'Shazaad' ko jeene kee dua dee jaaye.

For falling in love, let this heart be punished thus,
Let her portrait be hung (in a public place) for the gaze of every eye.
This time, as a letter send her a dry leaf,
And drawn on that leaf be an eye.
Let us drink to the extent, that all notions about 'I' and 'You' are wiped off,
Meaning, the wall of reason be demolished.
Reverse, seems to be the order of day the today,
Let us pray for an everlasting life to 'Shahzaad'.

'Farhat 'Shazaad'

जब साफ़गोई[1] को फ़ैशन बना लिया मैनें,
हर एक शख़्स[2] को दुश्मन बना लिया मैनें।
हुई न पूरी ज़रूरत जब चार पैसों की,
तो अपनी जेब को दामन बना लिया मैनें।
शबे-फ़िराक़[3] शबे-वस्ल[4] में हुई तब्दील[5],
ख़याले-यार[6] को दुल्हन बना लिया मैनें।
चमन में जब ना इजाज़त मिली रिहाइश की,
तो बिजलियों में नशेमन[7] बना लिया मैनें।

मुनव्वर राना

1.स्पष्टता 2.इन्सान 3.विरह की रात 4.मिलन की रात 5.बदलाव 6.प्रेयसी की याद 7.घोसला

Jab saafgoee ko faishan bana liya mainein,
Har ek shakhs ko dushman bana liya mainein.
Huee na pooree zaroorat jab chaar paison kee,
Tau apnee jeb ko daaman bana liya mainein.
Shabe-firaaq shabe-wasl mein huee tabdeel,
Khyaale-yaar ko dulhan bana liya mainein.
Chaman mein jab na ijaazat milee rihaaish kee,
Tau bijliyon mein nasheman bana liya mainein.

Since the day I adopted truthfulness as my personal style,
I have converted every person into an enemy of mine.
When my need for four paisas was not met,
I converted my pocket into a hem.
The 'night of separation' changed into 'the night of union',
(After) I assumed that the very thought of the beloved was my bride.
When I did not get permission to dwell in the garden,
I built up my nest in the lightning itself.

Munawwar Raana

बाग़ मे कैसी हवा चली अबके,
होश के पंछी उड़ गए सबके।
फूल जब फ़िक्र का शगूफ़ा[1] हुआ,
रह गया वो किताब में दबके।
सुलह की बात दुश्मनों से करो,
दोस्त तो हो गये ख़ुदा कबके।
बौने हो जाते हैं बुलन्दी[2] पर,
जाने ये लोग भी हैं किस ढब[3] के।

बेकल उत्साही

1.कली 2.ऊँचाई 3.तरह, प्रकार

Baagh mein kaisee hawa chalee abke,
Hosh ke panchhee udh gaye sabke.
Phool jab fikr ka shagoofa hua,
Rah gaya woh kitaab mein dabke.
Sulah kee baat dushmanon se karo,
Dost tau ho gaye khuda kabke.
Baune ho jaate hein bulandee par,
Jaane ye log bhee hain kis dhhhab ke.

What type of wind has been blowing in the garden this time,
All birds of consciousness have flown away.
When the flower turned into a bud of anxiety,
It was consigned to remain buried in a book.
About reconciliation, talk with the enemies,
(Because) Friends have become gods since long.
On reaching the heights, they become dwarfs,
What type of people are these.

Bekal 'Utsaahi'

मेरी नज़र के सलीके[1] में क्या नहीं आता,
बस इक तेरी ही तरफ़ देखना नहीं आता।
अकेले चलना तो मेरा नसीब[2] था कि मुझे,
किसी के साथ सफ़र बाँटना नहीं आता।
जगाना आता है उसको कई तरीकों से,
घरों पे दस्तख़ें देने ख़ुदा नहीं आता।
उधर तो जाते हैं रास्ते तमाम होने को,
उधर से होके कोई रास्ता नहीं आता।
पड़े रहो यूँ ही सहमे हुए दियों की तरह,
अगर हवाओं के पर[3] बाँधना नहीं आता।

वसीम बरेलवी

1.आचरण 2.भाग्य 3.पँख

Meree nazar ke saleeqe mein kya naheen aata,
Bas ek teree hee taraf dekhna naheen aata.
Akele chalna tau mera naseeb tha ki mujhe,
Kisee ke saath safar baantna naheen aata.
Jagaana aata hai usko kaee tareekon se,
Gharon pe dastakhein dene khuda naheen aata.
Udhar tau jaate hain raaste tamaam hone ko,
Udhar se hoke koee raasta naheen aata.
Padhe raho yoon hee sahme huye diyon kee tarah,
Agar hawaaon ke par baandhna naheen aata.

What all my eyes are not capable of doing,
Except than to look at you in the right way.
Walking alone was very much my destiny, for,
I do not know how to share the journey with anyone.
He knows many ways of giving the 'Wake-up' call,
God does not come knocking on individual doors.
All tracks go in that direction only for ending up.
No track comes from that direction.
Continue remaining subdued like the earthen lamps,
If you do not know how to tie the wings of the wind.

Waseem Bareilvi

वो हर जुम्ले[1] को आधा बोलता है,
फिर उसके बाद चेहरा बोलता है।
जहन्नुम[2] नाम लिखवा लेगा अपने,
बुजुर्गों से जो ऊँचा बोलता है।
ग़रीबी मारती है झक वतन में,
हर मस्तक पे पैसा बोलता है।

मलिकज़ादा जावेद

1.वाक्य 2.नरक

Woh har jumle ko aadha bolta hai,
Phir us ke baad chehra bolta hai.
Jahannum naam likhwaa lega apne,
Bujurgon se jo ooncha bolta hai.
Ghareebee maartee hai jhak watan mein,
Har mastak pe paisa bolta hai

He talks in half-sentences,
After that his face speaks.
He is sure to get the hell reserved in his name,
The one who talks in a raised voice to elderly people.
Poverty is kicked around all over in the motherland,
Money talks through every one's head.

Malikzaada Jaaved

बादल जब बरसा करते हैं रात ढले,
भीगे तन सुलगा करते हैं रात ढले।
मेरी ग़ज़लें पढ़कर वो तन्हाई[1] में
जाने क्या सोचा करते हैं रात ढले।
इनके रस्ते से बच कर रहना यारों,
दीवाने बहका करते हैं रात ढले।
'बेकल' को फिर एहदे-ज़वानी[2] याद आई,
छुप-छुप कर रोया करते हैं रात ढले।

बेकल उत्साही

1.अकेलापन, एकाँत 2.जवानी का समय

Baadal jab barsa karte hain raat dhale,
Bheege tan sulga karte hain raat dhale.
Merée ghazalein padhkar woh tanhaaee mein,
Jaane kya socha kartein hain raat dhale.
Inke raste se bach kar rahna yaaron,
Deewaane bahka karte hain raat dhale.
'Bekal' ko phir ahde-zawaanee yaad aaee,
Chhup-chhup kar roya karte hain raat dhale.

When the clouds rain in the late nights,
Soaked bodies (too) smoulder in the late nights.
After reading my poems in solitude,
What all she must be contemplating in the late nights.
Avoid crossing their tracks,O, friends!
Mad lovers go berserk in the late nights.
Again, 'Bekal' is reminded of days of (his) youth,
Hidden from all eyes he keeps crying late in the night

Bekal Utsaahi

सफ़र किन रास्तों पे कर रहा है,
ख़ुद अपने साये[1] से वो डर रहा है।
मै गहरी सोच में डूबा हुआ हूँ,
समन्दर मुझसे बातें कर रहा है।
न गिर जाये कहीं थक कर परिन्दा,
बहुत लम्बी उड़ाने भर रहा है।
हमें कम-कम मिला है साथ उसका,
हमारे साथ जो अक्सर रहा है।
वो ही 'मख़्मूर' मेरा हमक़दम था,
जो मेरी राह का पत्थर रहा है।

मख़्मूर सईदी

1.परछांई

Safar kin·raaston pe kar raha hai,
Khud apne saaye se wo dar raha hai.
Main gahree soch mein dooba hua hoon,
Samandar mujhse baatein kar raha hai.
Na gir jaaye kaheen thak kar parinda,
Bahut lambee udhaane bhar raha hai.
Humein kam-kam mila hai saath uska,
Humaare saath jo aksar raha hai.
Wohee 'Makhmoor' mera humqadam tha,
Jo meree raah ka patathar raha hai.

On what tracks he has been travelling,
Getting scared of his own shadow.
I am immersed in deep thoughts,
The ocean has been talking to me.
May the bird not fall down after getting exhausted,
It has been indulging in very high flights.
(Only) For short durations I have received her companionship,
The one, who has been in my thoughts often.
O, 'Makhmoor' she alone was my co-traveller,
The one who has been the stumbling block on my track.

'Makhmoor' Saeedee

ये मुमकिन[1] है, अँधेरा हार जाए,
अभी कुछ और जलना चाहता हूँ।
ज़रूरी तो नहीं सबसे मिलूँ मैं,
जरा सा बचके चलना चाहता हूँ।
शराफ़त कमज़ोरी सी लगने लगी है,
मैं रास्ता बदलना चाहता हूँ।

तुफ़ैल चतुर्वेदी

1.सम्भव

Ye mumkin hai, andhera haar jaaye,
Abhee kuchh aur jalna chaahta hoon.
Zarooree tau nahaeen sabse miloon main,
Jara sa bachke chalna chaahta hoon.
Sharaafat kamzoree see lagne lagee hai,
Main raasta badalna chaahta hoon.

This is possible that the darkness may give up,
(That is why) I wish to burn for some more time.
It is not mandatory that I must meet every body,
(I) Wish to walk keeping a slight distance.
My gentility seems to have become my weakness,
I want to change the track.

'Tufail' Chaturvedi

तेरा नाम कितना है मुख़्तसर[1],
तेरा ज़िक्र कितना तबील[2] है।
मुझे कौन तुझसे अलग करे,
मैं अटूट प्यास, तू झील है।
तेरे फैसलों से हूँ मैं मुतमईन[3],
ना मुक़दमा ना कोई अपील है
तेरी रहमतों[4] में कमी नहीं,
मेरी एहतियात[5] में ही ढील है।

अशोक साहिल

1.छोटा, संक्षिप्त 2.मुश्किल 3.संतुष्ट 4.कृपाएँ 5. सावधानी

Tera naam kitna hai mukhtsar,
Tera zikr kitna tabeel hai.
Mujhe kaun tujhse alag kare,
Main atoot pyaas, too jheel hai.
Tere faislon se hoon main mutmaeen,
Na muqadama, na koee apeel hai.
Teree rahmaton mein kamee naheen,
Meree aihtiyaat mein hee dheel hai.

How brief is your name,
How difficult is your description.
Who will dare to separate me from you,
I am unquenchable thirst, you are a lake.
I am quite satisfied with (all) your verdicts,
Neither there is any suit nor there is any appeal,
There is no lack in your mercies,
There is a sag in my caution alone.

Ashok 'Saahil'

कुछ इस तरह वह मेरी ज़िन्दगी में आया था,
कि मेरा होते हुए भी, बस एक साया[1] था।
हवा में उड़ने की धुन ने यह दिन दिखाया था,
उड़ान मेरी थी, लेकिन सफ़र[2] पराया था।
यह कौन राह दिखाकर चला गया मुझको,
मै ज़िन्दगी में भला किस के काम आया था।
मैं अपने वायदे पे क़ायम[3] न रह सका वर्ना,
वह थोड़ी दूर ही जाकर तो लौट आया था।
न अब वह घर है, न उस घर के लोग याद 'वसीम',
न जाने उसने कहाँ से मुझे चुराया था।

वसीम बरेलवी

1.परछाई 2.यात्रा 3.दृढ़

Kuchh is tarah wah meree zindgee mein aaya tha,
Ki mera hote huye bhee, bas ek saaya tha.
Hawa mein udhne kee dhun ne yah din dikhaaya tha,
Udhaan meree thee, lekin safar paraaya tha.
Yah kaun raah dikhakar chala gaya mujhko,
Main zindgee mein bhala kis ke kaam aaya tha.
Main apne waayde pe qaayam na rah saka warna,
Wah thodhee door hee jaakar tau laut aaya tha.
Na ab wah ghar hai, na us ghar ke log yaad 'Waseem',
Na jaane usne kahaan se mujhe churaaya tha.

She had come into my life in such a way,
That even after belonging to me, she was just a shadow.
The craze for flying in the wind had brought me to a state,
That the flight was mine, but the journey belonged to someone else.
Who was that, who showed me the way and left,
(After all) In my life time, I had not been able to be of any help to anyone.
I could not uphold my own promise, otherwise,
She had returned after taavelling a little distance only.
O, 'Waseem'! that house is no more, nor do I remember the people of that house.
God knows, where from she had stolen me.

Waseem Bareilvi

प्यादों[1] न ही दी कुर्बानियाँ[2] सब,
शहीदों में कोई राजा नही था।
मुझे झुकना पड़ा हर इक के आगे,
मेरे क़द से कोई नीचा नहीं था।
पशेमाँ[3] था गवाही दे के मैं तो,
वो क़ातिल होके शर्मिन्दा नहीं था।

राजेश रेडडी

1.सिपाही 2.बलिदान 3.शर्मिन्दा

Pyaadon ne hee dee qurbaaniyaan sab,
Shaheedon mein koee raaja naheen tha.
Mujhe jhukna pada har ik ke aage,
Mere qad se koee neecha naheen tha.
Pashemaan tha gawaahee de ke main tau,
Wo qaatil hoke sharminda naheen tha.

Only the foot soldiers made all the sacrifices,
No king was there amongst the martyrs.
I had to bow infront of everyone,
Nobody's stature was less than mine.
After giving evidence, I was shamefaced,
She, inspite of being a murderer, was not embarrassed (at all).

Rajesh Reddy

कभी कहा न किसी से तेरे फ़साने[1] को,
न जाने कैसे ख़बर हो गई ज़माने को।
सुना है ग़ैर की महफ़िल में तुम न जाओगे,
कहो तो आज सजा लूँ ग़रीबखाने[2] को।
दुआ बहार की माँगी तो इतने फूल खिले
कहीं जगह न रही मेरे आशियाने[3] को।
दबा के क़ब्र में सब चल दिये, दुआ न सलाम,
जरा सी देर में क्या हो गया ज़माने को

अब्दुल हमीद 'अदम'

1.कहानी 2.गरीब का घर 3.घोसला

Kabhee kaha na kisee se tere fasaane ko,
Na jaane kaise khabar ho gayee zamaane ko,
Suna hai ghair kee mehfil mein tum na jaaoge,
Kaho tau aaj saja loon ghareebkhaane ko.
Dua bahaar kee maangee tau itne phool khile,
Kaheen jagah na rahee mere aashiyaane ko,
Daba ke qabr mein sab chal diye, dua na salaam,
Jara see der mein kya ho gaya zamaane ko.

Never told anyone about your story,
Don't know how the world got the wind of it.
(I) Have heard that you would not go to the assembly of (my) rival,
If you permit, shall I decorate (my) poor man's dwelling.
When I prayed for the spring, so many flowers bloomed,
That there was no place left for my nest.
Having buried me in the grave, all of them departed without any pleasantries,
What had happened to the world in such a short time.

Abdul Hameed 'Adam'

देखा जो आईना, तो मुझे सोचना पड़ा,
ख़ुदसे न मिल सका तो मुझे सोचना पड़ा।
उसका जो ख़त मिला तो मुझे सोचना पड़ा,
आपना सा वो लगा तो मुझे सोचना पड़ा।
मुझको था ये गुमाँ कि मुझी में है इक अनाँ[1],
देखी तेरी अनाँ तो, मुझे सोचना पड़ा।
दुनियाँ समझ रही थी, कि नाराज़ मुझसे है,
लेकिन वो जब मिला तो, मुझे सोचना पड़ा।
इक दिन वो मेरे ऐब[2] गिनाने लगा 'फ़राग़',
जब ख़ुद ही थक गया तो, मुझे सोचना पड़ा।

फ़राग़ रूहवी

1.ख़ुद्दारी 2.दोष

Dekha jo aaeena tau mujhe sochna padha,
Khud se naa mil saka tau mujhe sochna padha.
Uska jo khat mila tau mujhe sochna padha,
Apna sa wo laga tau mujhe sochna padha.
Mujhko tha ye gumaan ki mujhee mein hai ik anaan,
Dekhee teree anaan tau mujhe sochna padha.
Duniyaan samajh rahee thee, ki naaraaz mujh se hai,
Lekin wo jab mila tau, mujhe sochna padha.
Ik din wo mere aib ginaane laga 'Faraagh',
Jab khud hee thak gaya tau, mujhe sochna padha.

When (I) looked at the mirror I had to think,
When could not meet myself then I had to think.
When (I) received her letter then I had to think,
When she looked as if she belonged to me, then I had to think,
I was confident that only I had this ego,
When confronted your ego, then I had to think.
The world was under the impression that (she) was angry with me,
But when she met me, then I had to think,
One day she started counting my vices to me O, 'Faraagh'!
When she herself got tired, then I had to think.

'Faraagh Roohvi'

लोग हर मोड़ पे रुक-रुक के सँभलते क्यों हैं,
इतना डरते हैं, तो फिर घर से निकलते क्यूँ हैं।
मैं न जुगनू हूँ, दिया हूँ न कोई तारा हूँ,
रौशनी वाले मेरे नाम से जलते क्यों हैं।
नींद से मेरा ताल्लुक़[1] ही नही बरसों से,
ख़्वाब[2] आ-आ के मेरी छत पे टहलते क्यों हैं।
मोड़ होता है ज़वानी का सँभलने के लिए,
और सब लोग यहीं आके फ़िसलते क्यों हैं।

राहत इन्दौरी

1.समबन्ध 2.स्वप्न, सपने

Log har modh pe ruk-ruk ke sambhalte kyon hain,
Itna darte hain, tau phir ghar se nikalte kyon hain.
Main na jugnoo hoon, diya hoon, na koee taara hoon,
Raushnee waale mere naam se darte kyon hain.
Neend se mera taalluq hee naheen barson se,
Khwwaab aa-aa ke meree chhat pe thahalte kyon hain.
Modh hota hai zawaanee ka sambhalne ke liye,
Aur sab log yaheen aake fisalte kyon hain.

Why do people repeatedly stop and steady themselves at every turn?
If (they) are so scared, then why do they come out of the house?
I am neither a firefly, nor a lamp, nor a star,
Why then the affluent ones are jealous of my name?
For years I have not even been in touch with the sleep,
Why then, the dreams come and keep strolling on my roof top.
The turn of youth is a pointer to become steady,
Why then all people come to this turn and keep slipping?

Raahat Indoree

तमाम उम्र जो की सबने बेरुख़ी[1] हमसे,
कफ़न मे हम भी अज़ीज़ों[2] से मुहँ छुपा के चले।
गलत है शिकवाए-दुश्मन[3], कि बाद मरने के,
मेरे अज़ीज़ मुझे ख़ाक में मिला के चले।
मिला जिन्हें उन्हें उफ्तादगी[4] से पूछ मिला,
उसी ने खाई है ठोकर जो, सर उठा के चले।
'अनीस' दम[5] का भरोसा नहीं है ठहर के जाओ,
चिराग़ लेके कहाँ सामने हवा के चले।

मीर अनीस

1.उदासीनता 2.मित्रगण 3.शत्रु की शिकायत 4.गिरावट 5.सांस

Tamaam umr jo kee sabne berukhee humse,
Kafan mein hum bhee azeezon se moohn chhupa ke chale.
Galat hai shikhwaaye-dushman, ki baad marne ke
Mere azeez mujhe khaak mein mila ke chale.
Mila jinhein unhein uftaadgee se pooch mila,
Usee ne khaayee hai thhokar, jo sar uthha ke chale.
'Anees' dam ka bharosa naheen hai thhahar ke jao
Chiraagh leke kahaan saamne hawa ke chale.

Since every one treated me indefferently throughout the life,
I too went away from the near and dear ones hiding my face in the shroud.
It is wrong to complaint against the enemy after the death,
For it were the friends who departed after covering me with the dust.
Those who got success, got by learning from the downfall,
"Only he gets tripped who walks with his head high."
O, " Anees"! rest a while before going as life is ephemeral,
What do you want to achieve by walking into the winds with a lighted earthen lamp (in hands),

'Meer Anees'

लहू न हो तो क़लम तरजुमाँ[1] नहीं होता,
हमारे दौर में, आँसू ज़बाँ नहीं होता।
जहाँ रहेगा वहीं रौशनी लुटायेगा,
किसी चराग़ का अपना मकाँ नहीं होता।
यह किस मुक़ाम पे लाई है मेरी तन्हाई,
कि मुझ से आज कोई बदगुमाँ[2] नहीं होता।
बस इक निगाह मेरी राह देखती होती,
यह सारा शहर मेरा मेज़बाँ[3] नहीं होता।
तेरा ख़्याल न होता तो कौन समझाता,
ज़मीं न हो तो कोई आसमाँ नहीं होता।
मैं उसको भूल गया हूँ, यह कौन मानेगा,
किसी चराग के बस में धुआँ नहीं होता।
'वसीम' सदियों की आँखों से देखिये मुझको,
वह लफ़्ज़[4] हूँ जो कभी दास्ता[5] नहीं होता।

वसीम बरेलवी

1.भाव बोधक 2.कुंठित 3.आतिथ्य 4.शब्द 5.कहानी

Lahoo na ho tau qalam tarjumaan naheen hota,
Hamaare daur mein, aansoo zabaan naheen hota.
Jahaan rahega waheen raushnee lutaayega,
Kisee charaagh ka apna makaan naheen hota.
Yah kis muqaam pe laaee hai meree tanhaaee,
Ki mujhse aaj koee badgumaan naheen hota.
Bas ik nigaah meree raah dekhtee hotee,
Yah saara shahar mera mezabaan naheen hota.
Tera khyaal na hota tau kaun samjhaata,
Zameen na ho tau koee aasmaan naheen hota.
Main usko bhool gaya hoon, yah kaun maanega,
Kisi charaagh ke bas mein dhuaan naheen hota,
'Waseem' sadiyon kee aankhon se dekhiye mujhko,
Wah lafz hoon jo kabhee daastaan naheen hota.

If the blood is not there then the pen is not expressive enough,
In our era, tear doesn't act like the tongue.
Wherever it remains, it will spread light lavishly there,
No earthen lamp has a house of its own.
At what stage this lonelines of mine has brought me,
That, now nobody becomes angry with me.
Only one particular eye should have been waiting for me,
The whole town should not have been my host.
But for you in mind, who would have explained (to me),
That if there were no earth, there would not be any sky either.
I have forgotten her, who will believe this,
No earthen lamp has any control our the smoke.
O! 'Waseem' ! look at me through the eyes of centuries,
I am that word which never turns into a tale.

'Waseem' Bareillvi

देखा तो मेरा साया भी मुझसे जुदा मिला,
सोचा तो हर किसी से मेरा सिलसिला मिला।
शहरे-वफ़ा[1] में अब किसे अहले-वफ़ा[2] कहें,
हमसे गले मिला तो वो ही बेवफ़ा मिला।
फ़ुरसत किसे थी जो मेरे हालात पूछता,
हर शख़्स[3] अपने ही बारे में कुछ सोचता मिला
उसने तो ख़ैर अपनों से मोड़ा था मुहँ 'अयाज़',
मैने ये क्या कि, मै ग़ैरों[4] से जा मिला।

अयाज़ झाँसवी

1.वफ़ादारों का शहर 2.खास वफ़ादार 3.आदमी, इन्सॉन 4.पराए

Dekha tau mera saaya bhee mujhse juda mila,
Socha tau har kisee se mera silsila mila.
Shahare-wafa mein ab kise aihle-wafa kahein,
Humse gale mila tau wo hee bewafa mila.
Fursat kise thee jo mere haalaat poochhta,
Har shakhs apne hee baare mein kuchh sochta mila.
Usne tau khair apnon se modha tha muhn 'Ayaaz'
Maine ye kya kiya ki, main ghairon se ja mila.

When looked (closely), my own shadow was away from me,
When thought (deeply) I found myself connected with everyone.
Whom should (I) proclaim as faithful in the city of faithfuls,
The only one who came and embraced me was that unfaithful one.
Who had the time to bother about my plight,
Every person was found thinking about himself.
O! 'Ayaaz', she had turned away from her people only,
But what have I done? I have gone and connived with the adversaries.

Ayaaz Jhanswi

अपने चेहरे से जो ज़ाहिर[1] है, छुपाऐं कैसे,
तेरी मरज़ी के मुताबिक़[2] नज़र आयें कैसे?
घर सजाने का तसव्वुर[3] तो बहुत बाद का है,
पहले ये तय हो कि इस घर को बचायें कैसे।
लाख तलवारें बढ़ी आती हों गरदन की तरफ़,
सर झुकाना नहीं आता तो झुकायें कैसे।
क़हक़हा आँख का बर्ताव बदल देता है,
हँसने वाले तुझे आसूँ नज़र आयें कैसे?
फूल से रंग जुदा होना कोई खेल नहीं,
अपनी मिटटी को कहीं छोड़ के जायें कैसे।
कोई अपनी ही नज़र से तो हमें देखेगा,
एक क़तरे[4] को समन्दर नज़र आयें कैसे?
जिसने दानिस्ता किया हो नज़र अन्दाज़ 'वसीम',
उसको कुछ याद दिलायें तो दिलायें कैसे।

वसीम बरेलवी

1.स्पष्ठ 2.अनुसार 3.कल्पना 4.बूंद

Apne chehre se jo zaahir hai, chhupaayein kaise,
Teree marzee ke mutaabiq nazar aayein kaise?
Ghar sajaane ka tasawwur tau bahut baad ka hai,
Pahle ye tai ho ki is ghar ko bachaayein kaise
Lakh talwaarein badhhee aatee hon gardan kee taraf,
Sar jhukaana naheen aata tau jhukaaein kaise.
Qahqaha aankh ka bartaab badal deta hai,
Hansne waale tujhe aansoon nazar aayein kaise?
Phool se rang juda hona koee khel naheen,
Apnee mittee ko kaheen chhodh ke jaaein kaise.
Koyee apnee hee nazar se tau humein dekhega,
Ek qatre ko samandar nazar aayein kaise?
Jisne daanista kiya ho nazar andaaz 'Waseem',
Usko kuchh yaad dilaayein tau dilaayein kaise.

How to hide that, which is obvious from (my face)?
How can I appear to thee as thou desire?
The fancy of beautifying the 'home' is farfetched,
First, let us decide, how to save this home.
Millions of swords may be advancing towards my neck,
once, I do not know how to bow (my) head, then how do I bow it.
Guffaw changes the perception of (one's) eyes,
O, laughing one, how can you see the tears?
Separation of colour from the flower is no joke,
leaving the soil of one's roots, where can one go.
Someone would perceive me with his own eyes (yardstick) only,
How can (I) appear like an ocean to a droplet?
O, 'Waseem'! how can you remind something of the past to the one,
who has delibrately turned her eyes away from (you).

Wassem Bareilvi

फ़ासिला[1] तो है मगर कोई फ़ासिला नहीं,
मुझसे तुम जुदा[2] सही, दिल से तो जुदा नहीं।
आसमाँ की फ़िक्र क्या, आसमाँ खफ़ा सही,
आप ये बताईये, आप तो खफ़ा[3] नहीं।
कश्तियाँ नहीं तो क्या, हौसलें[4] तो पास हैं,
कह दो नाखुदाओं[5] से, तुम कोई ख़ुदा नहीं।
लीजिए, बुला लिया आपको ख़याल में,
अब तो देखिये हमें, कोई देखता नहीं।
आइए चिरागे़-दिल[6] आज ही जलाएँ हम,
कैसी कल हवा चले, कोई जानता नहीं।

शामीम कराहनी

1.दूरी 2.अलग 3.नाराज 4.हिम्मत 5.मल्लाहलोग 6.हदय का दीपक

Faasila tau hai magar, koyee faasila naheen,
Mujhse tum juda sahee, dil se tau juda naheen.
Aasmaan kee fikr kya, aasmaan khafa sahee,
Aap ye bataayeeye, aap tau khafa naheen,
Kashtiyaan naheen tau kya, haunslein tau paas hain,
Kah do naakhudaaon se, tum koyee khuda naheen.
Leejiye bula liya aap ko khyaal mein,
Ab tau dekhiye humein, koyee dekhta naheen.
Aayeeye chiraaghe-dil aaj hee jalaayein hum,
Kaisee kal hawa chale, koyee jaanta naheen.

Yes distance is there, yet there is no distance,
Agreed you are away from me, but not away from (my) heart.
Let the heavens be angry, who cares for the heavens,
You tell me this, at least you aren't angry (with me).
Never mind if the boats are not there, our courage is with us,
Tell the boatmen, you, are not the God.
Ok, now I have invited you in my thoughts,
At least, now have a close look at me, no one is watching.
Come, let us kindle the lamp of heart tonight itself,
Who knows what sort of wind will blow tomorrow.

Shameem Karaahni

अबकी बरसात की रुत और भी भड़कीली है,
जिस्म[1] से आग निकलती है, कबा[2] गीली है।
सोचता हूँ कि अब अन्ज़ामे-सफ़र[3] क्या होगा,
लोग भी काँच के है, राह भी पथरीली है।
पहले रग-रग से मेरी खून निचोड़ा उसने,
अब ये कहता है कि रंगत[4] ही मेरी पीली है।
मुझको बेरंग ही कर दे न कहीं रंग इतने,
सब्ज़[5] मौसम है, हवा सुर्ख़, फ़िज़ा[6] नीली है।

मुज़फ़्फ़र वारसी

1.शरीर 2.कोट 3.यात्रा का अन्त/नतीजा 4.सूरत,रंग 5.हरा 6.आसमान

Abkee barsaat kee rut aur bhee badhkeelee hai,
Jism se aag nikaltee hai kaba geelee hai.
Sochta hoon ki ab anzaame-safar kya hoga,
Log bhee kaanch ke hain, raah bhee pathreelee hai.
Pahle rag-rag se meree khoon nichodha usne,
Ab ye kahta hai ki rangat hee meree peelee hai.
Mujhko berang hee na kardein kaheen rang itne,
Sabz mausam hai, hawa surkh, fiza neelee hai.

This time the rainy season is even more flaunting,
Fire is oozing out of the body and the gown is drenched.
I am thinking as to what will be the end of trek,
For, people are made of glass, and the track too is stony.
First he drained out the blood slowly from all my veins,
Now he asserts that my complexion itself is ashen.
I fear lest so many colours may decolour my ownself,
Weather is green, atmosphere is red and the sky is blue.

'Muzaffar Waarsee'

लबे-ख़ामोश[1] से इज़हारे-तमन्ना[2] चाहें,
बात करने को भी तस्वीर का लहज़ा[3] चाहें।
तू चले साथ तो आहट भी न आए अपनी,
दरमियाँ[4] हम भी न हों, यूँ तुझे तन्हा[5] चाहें।
ख़्वाब में रोयें तो एहसास हो सैलाबी[6] का,
रेत पर सोएँ, मगर आँख में दरिया चाहें।
ऐसे तैराक भी देखे हैं 'मुज़फ़्फ़र' हमने,
ग़र्क़[7] होने के लिए भी जो सहारा चाहें।

मुज़फ़्फ़र वारसी

1.बन्द होंठ 2.इच्छा का प्रकटीकरण 3.बोलने का ढंग 4.बीच मे 5.अकेला 6.झरना 7.डूबने के लिए

Labe-khaamosh se izhaare-tamanna chaahein,
Baat karne ko bhee tasweer ka lahza chaahein.
Too chale saath tau aahat bhee na aaye apnee,
Darmiyaan hum bhee na hon, yoon tujhe tanha chaaein,
Khwwaab mein royein tau aihsaas ho sailaabee ka,
Ret par soyein magar aankh mein dariya chhahein.
Aise tairaak bhee dekhe hain 'Muzaffar' humne,
Gharq hone ke liye bhee jo sahaara chhahein.

(I) Want expression of desire through closed lips,
Want, talking too to be done in the tone of a picture.
Whenever you are walking with me, I do not wish to hear even my own rustle,
I too should not be in-between, to this extent I want you alone (with me).
When I weep in the dream then I should sense a water fall,
Even while sleeping on sand, I wish a river in (my) eyes.
I have seen such ace swimmers too, O, 'Muzaffar'!
Even for drowning (themselves) who look for support.

'Muzaffar Waarsee'

याद में तेरी जहाँ को भूलता जाता हूँ मैं,
भूलने वाले कभी तुझको भी याद आता हूँ मैं।
एक धुंधला-सा तसव्वुर[1] है कि दिल भी था यहाँ,
अब तो सीने में फ़क़त इक ठीस[2] सी पाता हूँ मैं।
ओ वफ़ा-ना-आशना[3] कब तक सुनूँ तेरा गिला[4],
बेवफ़ा कहते हैं तुझको और शर्माता हूँ मैं।
जिस तरह ऊपर से नीचे को गिरे पानी की धार।
तेरे क़दमों की तरफ यूँहीं बहा जाता हूँ मैं।
आरज़ूओं का शबाब[5] और मर्गे-हसरत[6] हाय-हाय।
जब बहार आती है गुलशन में तो मुर्झाता हूँ मैं।
दिल की धड़कन जिसकी लय है, अश्क सम और आह ताल,
फिर वो नग़मा आज साज़े-रूह[7] पर गाता हूँ मैं।
'हश्र' मेरी शैरगोई[8] है फ़क़त फ़रियादे-शौक़[9],
अपना ग़म दिल की ज़बाँ मे दिल को समझाता हूँ मैं।

आगा हश्र कशमी

1.याद कल्पना 2.दुखन, दर्द 3.बेवफा 4.शिकायत 5.जवानी 6.मौत की आकांक्षा
7.आत्मा के बाजे पर 8.शायरी 9.सुखद शिकायत

Yaad mein teree jahaan ko bhoolta jaata hoon main,
Bhoolne waale kabhee tujh ko bhee yaad aata hoon main.
Ek dhundhla sa tasawwur hai ki dil bhee tha yahaan,
Ab tau seene mein faqat ek tees see paata hoon main.
O! wafa-na-aashna kab tak sunoon tera gila,
Bewafa kahte hain tujhe ko, aur sharmaata hoon main.
Jis tarah oopar se neeche ko gire paanee kee dhaar,
Tere qadmon kee taraf yoon heen baha jaata hoon main.
Aarzuon ka shabaab aur marge-hasrat haai-haai,
Jab bahaar aatee hai gulshan mein tau murjhaata hoon main.
Dil kee dhadhkan jiskee lai hai, ask sam aur aah taal,
Phir wo naghma aaj saaze-rooh par gaata hoon main.
'Hashr' meree shairgoee hai faqat fariyaade-shauq,
Apna gham dil kee zabaan mein dil ko samjhaata hoon main.

In your remembrance, I keep forgetting the world,
O, forgetful one! do you also remember me ever.
A hazy memory exists that sometime back here was a heart too,
Now I find only a pang like thing in my chest.
O, unfaithful one! how long can I listen to the complaints against you,
They call you disloyal and I feel ashamed.
The way the stream of water falls from top to down,
Same way I keep flowing towards your foot-steps.
Desires full of youth and wish for death, alas-alas,
When the spring arrives, I start fading.
Pulsation of heart is its tune, tears its metre and sighs its beat,
once again today I am singing such a song on the instrument of my soul.
O, 'Hashr', my couplet-composing is just the outcry of delight,
I am trying to explain my sorrow to (my) heart in the language of heart

'Aagha Hashr Kashmeeri'

क्या बताऊँ कैसा खुद को दर-ब-दर मैंने किया,
उम्र भर किस-किस के हिस्से का सफ़र मैंने किया।
तू तो नफ़रत भी न कर पाएगा इस शिद्दत[1] के साथ,
जिस बला का प्यार तुझसे बेख़बर मैंने किया।
कैसे बच्चों को बताऊँ, रास्तों के पेचों-ख़म[2],
ज़िन्दगी भर तो किताबों का सफ़र मैंने किया।
किसको फ़ुर्सत थी कि बतलाता उसे इतनी सी बात,
खुद से क्या बर्ताव तुझ से छूट कर मैंने किया।
चन्द ज़ज्बाती[3] से रिश्तों के बचाने को 'वसीम',
कैसा-कैसा जब्र[4] अपने आप पर मैंने किया।

वसीम बरेलवी

1.तीव्रता 2.घुमाव-फिराव 3.भावुक 4.अत्याचार

Kya Bataoon kaisa khud ko dar-ba-dar maine kiya,
Umr bhar kis-kis ke hisse ka safar maine kiya.
Too tau nafrat bhee na kar paayega is shiddat ke saath,
Jis bala ka pyaar tujhse bekhabar maine kiya.
Kaise bachchon ko bataoon, raaston ke pechon-kham,
Zindgee bhar tau kitaabon ka safar maine kiya.
Kisko fursat thee ki batlaata use itnee see baat,
Khud se kya bartaab tujh se chhoot kar maine kiya.
Chand zajbaatee se rishton ke bachaane ko 'Waseem',
Kaisa-kaisa jabr apne aap par maine kiya.

What to say, how I made myself go from pillar to post,
Throughout the life, how many people's share of journey I undertook.
You will not be able to even hate with the intensity,
With which I loved you, o, ignorant one!.
How do I explain the twists and turns of the tracks to the kids,
Throughout the life I travelled through the books only.
Who had the time to tell her this small thing,
That having parted from her, how (savagely) I treated myself.
To safeguard a few emotional relationships, O, 'Waseem'!,
What all atrocities I showered upon myself.

'Waseem' Bareilvi

मेरी ज़िन्दगी है ज़ालिम तेरे गम से आशकारा[1],
तेरा ग़म है दर हक़ीक़त[2] मुझे ज़िन्दगी से प्यारा।
तू अगर बुरा ना माने तो जहाने-रगों-बू[3] में,
मैं सकूने-दिल[4] की ख़ातिर कोई ढूंड लूँ सहारा।
मुझे तुझसे खास निस्बत[5], मैं रहीने-मौजे-तूफ़ां[6],
जिन्हें ज़िन्दगी थी प्यारी उन्हें मिल गया किनारा।
मुझे आ गया यकीं-सा कि यही है मेरी मंज़िल,
सरे-राह[7] जब किसी ने मुझे दफ़अतन[8] पुकारा।
मै बताऊँ फ़र्क नासेह[9], जो है मुझमें और तुझमें,
मेरी ज़िन्दगी तलातुम[10] तेरी ज़िन्दगी किनारा।
मुझे गुफ़्तगू से बढ़कर ग़मे-इज़्ने गुफ़्तगू[11] है,
वही बात पूछते हैं जो न कह सकूँ दुबारा।
कोई ऐ 'शकील' देखे, ये जुनूँ[12] नहीं तो क्या है,
कि उसी के हो गए हम, जो न हो सका हमारा।

शकील बदायूनी

1.प्रकाशमान 2.सच्चाई में 3.रंग और खुशबू भरा संसार 4.दिल की शांती 5.लगाव 6.तूफानी लहर की बन्दी 7.खुले आम 8.अचानक 9.उपदेशक 10.तूफान 11.बात करने की इजाजत का दुख 12.पागलपन

Meree zindagee hai zaalim tere gham se aashkaara,
Tera gham hai dar haqeeqat mujhe zindagee se pyaara.
Too agar bura na maane tau jahaane-rango-boo mein,
Main sukoone-dil kee khaatir koee doondhh loon sahaara.
Mujhe tujh se khaas nisbat, mein raheene-mauje-toofaan,
Jinhe zindagee thee pyaaree unhein mil gaya kinaara.
Mujhe aagaya yakeen-sa-ki yahee hai meree manzil,
Sare-raah jab kisee ne mujhe dafatan pukaara.
Main bataaoon fark naaseh! jo hai mujhmein aur tujhmein,
Meree zindagee talaatum, teree zindagee kinaara.
Mujhe guftgoo se badhhkar ghame-izne-guftgoo hai,
Wahee baat poochhte hain jo na kah sakoon dubaara,
Koee aye 'Shakeel' dekhe, ye junoon naheen tau kya hai,
Ki usee ke ho gaye hum, jo na ho saka humaara.

O, cruel one, my life is lit by your sorrow,
In fact, your sorrow is dearer to me than life (itself).
If you do not mind, then in this world of fragrance and colours,
May I seek some support for the peace of (my) heart.
There is a unique relationship, O, cyclonic wave! I have been pledged with you,
Those who were attatched to life, have found the shore.
I almost believed that this was my destination,
When on the thoroughfare some one called me all of a sudden.
Let me explain the difference between me and you, O preacher!
My life is the tempest and your life is the shore.
More than the talks, I am sad about being given permission to talk,
(For) She asks me to say the samething which I can not repeat.
Let someone judge, O 'Shakeel'! what else it is, if not sheer madness,
That I have allowed my self to be totally possessed by the one who would not belong to me.

Shakeel Badayoonee"

मैं आप अपनी तलाश में हूँ, मेरा कोई रहनुमा[1] नहीं है,
वो क्या बताएगें राह मुझको, जिन्हें कुछ अपना पता नहीं है।
मर्सरतों[2] की तलाश में है, मगर ये दिल जानता नहीं है,
अगर ग़मे-जिन्दगी[3] नहीं है, तो ज़िन्दगी का मज़ा नहीं है।
आतिशे-ग़म[4] भड़क रही है, तो क्या हुआ मुतमईन[5] रहो तुम,
ये आँच सिर्फ मुझ पर आई है, तुम्हारा दामन जला नहीं है।
बहुत दिनो से मैं सुन रहा था, सज़ा वो देते हैं हर ख़ता पर,
मुझे तो इसकी सज़ा मिली है, कि मेरी कोई ख़ता नहीं है।
तू मेरे सज़दों[6] की लाज रखले, शऊरे-सज़दा नहीं है मुझको,
ये सर तेरे आस्ँता[8] से पहले, किसी के आगे झुका नहीं है।
अगर कभी मिल गए इत्तिफ़ाक़[9] से, तो 'राज़' उनसे मैं ये कहूँगा,
तेरे सितम[10] तो भुला चुका हूँ, तेरा करम[11] भूलता नहीं है।

राज़ इलाहाबादी

1.रास्ता दिखाने वाला 2.शान्ती 3.जीवन के दुख 4.दुखों की आग
5.आश्वस्त 6.सरझुकाने की 7.सरझुकाने का तरीका 8.दरवाज़े 9.अचानक 10. .ज़ुल्म 11.दया

Main aap apnee talaash mein hoon, mera koee rahnuma naheen hai,
Wo kya bataayenge raah mujhko, jinhe kuchh apna pata naheen hai.
Masarraton kee talaash mein hai, magar ye dil jaanta naheen hai,
Agar ghame-zindagee naheen hai, tau zindagee ka maza naheen hai,
Aatishe-gham bhadhhak rahee hai, tau kya hua mutmaeen raho tum,
Ye aanch sirf mujh par aaee hai, tumhaara daaman jala naheen hai.
Bahut dinoon se main sun raha tha, saza wo dete hain har khata par,
Mujhe tau iskee saza milee hai, ki meree koee khata naheen hai.
Too mere sazdon kee laaj rakhle, shaoore-sazda naheen hai mujhko,
Ye sar tere aastaan se pahle, kisee ke aage jhuka naheen hai.
Agar kabhee mil gaye ittifaaq se, tau 'Raaz' unse main ye kahoonga,
Tere sitam tau bhula chuka hoon, tera karam bhoolta naheen hai.

I myself am in search of my ownself, I have no guide,
How they will show me the way, (those) who don't know their own where abouts.
It is in the search of worldly pleasures but, the heart doesn't know,
That, there is no fun in life if it is bereft of sorrow.
Never mind the blaze, be rest assured,
This fire is after me alone, your hem has remain unharmed by her.
Since long I have been hearing that she gives punishment for every mistake.
(But) I have been punished for the fact, that I have committed no mistake.
Keep the honour of my prostrations, I am not well versed with the art of prostrating,
Prior to bowing before your door, this head of mine had not bowed before anyone.
'Raaz' if ever I happen to meet her, then I shall tell her,
That I have already forgotten your atrocities, but am unable to forget your benevolence.

'Raaz' Allahabaadi.

आज नागहा[1] हम किसी से मिले,
बाद मुद्दत[2] के ज़िन्दगी से मिले।
ख़ुद से मिलने को उम्र भर तरसे,
यूँ तो मिलने को हम सभी से मिले।
फूल करलें निबाह काटों से,
आदमी ही न आदमी से मिले।
शम्मा क्या, चाँद क्या, सितारे क्या,
सिलसिले सबके तीरगी[3] से मिले।
हम पे गुज़रा है वो भी वक्त 'ख़ुमार'
जब शनासा[4] भी अजनबी से मिले।

ख़ुमार बाराबंकवी

1.अचानक 2.वर्षों के बाद 3.अंधेरा 4.मित्र, परिचित

Aaj naagaha hum kisee se mile,
Baad muddat ke zindagee se mile,
Khud se milne ko umr bhar tarse,
Yoon tau milne ko hum sabhee se mile.
Phool karlein nibaah kaanton se,
Aadmee hee na aadmee se mile.
Shamma kya, chaand kya, sitaare kya,
Silsile sab ke teergee se mile
Hum pe guzra hai wo bhee waqt 'Khumaar'
Jab shanaasa bhee ajnabee se mile.

Today I happened to come across someone,
Met with life after ages.
Kept craving throughout the life to meet my ownself,
Otherwise, for the sake of meeting, I did meet everyone.
The flower gets along (even) with the thorns,
It is only the homosapien who doesn't get along with his own kind.
Be it the candle, be it the moon, be them the stars,
They all end up merging with the darkness.
O, 'Khumaar' I have passed through such phase also,
During which friends have met (me) like strangers.

Khumaar' Baaraabankvi

शम्मा-ए-मज़ार[1] थी, न कोई सोगवार[2] था,
तुम जिस पे रो रहे थे, वो किसका मज़ार था।
तड़पूँगा उम्र भर दिले-मरहूम[3] के लिए,
कमबख़्त, नामुराद, लड़कपन का यार था।
सौदा-ए-इश्क़ और है, वहशत कुछ और शै[4],
मजनूं का कोई दोस्त फ़साना-निगार था।
जादू है या तिलिस्म तुम्हारी ज़बान में,
तुम झूठ कह रहे थे, मुझे एतिबार था।
क्या-क्या हमारे सिजदे की रुसवाइयाँ हुईं,
नक़्शे-क़दम किसी का सरे-रहगुज़ार था।
इस वक़्त तक तो वज़्अ में आया नही है फ़र्क़,
तेरा करम शरीक़ जो परवरदिगार था।

बेख़ुद देहलवी

1.कब्र की मोमबती 2.दुख प्रकट करने वाला 3.मरा हुआ दिल 4.वस्तु,चीज 5.रंग-ढंग

Shamma-e-mazaar thee, na koee sogwaar tha,
Tum jis pe ro rahe the, wo kis ka mazaar tha.
Tadhpoonga umr bhar dile-marhoom ke liye,
Kambaqt, naa muraad, ladhakpan ka yaar tha.
Sauda-e-ishq aur hai ,wahshat kuchh aur shai,
Majnoon ka koee dost fasaana-nigaar tha.
Jaadoo hai ya tilism tumhaaree zabaan mein,
Tum jhoothh kah rahe the, mujhe aitbaar tha.
Kya-kya humaare sizde kee ruswaaeeyaan hueen,
Naqshe-qadam kisee ka sare-rahguzaar tha.
Is waqt tak tau wazai mein aaya naheen hai fark,
Tera karam shareek jo parwardigaar tha.

Neither there was a candle on the tomb, nor there was any sympathiser,
Where you were weeping, whose tomb was that?
Throughout the life (I) will lament for the dead heart,
The wretched, the unwanted one was my childhood friend.
Business of love is different, madness is a separate thing,
Perhaps some friend of 'Majnoon' must have been a story-maker.
Is there magic or some incantation in your tongue,
You were telling lies and I was believing.
What all humiliations had to be undergone by my prostrations,
(Because) Foot prints of my beloved were all over on the thoroughfare.
Till now there has been no change in
Your benevolence (Which has always been on me) O, gracious God.

Bekhud Dehalvi

उदास एक मुझी को तो कर नहीं जाता,
वह मुझसे रूठ के अपने भी घर नहीं जाता।
वह दिन गये, कि मुहब्बत थी जान की बाज़ी,
किसी से अब कोई बिछड़े, तो मर नहीं जाता।
तुम्हारा प्यार तो सांसों में सांस लेता है,
जो होता नशशा तो इक दिन उतर नहीं जाता?
पुराने रिश्तों की बेग़रज़ियां[1] न समझेगा,
वह अपने ओहदे[2] से जब तक उतर नहीं जाता।
'वसीम' उसकी तड़प है, तो उसके पास चलो,
कभी कुँआ किसी प्यासे के घर नहीं आता।

वसीम बरेलवी

1.निस्वार्थ 2.पद

Udaas ek mujhee ko tau kar naheen jaata,
Wah mujhse roothh ke apne bhee ghar naheen jaata.
Wah din gaye, ki muhabbat thee jaan kee baazee,
Kisi se ab koee bichhdhe, tau mar naheen jaata.
Tumhaara pyaar tau saanson mein saans leta hai,
Jo hota nashsha tau ik din utar naheen jaata?
Puraane rishton kee begharziyaan na samjhega,
Wah apne ohde se jab tak utar naheen jaata.
'Waseem' uskee tadhap hai, tau uske paas chalo,
Kabhee kuaan kisee pyaase ke ghar naheen jaata.

I am not the only one whom she leaves behind sad,
After getting angry with me, she doesnot return to her home even.
Those days have gone when love used to be a matter of life and death,
These days, after separation, noone ever dies.
For sure, your love breathes through my breath,
Had it been intoxication, it would have faded one day.
He will not understand the selfless culture of old relationships,
Until he relinquish the high-office.
O, 'Waseem' if you are desperate for her, then go to her place,
No well ever comes to the home of a thirsty peron.

'Waseem' Bareilvi

और काँटों को लहू किसने पिलाया होगा,
हमसा दीवाना चमन[1] मे कोई आया होगा।
बे-सबब[2] कोई उलझता है भला कब किस से,
तुम ने गुज़रा हुआ कल याद दिलाया होगा।
जुज़[3] हमारे ऐ! सुलगती हुई तन्हाई तुझे,
ऐसे सीने से भला किसने लगाया होगा।
कोई आया है ना 'शहज़ाद' कोई आएगा,
वहम ने याद के पर्दे को हिलाया होगा।

फ़रहत शहज़ाद

1.बाग 2.बिना कारण 3.सिवा

Aur kaanton ko lahoo kisne pilaaya hoga,
Humsa deewaana chaman mein koee aaya hoga.
Be-sabab koee ulajhta hai bhala kab kis se,
Tumne guzra hua kal yaad dilaaya hoga.
Juz humaare aye! sulagtee huee tanhaaee tujhe,
Aise seene se bhala kisne lagaaya hoga.
Koee aaya hai, na 'Shahzaad' koee aayega,
Waham ne yaad ke pardon ko hilaaya hoga.

Who else must have offered blood to the thorns,
Some mad man like me must have visited the garden.
Without any reason who confronts whom,
You must have reminded about the days gone by.
O, smouldering loneliness!, who else but I,
Would have embraced you so close to the heart.
No one has come, no one will come, O 'Shahzaad'!
misconception must have stirred the curtain of memory.

'Farhat Shahzaad

अब मैं राशन की कतारों में नजर आता हूँ,
अपने खेतों से बिछड़ने की सज़ा पाता हूँ।
इतनी मँहगाई, कि बाज़ार से कुछ लाता हूँ,
अपने बच्चों मे उसे बाँट के शरमाता हूँ।
अपनी नीदों का लहू पूछने की कोशिश में,
जागते-जागते थक जाता हूँ, सो जाता हूँ।
कोई चादर समझ के ख़ींच ना ले फिर से 'ख़लील'
मै कफ़न ओढ़ के फुटपाथ पे सो जाता हूँ।

ख़लील धनतेज़वी

Ab main raashan kee kataaron mein nazar aata hoon,
Apne kheton se bichhadhne kee saza paata hoon.
Itnee mahngaaee ki baazaar se kuchh laata hoon,
Apne bachchon mein use baant ke sharmaata hoon.
Apnee neendon ka lahoo poochhne kee koshish mein,
Jaagte-jaagte thak jaata hoon, so jaata hoon.
Koee chaadar samajh ke kheench na le phir se 'Khaleel'
Main qafan odhh ke futpaath pe so jaata hoon.

These days I am seen in the queues for rations,
(I'm) Getting punished for leaving my fields behind.
Dearness is so much that when I bring something from the market,
I feel Ashamed while distributing it among my children.
I continue remaining awake in the effort of wiping off blood from my sleeps,
(Finally) When tired, I go to sleep.
Lest somebody should again take it to be a sheet and pull it off my body, O, "Khaleel"!
I cover myself with the shroud and go to sleep on the footpath.

Khaleel Dhantejvi.

आज के दौर मे ऐ! दोस्त ये मंज़र[1] क्यूँ है,
ज़ख़्म हर सर पे, हर इक हाथ में पत्थर क्यूँ है।
जब हकीक़त[2] है कि हर ज़र्रे में तू रहता है,
फिर ज़मी पर कहीं मस्ज़िद कहीं मन्दिर क्यूँ है।
अपना अन्ज़ाम[3] तो मालूम है सबको फिर भी,
अपनी नज़रों में हर इन्सान सिकन्दर क्यूँ है।
ज़िन्दगी जीने के क़ाबिल ही नही है अब 'फ़ाकिर'
वरना हर आँख में अश्कों[4] का समन्दर क्यूँ है।

सुदर्शन फ़ाकिर

1.हष्य 2.सच्चाई 3.नतीजा,अंत 4.आँसूओं

Aaj ke daur mein aye! dost ye manzar kyoon hai,
Zakhm har sar pe, har ik haath mein patthar kyoon hai.
Jab haqeeqat hai ki har zarre mein too rahta hai,
Phir zameen par kaheen maszid kaheen mandir kyoon hai,
Apna anzaam tau maloom hai sabko phir bhee,
Apnee nazroon mein har insaan Sikandar kyoon hai,
Zindage jeene ke qaabil hee nahee hai ab 'Faakir'
Warna har aankh mein ashkon ka samandar kyoon hai.

O, Friend! in the present era why there is such a spectacle,
Wound on every head and every hand is holding a stone
When the reality is, that you (God) dwell in every particle,
Then on the earth why there is mosque somewhere and temple somewhere.
Every one knows his own end, yet why,
In his own eyes every one is the 'Alexender'.
Life is no more worth living O, Faakir!
Why else there is an ocean of tears in every eye.

Sudarshan Faakir

मेरी दास्ताँ[1] का ऊरूज[2] था, तेरी नर्म पलकों की छाँव में,
मेरे साथ था तुझे जागना, तेरी आँख कैसे झपक गई।
तेरे हाथ से मेरे होठ तक, वो ही इन्तिज़ार की प्यास है,
मेरे नाम की जो शराब थी, कहीं रास्ते में छलक गई।
तुझे भूल जाने की कोशिशें कभी कामयाब[3] न हो सकीं,
तेरी याद शाखें-गुलाब[4] है जो हवा चली तो लचक गई।
कोई दर्द जाँ का बताए क्या, कोई चोट दिल की दिखाए क्या,
ये बहार कितनी अजीब है, मेरे ज़ख़्म फूलों से ढक गई।
कभी हम मिले भी तो क्या मिले, वो ही दूरियाँ वो ही फासलें,
न कभी हमारे क़दम बढ़े न कभी तुम्हारी झिझक गई।

बशीर बद्र

1.कहानी 2.पराकाष्टा 3.सफल 4.गुलाब की टहनी

Meree daastaan ka oorooj tha, teree narm palkon kee chhaaon mein,
Mere saath tha tujhe jaagna, teree aankh kaise jhapak gayee,
Tere haath se mere honth tak, wo hee intizaar kee pyaas hai,
Mere naam kee jo sharaab thee, kaheen raaste mein chhalak gayee.
Tujhe bhool jaane kee koshishein, kabhee kaamyaab na ho sakeen,
Teree yaad shaakhe-gulaab hai, jo hawa chalee tau lachak gayee,
Koee dard jaan ka bataaye kya, koee chot dil kee dikhaaye kya,
Ye bahaar kitnee ajeeb hai, mere zakhm phoolon se dhak gayee.
Kabhee hum mile bhee tau kya mile, wo hee dooreeyaan wohee faaslein,
Na kabhee humaare qadam badhe, na kabhee tumhaaree, jhijhak gayee.

The climax of my story was in the shade of your delicate eyelids,
You were supposed to remain awake with me, how come your eyes got winked?
From thy hand to my lips was the same thirst of waiting,
The wine that was earmarked for me, got spilled some where on the way.
Efforts to forget you, never succeeded,
Your memory is a branch of rose which swayed when the breeze blew.
How should one explain the pain of living, how should one show the injury of heart,
How crazy is this spring which left my wounds covered with flowers.
even when we met of what use those meetings were, same distances, same separations,
Neither my steps could advance, nor you could overcome your hesitation.

'Bashir Badr'

दाग़ आँसुओं से दिल के क्या-क्या धो लिए,
मंज़िल के अपनी आप निशाँ हमने खो दिए।
वो क्या करेगें मेरे शबिस्ताँ[1] में रौशनी,
बुझ जाएँ आँधियों के तसव्वुर[2] से जो दिए।
हम ग़मनवाज़[3] आपकी महफ़िल को क्या कहें,
हँसते हुए जो लोग गये थे वो रो दिये,
मालिक ने तो कराई फ़रिशतों[4] से बन्दगी[5],
अपने मुक़ाम[6] आप ही इन्साँ ने खो दिये।
थी राहे-शब[7] तो बज़्म[8] में रौशन था एक-एक,
थे मंज़िले-सहर[9] पे मगर एक-दो दिए।
रूमानियत के साये में उभरे थे जो 'वसीम',
तुमने वो शेर ख़ूने-जिगर[10] में डुबो दिये।

वसीम बरेलवी

1.शयनकक्ष 2.कल्पना 3.दुखग्रस्त 4.देवतागण 5.पूजा 6.मंजिलें 7.अंधेरे रास्ते
8.महफ़िल 9.सुबह के वक़्त 10.हदय का ख़ून

Daagh aansuon se dil ke kya-kya dho liye,
Manzil ke apnee aap nishaan humne kho diye.
Woh kya kareinge mere shabistaan mein raushnee,
Bujh jaayein aandhiyon ke tasawwur se jo diye.
Hum gham nawaaz aapkee mehfil ko kya kahein,
Hanste huye jo log gaye the woh ro diye.
Maalik ne tau karaaee farishton se bandgee,
Apne muqaam aap hee insaan ne kho diye.
Thee raahe-shab tau bazm mein raushan tha ek-ek,
The manzile-sahar pe magar ek-do diye.
Roomaaniyat ke saaye mein ubhre the jo 'Waseem',
Tumne wo shair khoone-jigar mein dubo diye.

I wiped off all blots of heart with tears,
Deliberately I (myself) lost all signs of my destination.
What lighting will they do in my bed room,
The lamps which get extinguished by the mere thought of gusty winds.
What can we depressed ones say of your assembly,
Even the smiling ones have returned crying.
God made even the angels do worship,
(Whereas) Human beings themselves lost their own destinations.
When it was dark on way, then every lamp was fully lit up,
By the time the morning arrived, there were only one or two burning.
O, 'Waseem'! which had cropped up in the Shade of romanticism,
You have immersed those couplets in the blood of (your) heart.

'Waseem' Bareilvi

आप क्यों हो गए अजनबी की तरह,
बात तो कीजिए आदमी की तरह।
फूल बरसते थे कल जिनकी गुफ़्तार[1] से,
आज वो हो गए फुलझड़ी की तरह।
बेवफ़ा, आप अगर यूँ ही कहते रहे,
हम भी हो जाएगें आप ही की तरह।
मंज़िलों ने ही लूटे हैं ख़ुद क़ाफ़िले[2],
रहबरी[3] हो गई रहजनी[4] की तरह।
हम परिंदों की मानिन्द[5] उड़ने लगे,
चल न पाए मगर आदमी की तरह।
'राज़' को आज तक कोई समझा नहीं,
ग़ौर करते रहे फलसफ़ी[6] की तरह।

राज़ इलाहाबादी

1.बातों से 2.कारवाँ 3.पथप्रदर्शन 4.ठगी 5.तरह 6.दर्शनशास्त्र

Aap kyon ho gaye ajnabee kee tarah,
Baat tau keejiye aadmee kee tarah.
Phool baraste the kal jinkee guftaar se,
Aaj wo ho gaye phuljhadhee kee tarah.
Bewafa, aap agar yoon hee kahte rahe,
Hum bhee ho jaayenge aap hee kee tarah.
Manzilon ne hee loote hain khud qaafile,
Rahbaree ho gayee rahjanee kee tarah.
Hum parindon kee maanind udhne lage,
Chal na paaye magar aadmee kee tarah.
'Raaz' ko aaj tak koee samjha naheen.
Ghaur karte rahe phalsafee kee tarah.

Why are you behaving like a stranger,
At least talk like a human being.
From whose talks flowers used to rain till yesterday,
Today she has become like a sparkler.
If you continue calling me unfaithful in this way,
I too will become like yourself (someday).
The destinations (themselves) have looted the caravans,
Guiding has become like thuggery,
We started flying like the birds,
But could not walk like human beings.
Till date no one has been able to understand the real 'Raaz',
All of them have been trying to read (me) like a philosophy.

Raaz' Allahabaadi

उसे पाक[1] नज़रों से चूमना भी, इबादतों[2] में शुमार है,
कोई फूल लाख क़रीब हो, कभी मैने उसको छुआ नहीं।
ये ख़ुदा की देन अजीब है, कि उसी का नाम नसीब[3] है,
जिसे तूने चाहा वो मिल गया, जिसे मैने चाहा मिला नहीं।
इसी शहर मे कई साल से, मिरे कुछ क़रीबी-अज़ीज़[4] हैं,
उन्हें मेरी कोई ख़बर नहीं, मुझे उनका कोई पता नहीं।

बशीर बद्र

1.पवित्र 2.पूजाओं में 3.उभाग्य 4.घनिष्ठ मित्र

Use paak nazron se choomna bhee, ibaadaton mein shumaar hai,
Koee phool laakh qareeb ho, kabhee maine usko chhua naheen.
Ye khuda kee den ajeeb hai, kee usee ka naam naseeb hai,
Jise toone chaaha wo milgaya, jise maine chaaha mila naheen.
Isee shahar mein kayee saal se, mere kuchh qareebee-azeez hain,
Unhein meree koee khabar naheen, mujhe unka koee pata naheen.

Looking at her with devout eyes, too is counted as worship,
However close a flower might have been, I never touched it,
This grace of God is quite strange and is known as fate,
Whom you wanted you got him, whom I wanted I did not get her.
In this very city, for last many years, many near and dear ones of mine have been residing,
(But Alas!) Neither they have any news of mine, nor I know their whereabouts.

'Bashir Badr'

सामने है जो, उसे लोग बुरा कहते हैं,
जिसको देखा ही नहीं, उसको ख़ुदा कहते हैं।
ज़िन्दगी को भी सिला[1] कहते हैं कहनेवाले,
जीनेवाले तो गुनाहों की सजा कहते है।
फ़ासलें उम्र के कुछ और बढ़ा देती है,
जाने क्यों लोग उसे फिर भी दवा कहते हैं।
चन्द मासूम से पत्तों का लहू है 'फ़ाकिर',
जिसको महबूब के हाथों की हिना[2] कहते हैं।

सुदर्शन फ़ाकिर

1.ईनाम 2.महँदी

Saamne hai jo, use log bura kahte hain,
Jisko dekha hee naheen, usko khuda kahte hain,
Zindagee ko bhee sila kahte hain kahne waale,
Jeene waale tau gunaahon kee saza kahte hain.
Faaslein umr ke kuchh aur badhha detee hai,
Jaane kyon log use phir bhee dawa kahte hain
Chand maasoom se patton ka lahoo hai 'Faakir'
Jisko mahboob ke haathon kee hina kahte hain,

The one who is infront, people call him bad,
The one who has never been seen, (they) call him God.
For the sake of saying, people call life a reward,
Those who really live life, call it a punishment for their (past) sins.
It increases the distances of age some more,
And yet, God knows why people call it medicine.
'Faakir' (it) is the blood of a few innocent leaves,
Which is called the henna of the beloved's palms.

Sudarshan 'Faakir'

सारे बदन का ख़ून पसीने में जल गया,
इतना चले कि जिस्म हमारा पिघल गया।
चलते थे गिन रहे थे, मुसीबत के रात-दिन,
दम लेने हम जो बैठ गए, दम निकल गया।
अच्छा हुआ जो राह मे ठोकर लगी हमें,
हम गिर पड़े तो सारा ज़माना सँभल गया।
वहशत[1] मे कोई साथ हमारा न दे सका,
दामन की फ़िक्र की तो गरेवाँ निकल गया।

महमूद दुर्रानी

1.घबराहट, डर

Saare badan ka khoon paseene mein jal gaya,
Itna chale ki jism humaara pighal gaya.
Chalte the gin rahe the, museebat ke raat-din,
Dam lene hum jo baith gaye, dam nikal gaya.
Achha hua jo raah mein thhokar lagee humein,
Hum gir padhe tau saara zamaana sambhal gaya.
washat mein koee saath humaara na de saka,
Daaman kee fikr kee tau garewaan nikal gaya.

Entire blood of (my) body got burnt in sweat,
Have walked so much that my body has melted.
While walking, I was counting the days and nights of misfortune,
The moment I stopped for a breather, the breath went out of the body.
Good, that I got tripped enroute,
After I stumbled, the entire world became steady.
In nervousness, nobody came to my rescue,
When tried to retrieve the hem, the collar got exposed

'Mahmood Durranee'

दोनों की निगाहों में है अज़मते-मयखाना[1],
वो हमको सँभाले हैं, हम उनको सँभाले हैं।
इक झूँठ को सच हमने जिस दिन से कहा यारों,
चान्दी के कटोरे हैं, सोने के निवाले है।
ये दिन भी दिखाए हैं, इस दौर-तरक्क़ी[2] ने,
पुरनूर[3] अँधेरे हैं, बेनूर[4] उजाले हैं।
ऐ! 'राज़' कहाँ तक वो अपने को छुपाएगें,
अब सामने आजाएँ, हम दिल को संभाले हैं।

'राज़ इलाहाबादी'

1.शराब-खाने की इज़्ज़त का ख़याल 2.उन्नती का युग 3.प्रकाशमान 4.प्रकाशहीन

Donon kee nigaahon mein hai azmate-maikhaana,
Wo humko sambhaale hain, hum unko sambhaale hain.
Ik jhoonthh ko sach humne jis din se kaha yaaron,
Chaandee ke katore hain, sone ke niwaale hain.
Ye din bhee dikhaayein hain is daure-taraqqee ne,
Purnoor andhere hain, benoor ujaale hain.
Aye! Raaz' kahaan tak wo apne ko chhupaayenge,
Ab saamne aa jaayein, hum dil ko sambhaale hain.

Both of us are sensitive about the dignity of the bar,
She has been steadying me, and I have been steadying her.
Friends! Since the day I proclaimed the lie as the truth,
silver bowls and golden morsels have been at my disposal.
This progressive era has pushed us into the days,
Wherein darkness is fully lit and the lighting is devoid of light.
O, 'Raaz'! how far she will hide herself,
Now let her show up, I have braced up my heart.

'Raaz Allahabaadi'

गर्चे[1] सौ बार ग़मे-हिज्र[2] से जाँ गुज़री है,
फिर भी जो दिल पे गुज़रनी थी कहाँ गुज़री है।
आप ठहरे हैं तो चेहरा है निज़ामे-आलम[3],
आप गुज़रे हैं तो, इक मौजे-खाँ गुज़री है।
होश मे आए तो बतलाए तेरा दीवाना,
दिन गुज़ारा है कहाँ रात कहाँ गुज़री है।
हश्र[4] के बाद भी, दीवाने तेरे पूछते हैं,
वो क़यामत[5] जो गुज़रनी थी, कहाँ गुज़री है?

'सैफ़ उद्दीन सैफ़'

1.यध्यपी 2.विरह के दुख से 3.ससौंर का राज्यपाल 4.प्रलय का दिन 5.प्रलय

Garche sau baar ghame-hijr se jaan guzree hai,
Phir bhee jo dil pe guzarnee thee, kahaan guzree hai,
Aap thhahre hain tau, chehara hai nizaame-aalam,
Aap guzre hain tau, ik mauje-rawaan guzree hai.
Hosh mein aaye tau, batlaaye tera deewaana,
Din guzaara hai kahaan, raat kahaan guzree hai.
Hashr ke baad bhee, deewaane tere poochhte hain,
Wo qayaamat jo guzarnee thee, kahaan guzree hai.

Even though life has passed through the pain of separation for (more than) hundred times,
Yet the heart is yet to suffer the ultimate (real thing).
During your stay (my) face appears to be on top of the world,
Once you have gone away, it appears a wave has passed.
Let him become conscious, then only your mad lover will be able to tell,
Where (he) had passed the day, and where (his) night had been spent.
Even after the day of reckoning, your crazy lovers have been asking,
That doomsday which was to come, where it is ?

'Saif-ud-deen-saif'

जब तेरी याद का तूफ़ान गुज़र जाएगा,
दिल किसी और समन्दर में उतर जाएगा।
दश्त[1] से दूर सही साया-ए-दीवार[2] तो है,
हम न ठहरेगें कोई और ठहर जाएगा।
अपने हालात से मैं सुलह तो कर लूँ लेकिन,
मुझमे रूहपोश[3] जो इक शख़्स[4] है, मर जाएगा।
दाग़ रहने के लिए होते है, रह जाएगें,
वक़्त का काम गुज़रना है गुज़र जाएगा।

रईस फ़रोग़

1.रेगिस्तान 2.दीवार का साया 3.आत्मा में छिपा हुआ 4.आदमी

Jab teree yaad ka toofaan guzar jaayega,
Dil kisee aur samandar mein utar jaayega.
Dasht se door sahee, saaya-e-deewaar tau hai,
Hum na thhahreinge, koyee aur thhahar jaayega.
Apne haalaat se main sulah tau karloon lekin,
Mujhme roohposh jo ik shakhs hai, mar jaayega.
Daagh rahne ke liye hote hain, rah jaayenge,
Waqt ka kaam guzarna hai, guzar jaayega.

When the storm of your rememberance has passed,
The heart will get into some other ocean.
Agreed, it is far from the desert, yet here it is, a shadow of a wall,
If I do not rest here, someone else will.
I may compromise with my present state but,
The person who is latent in my soul, will die.
Scars are meant to remain, they will remain,
Time's job is to pass, it will pass.

'Raees farogh'

वो भी सूरज का सताया होगा,
खुद से बिछुड़ा हुआ साया[1] होगा।
खुश्क आँखो को दिखा कर अपनी,
उसने सहरा[2] को रुलाया होगा
क़ब्र सूनी थी कफ़न कोरा था,
इसलिए लाश वो लाया होगा।
किसकी आहट से ये चौंका 'आदम',
ख़्वाब[3] में कौन ये आया होगा।

शेख़ आदम अबूवाला

1.परछाई 2.रेगिस्तान 3.सपना

Wo bhee sooraj ka sataaya hoga,
Khud se bichhudha huya saaya hoga.
Khushk aankhon ko dikha kar apnee,
Usne sahraa ko rulaaya hoga.
Qabr soonee thee qafan kora tha,
Is liye laash wo laaya hoga.
Kiskee aahat se ye chaunka 'Aadam',
Khwwaab mein kaun ye aaya hoga.

She too must have been tortured by the sun,
Must have been the separated shadow of herself.
By showing her dry eyes,
She must have made the desert cry.
The grave was unoccupied, the shroud was brand new,
That's why she must have brought the dead body.
By whose foot falls 'Adam' has stirred,
Who would have come in the dream

Shaikh Aadam Aboowaala

आपके सामने कहते क्या,
टूट गया दिल रह गई बात।
इतने हैं कि याद नहीं हैं,
दुनिया तेरे अहसानात[1]।
राहों मे क्या खोया हूँ,
मंज़िल-मंज़िल पहुँची बात।
कितनी बड़ी मजबूरी को,
दुनियाँ वाले समझे हयात[2]।
कैसे गुज़री होगी 'वसीम'
मयख़ाने की पहली रात।

वसीम बरेलवी

1.कृपाएँ 2.जीवन

Aapke saamne kahte kya,
Toot gaya dil rah gaee baat,
Itne hain ki yaad naheen hain,
Duniyaan tere aihsaanaat.
Raahon mein kya khoya hoon,
Manzil-manzil pahunchee baat.
Kitnee badee majbooree ko,
Duniyaan waale samjhe hayaat.
Kaise guzree hogee 'waseem'
Maikhaane kee pahlee raat.

What could have I said in front of you,
The heart got shattered, the talk remained,
So many are there that I can not remember,
O, World! Your kind acts.
Since the moment I got lost on way,
The information has reached varied destinations.
It was hell of a helplessness,
Which the living-ones mistook for life.
O 'Wassem' how (you) must have coped up with the first night of tavern.

'Waseem' Bareilvi

तुम्हारी अजुंमन[1] से उठके दीवाने कहाँ जाते,
जो बाबस्ता[2] हुए तुमसे वो अफ़साने कहाँ जाते।
निकल कर दैर-ओ-काबा[3] से अगर मिलता न मयख़ाना।
तो ठुकराए हुए इन्सां ख़ुदा जाने कहाँ जाते।
चलो अच्छा हुआ काम आ गई दीवानगी अपनी,
बगरना हम ज़माने भर को समझाने कहाँ जाते।
तुम्हारी बेरुख़ी ने लाज रखली बादाख़ाने[4] की।
तुम आँखों से पिला देते तो मयख़ाने कहाँ जाते।
'क़तील' अपना मुक़द्दर[5] गम से बेगाना[6] अगर होता,
तो फिर अपने-पराए हमसे पहचाने कहाँ जाते।

क़तील शिफ़ाई

1.महफ़िल 2.समबन्धित 3.मन्दिर और मस्जिद 4.शराबखाना 5.भाग्य 7.अपरिचित

Tumhaaree anjuman se uthh ke deewaane kahaan jaate,
Jo baabasta huye tumse wo afsaane kahaan jaate.
Nikal kar dair-o-kaaba se agar milta na maikhaana,
Tau thhukraaye huye insaan khuda jaane,kahaan jaate.
Chalo achchha huya kaam aagayee deewaangee apnee,
Bagarna hum zamaane bhar ko samjhaane kahaan jaate.
Tumhaaree berukhee ne laaj rakhlee baadaakhaane kee,
Tum aankhon se pila dete tau maikhaane kahaan jaate.
'Qateel' apna muqaddr gham se begaana agar hota,
Tau phir apne-paraaye humse pahchaane kahaan jaate.

After leaving your assembly, where the crazy lovers could have gone,
All those stories related to you, where those could have gone.
Forced out of the temple and mosque, if they hadn't found the tavern,
God only knows where these banished ones would have gone.
Thanks heavens, our madness had come to our rescue,
Otherwise whereall we would have to go to make the entire world understand.
Your indifference had saved the esteem of the tavern,
If you were to make (people) drunk from your eyes, what would have been the fate of the taverns.
O, 'Qateel'! if my fate were to be bereft of sorrows,
Then how could I have distinguished between friends and foes.

'Qateel' Shifaai

दिल में किसी के राह किये जा रहा हूँ मैं,
कितना हँसी गुनाह किये जा रहा हूँ मैं।
फ़र्दे-अमल[1] सियाह[2] किये जा रहा हूँ मैं,
रहमत को बेपनाह किये जा रहा हूँ मैं।
ऐसी भी एक निगाह किये जा रहा हूँ मैं।
ज़र्रों[3] को मेहरो-माह[4] किये जा रहा हूँ मैं।
उठती नही है आँख मगर उसके रूबरू[5]।
नादीदा एक निगाह किये जा रहा हूँ मैं।
गुलशन-परस्त[6] हूँ मुझे गुल ही नही अज़ीज़[7],
काटों से भी निबाह किये जा रहा हूँ मैं।
यूँ ज़िन्दगी गुज़ार रहा हूँ तेरे बग़ैर,
जैसे कोई गुनाह किये जा रहा हूँ मैं।
मुझसे लगे है इश्क़ की अज़्मत को चार चाँद,
ख़ुद हुस्न को गवाह किये जा रहा हूँ मैं।

जिगर मुरादाबादी

1.खुद के कार्य 2.काला 3.कणों 4.सूरज-चाँद 5.सामने 6.बाग का पुजारी 7.प्रिय 8.महानता

Dil mein kisee ke raah kiye jaa raha hoon main,
Kitna hansee gunaah kiye jaa raha hoon main.
Farde-amal siyaah kiye jaa raha hoon main.
Rahmat ko bepanaah kiye jaa raha hoon main,
Aisee bhee ik nigaah kiye jaa raha hoon main,
Zarron ko mehro-maah kiye jaa raha hoon main.
Uthhtee naheen hai aankh, magar us ke roobaroo,
Naadeeda ik nigaah kiye jaa raha hoon main.
Gulshan-parast hoon, mujhe gul hee naheen azeez,
Kaanton se bhee nibaah kiye jaa raha hoon main.
Yoon zindagee guzaar raha hoon tere baghair,
Jaise koee gunaah kiye jaa raha hoon main
Mujhse lage hain ishq kee azmat ko chaar chaand,
Khud husn ko gawaah kiye jaa raha hoon main

I have been making a place in someone's heart,
What a lovely sin I have been committing.
I have been blackening my own deeds (and),
Have been stretching the benevolence to the limits.
I have been perceiving thing with such eyes,
That small particles appear like sun and moon.
These eyes dare not (my) lift in front of her
Yet I continue to cast a glance inadvertently.
I am addicted to the garden, not just the flowers are dear to me,
I have been at home with the thorns too.
I have been spending life without you in such a way,
As if I have been committing a sin nonstop.
because of me the greatness of love has been increased, manifold,
I have made the beauty itself to stand as a witness.

Jigar Muradabadi

शामे-ग़म कुछ उस निगाहे-नाज़[1] की बातें करो,
बेख़ुदी[2] बढ़ती चली है राज़ की बातें करो।
नकहते-.जुल्फ़े-परीशां[3], दास्ताने-शामे-ग़म,
सुबह होने तक इसी अदांज़ की बातें करो।
ये सुकूते-यास[4] ये दिल की रगों का टूटना,
ख़ामशी में कुछ शिकस्ते-साज़[5] की बातें करो
हर रगे-दिल वज्द[6] में आती रहे दुखती रहे,
यूँ ही उसके जा-ओ-बेजा नाज़[7] की बातें करो।
कुछ क़फ़स[8] की तीलियों से छन रहा है नूर[9] सा,
कुछ फ़ज़ा कुछ हसरते-परवाज़[10] की बातें करो।
जिसकी .फुरकत[11] ने पलट दी इश्क़ की काया 'फ़िराक़',
आज उस ईसा-नफ़स-दमसाज़[12] की बातें करो।

फ़िराक़ गोरखपुरी

1.प्रेमिका की घमंडी नज़र 2.आत्मविसर्जन 3.बिखरेबालों की खुशबू 4.निराशा की चुप्पी 5.टूटा हुआ साज़ 6.उन्माद 7.उचित-अनुचित नख़रे 8.पिजैंरा 9.रौशनी 10.उड़ने की इच्छा/लालसा 11.जुदाई 12.ईसा रुपी दोस्त

Shaame-gham kuchh us nigaahe-naaz kee baatein karo,
Bekhudee badhhtee chalee hai, raaz kee baatein karo.
Nakhate-zulfe-pareeshaan, daastaane shaame-gham,
Subah hone tak isee andaaz kee baatein karo.
Ye sukoote-yaas, ye dil kee ragon ka tootna,
Khaamshee mein kuchh shikaste-saaz kee baatein karo.
Har rage-dil wajd mein aatee rahe, dukhtee rahe,
Yoon hee uske jaa-o-beja naaz kee baatein karo.
Kuchh qafas kee teeliyon se chhan raha hai noor sa.
Kuchh fazaa kuchh hasrate-parwaaz kee baatein karo.
Jiskee furqat ne palat dee ishq kee kaaya 'Firaaq'
Aaj us eesaa-nafas-damsaaz kee baatein karo.

It is the evening of sorrows, let us talk about the one with high-headed looks,
Forgetfulness is on the increase, let us talk about things secret.
Fragrance of dishevelled tresses, tales of sorrowful evenings,
Let us talk on these lines till the daybreak.
This silence of despair, this breakdown of heart's nerves,
In the serenity, let us talk about the shattered musical instrument.
Let the heart's nerve get crazy, let it get hurt,
Just for the heck of it, talk about her justified or unjustified disdain.
Something like the light has been filtering through the spokes of the cage,
Let us talk about the sky and the yen for flying.
Whose separation has completely changed the very being of love O, 'Firaaq'!
Let us talk about such christ like saviour of a friend.

'Firaaq' Gorakhpuri

हम ही में थी न कोई बात, याद न तुमको आ सके।
तुमने हमें भुला दिया, हम न तुम्हें भुला सके।
तुम ही न सुन सके अगर, क़िस्सा-ए-ग़म सुनेगा कौन,
किसकी ज़बां खुलेगी फिर, हम न अगर सुना सके।
होश में आ चुके थे हम, जोश में आ चुके थे हम,
बज़्म[1] का रंग देखकर सर न मगर उठा सके।
रौनके-बज़्म-बन गये, लब पे हिकायतें[2] रहीं,
दिल में शिकायतें रहीं, लब न मगर हिला सके।
शौक़े-विसाल[3] है यहाँ, लब पे सवाल है यहाँ,
किसकी मजाल है यहाँ, हम से नज़र मिला सके।
ऐसा भी हो कोई नामाबर[4], बात पे कान धर सके,
सुन के यकीन कर सके, जाके के उन्हें सुना सके।
इज्ज़[5] से और बढ़ गई बरहमी-ए-मिज़ाजे[6] दोस्त,
अब वो करे इलाजे-दोस्त जिसकी समझ मे आ सके।
अहले-ज़बां[7] तो हैं बहुत, कोई नही है अहले दिल,
कौन तेरी तरह 'हफ़ीज़' दर्द के गीत गा सके।

हफ़ीज़ जलन्धरी

1.महफ़िल 2.कहानियाँ 3.प्रेमिका से मिलने का शौक़ 4.पत्रवाहक 5.विनम्रता 6.दोस्त की क्रूरता 7.भाषा के विशेषज्ञ

Hum hee mein thee na koee baat, yaad na tumko aasake,
Tumne humein bhula diya, hum na tumhein bhula sake.
Tum hee na sun sake agar, qissa-a-gham sunega kaun,
Kiskee zabaan khulegee phir, hum na agar suna sake .
Hosh mein aa chuke the hum, josh mein aa chuke the hum.
Bazm ka rang dekhkar sar na magar uthha sake.
Raunke-bazm ban gaye, lab pe hikaayatein raheen,
Dil mein shikaayatein raheen, lab na magar hila sake.
Shauqe-wisaal hai yahaan, lab pe sawaal hai yahaan,
Kiskee majaal hai yahaan, hum se nazar mila sake.
Aisa bhee ho koee naamaabar, baat pe kaan dhar sake,
Sun ke yakeen kar sake, jaake unhein suna sake.
Ijz se aur badhh gayee, barhamee-e-mizaaje-dost,
Ab wo kare ilaaje-dost, jiskee samajh mein aasake.
Ahle-zabaan tau hain bahut, koee naheen hai aihle-dil,
Kaun teree tarah 'Hafeez' dard ke geet gaa sake.

There was nothing of worth in me for which you would have remembered me,
You have forgotten me, but I have not been able to forget you.
If you can not listen then who else will listen to my sad story,
Who else will dare to recount it, if I am unable to do so.
I had become aware and was raring to open up,
But after seeing the atmosphere of the assembly, I could not lift my head.
(I) Became the attraction of assembly with stories remaining on the lips,
Complaints were there in the heart, but could not dare to open the lips.
Desire to meet is here (in the heart), questions are here on the lips,
Who has the gumption here, to look directly in my eyes.
There ought to be a messenger, capable of comprehending (my) message,
Believe it after hearing and then go and recount to her.
Excess of humility (on my part) has intensified the cruel intent in (my) friend's attitude,
Now, she can be treated only by those who can understand this malady.
There are lot of linguists here but none expert enough to understand the language of heart,
O, 'Hafeez' ! who else can render sad songs of love like you.

'Hafeez' Jalandhari

हर एक अश्क[1] है मेरा तेरी ख़ुशी के लिए,
मैं रो रहा हूँ तेरे ग़म की ज़िन्दगी के लिए।
ये कैसी रात है जिसमे हमारा ज़िक्र ही क्या,
तरस रहे हैं सितारे भी रौशनी के लिए।
मैं मुस्कराहटें क्या माँगता, मगर ऐ दोस्त।
कुछ सहारे भी ज़रूरी हैं ज़िन्दगी के लिए।
किस अहतमाम[2] से गुज़री है ज़िन्दगी मेरी,
न कोई मेरे लिए था न मैं किसी के लिए।
किसी को मर्गे-मुसलसल[3] में जो मिले होगें,
वो लुत्फ़[4] मैनें 'वसीम' इस जहाँ में जी के लिए।

वसीम बरेलवी

1.आसूँ 2.इन्तिज़ाम 3.लगातर मत्यु 4.मजे

Har ek ashk hai mera teree khushee ke liye,
Main ro raha hoon tere gham kee zindagee ke liye.
Ye kaisee raat hai jisme humaara zikr hee kya,
Taras rahe hain sitaare bhee raushanee ke liye.
Main muskraahatein kya maangta, magar aye dost!
Kuchh sahaare bhee zaroorее hain zindagee ke liye.
Kis aihtmaam se guzree hai zindagee meree,
Na koee mere liye tha na main kisee ke liye.
Kisee ko marge-musalsal mein jo mile honge,
Wo lutf maine 'Waseem' is jahaan mein jee ke liye.

Every tear of mine is for your happiness,
I am weeping for the life of the sorrow given by you.
What sort of night is this, in which what to talk of me,
Even the stars have been yearning for the light.
Why would have I asked for smiles, but O, Friend!
Some succours too are necessary for the life.
Under what strange arrangement my life has passed,
(Wherein) No one was for me and I was for no one.
What someone might have experienced in continuous death,
The same pleasures I experienced while living.

Waseem Bareilvi

एहले-दैरो-हरम[1] रह गये,
तेरे दीवाने कम रह गये।
मिट गये मंज़िलों के निशाँ,
सिर्फ नक़्शे क़दम[2] रह गये।
हमने हर शै[3] सवाँरी मगर,
तेरी ज़ुल्फ़ों के खम[4] रह गये।
मज़िंले दूर तर हो गईं,
फ़ासलें कम से कम रह गये।
देखकर उनकी तस्वीर को,
आईना बनके हम रह गये।
बेतकल्लुफ़[5] वो औरों से है,
नाज़[6] उठाने को हम रह गये।
हक़ बहारों पे गुलचीं[7] का है,
बाग़बानी को हम रह गये।
जान थे मयकदे की हमीं,
और तरसते हम ही रह गये।
ऐ 'फ़ना' तेरी तक़दीर में,
सारी दुनियाँ के ग़म रह गए।

फ़ना कानपुरी

1.मन्दिर और मस्जिद के विशेषज्ञ 2.पद चिन्ह 3.वस्तु 4.धुँधरालापन 5.अनौपचारिक 6.नख़रे 7.माली, फूलतोड़नेवाला

Aihle-dairo haram rah gaye,
tere deewane kam rah gaye,
Mit gaye manzilon ke nishaan,
Sirf naqshe-qadam rah gaye.
Humne har shai samwaaree magar,
Teree zulfon ke kham rah gaye.
Manzilein door tar ho gayeen,
Faaslein kam se kam rah gaye.
Dekh kar unkee tasweer ko,
Aaina ban ke hum rah gaye.
Haq bahaaron pe gulcheen ka hai,
Baaghbaanee ko hum rah gaye.
Jaan the maikade kee humhee,
Aur taraste hum hee rah gaye.
Aye 'Fana'! teree taqdeer mein,
Saaree duniyaan ke gham rah gaye.

Ardent devotees of temples and mosques remain now,
Number of your mad lovers has decreased (considerably).
All signs of destinations have been wiped off,
Only the foot-prints are remaining.
I did tidy up everything,
The curls of your tresses still remain.
Destinations have gone farther away,
(Whereas) The distances have been reduced to bare minimum.
After seeing her portrait,
I have been transformed into a mirror.
She is quite informal while dealing with others,
Only I have been left to be at her beck and call.
The flower-plucker has all the rights on the springs,
(Whereas) Nurturing of the garden has been left to me.
I was the very life of the tavern,
And I alone remained craving (for a drink).
O, 'Fana' your fate has been destined,
With all the woes of the world.

'Fana' Kaanpuri

जान आँखों में रही, जी से गुज़रने न दिया,
अच्छी दीदार[1] की हसरत[2] थी कि मरने न दिया।
मुद्दतों[3] कशमकशे-यास-ओ-तमन्ना[4] में रहे,
ग़म ने जीने न दिया, शौक़ ने मरने न दिया।
नाख़ुदा[5] ने मुझे दलदल में फ़साँये रख़्ख़ा,
डूब मरने न दिया, पार उतरने न दिया।
कोई तो बात है जो ग़ैर के आगे उसने,
शिक़वा[6] कैसा कि मुझ शुक्र[7] भी करने न दिया।

तपिश

1.दर्शन 2.लालसा 3.वर्षों 4.आशा और निराशा की रस्साकशी 5.मल्लाह,नाविक 6.शिकायत 7.धन्यवाद

Jaan aankhon mein rahee, jee se guzarne na diya,
Achchhee deedaar kee hasrat thee ki marne na diya.
Muddaton kashamkashe-yaas-o-tamanna mein rahe,
Gham ne jeene na diya, shauq ne marne na diya.
Naakhuda ne mujhe daldal mein fansaaye rakhkha,
Doob marne na diya, paar utarne na diya .
Koee tau baat hai jo ghair ke aage usne,
Shiqwaa kaisa ki mujhe shukr bhee karne na diya.

Life got stuck in the eyes, did not allow (me) to cross the ultimate limit,
Strange was the desire to see her that it did not allow me to die.
For years (I) remained stranded in the tug of war between hope and despair,
Sorrow did not allow (me) to live, craze did not allow to die.
The boatman kept me stranded in the swamp,
Did not let me drown nor let me go across.
There definitely is some angle (to it), that infront of an outsider,
Let alone the complaint, she did not allow me even to say 'thanks'.

'Tapish'

अंगड़ाई पर अंगड़ाई लेती है रात जुदाई[1] की
तुम क्या समझो, तुम क्या जानो बात मेरी तन्हाई की।
कौन सियाही[2] घोल रहा है वक़्त के बहते दरिया में
मैने आँख झुकी देखी है, आज किसी हरजाई[3] की।
टूट गये सय्याल[4] नगीने, फूट बहे रुख़्सारों[5] पर,
देखो मेरा साथ न देना, बात है ये रुसवाई[6] की
वस्ल[7] की रात न जाने क्यों इसरार[8] था उनको जाने पर,
वक़्त से पहले डूब गये तारों ने बड़ी दानाई[9] की।
आपके होते दुनियाँ वाले मेरे दिल पर राज करें,
आपसे मुझको शिकवा[10] है खुद आपने वेपरवाही की।
उड़ते-उड़ते आस का पछीं दूर उफ़क[11] में डूब गया,
रोते-रोते बैठ गई आवाज़ किसी सौदाई की।

क़तील शिफ़ाई

1.विरह 2.कालारंग 3.बेवफ़ा सुन्दरी 4.तरल 5.गाल 6.बदनामी 7.मिलन 8.ज़िद 9.कृपा 10.शिकायत,गिला 11.क्षितिज

Angdhaayee par angdhaayee letee hai raat judaayee kee.
Tum kya samjho, tum kya jaano baat meree tanhaaee kee.
Kaun sihaayee ghol raha hai waqt ke bahte dariya mein,
Maine aankh jhukee dekhee hai aaj kisee harjaaee kee.
Toot gaye sayyaal nageene, phoot bahe rukhsaaro par,
Dekho mera saath na dena, baat hai ye ruswaaee kee.
Wasl kee rat na jaane kyon israar tha unko jaane par,
Waqt se pahle doob gaye, taaron ne badhee daanaaee kee.
Aap ke hote duniyaan waale mere dil par raaj karein ,
Aap se mujhko shikwaa hai, khud aapne beparwaahee kee.
Udhte-udhte aas ka panchhee door ufak mein doob gaya,
Rote-rote baith gayee aawaaz kisee saudaaee kee

The night of separtion has been stretching again and again,
How can you understand, what do you know of the plight of my loneliness.
Who has been pouring black colour in the running stream of time,
Today I have seen that unfaithful beauty with eyes bowed.
The liquid gems having collapsed, are flowing down on (her) cheeks,
Do not look at this sight with me, (as) it is a matter of infamy.
Do not know why she was insisting on leaving on the night of union,
The stars acted smart and sat down before time.
With you around, why rest of the people have been ruling my heart,
I have a complaint, you yourself have been acting indifferent.
The bird of hope kept flying and flying and went down the horizon,
The voice of some mad man got drowned after continuous weeping.

Qateel Shifaai

हम तुझसे बिछड़ कर जाने क्यों वो अहद[1] वो पैमां[2] भूल गए,
जीने की कुछ ऐसी चाट लगी, मरने के सब अर्मा[3] भूल गए।
देखी जो कहीं इक श्मअे-हया[4], कुछ हमको भी जैसे याद आया,
ख़ुद अपने ही पहलू में रखकर इक शोला-ए-उरियां[5] भूल गये।
हम अपनी कहानी किस से कहें, ख़ुद हमको झूटी लगती है,
वो कौन था, किसको चाहा था, ए उम्रे-गुरेज़ां[6] भूल गये।
गर तुझको मिले ओ बादे-सबा[7] हम जैसा कोई ख़ाकबसर[8],
कहना कि नहीं अपना कोई, घर और बियाबां[9] भूल गए।
यूँ हमने उम्र बसर की है दुनिया-ए-विसालो-हिज्रा[10] में,
इक ग़म की रफ़ाक़त[11] याद रही और सारे उनवां[12] भूल गए।

'ख़लील-उर-रहमान'

1.कसमें 2.शराब के प्याले 3.इच्छाएँ, मनोकामनाएँ 4.शर्माती हुई मोमबत्ती 5.नैंगा शोला 6.गुज़री हुई उम्र 7.सुबह की हवा 8.राख में बसनेवाला 9.जंगल 10.मिलन और विरह का संसार 11.दोस्ती 12.शीर्षक

Hum tujhse bichhadh kar jaane kyon wo aihad wo paimaan bhool gaye,
Jeene kee kuchh aisee chaath lagee, marne ke sab armaan bhool gaye.
Dekhee jo kaheen ek shame-haya, kuch humko bhee jaise yaad aaya,
Khud apne pahloo mein rakhkar ek shola-e-uriyaan bhool gaye.
Hum apnee kahaanee kis se kahein, khud humko jhoothhee lagtee hai,
Wo kaun tha, kisko chaaha tha, aye umre-gurezaan bhool gaye.
Gar tujhko mile o baade-saba! hum jaisa koee khaakbasar,
Kahna ki naheen apna koee, Ghar aur biyaabaan bhool gaye.
Yoon humne umr basar kee hai, duniyaa-e-wisaalo hijraan mein,
Ek gham kee rafaaqat yaad rahee aur saare unwaan bhool gaye.

After parting from you, don't, know why I forgot all those pledges, all those goblets,
Started relishing life so much, that I forgot all desires for dying.
Whenever I noticed a subdued candle, I was reminded that,
I had forgotten all about the naked flame which I had once kept in my own lap.
Whom do I tell my story to, it sounds false to myself too,
Who was that, whom I had craved for, O,age gone by! I have forgotten (all).
O, morning breeze! If you meet some destitute like me,
Tell him, "there is no one my own, have forgotten about the home and ruins".
I have spent the life in this world of union and separation in such a way,
That I remember only the friendship with pain and have forgotten all other issues.

'Khaleel-ur-Rehmaan'

वो जो हममें तुममें क़रार था, तुम्हें याद हो कि न याद हो,
वही यानी वादा निबाह का तुम्हें याद हो कि न याद हो।
वो जो लुत्फ़ मुझ पे थे पेशतर[1] वो करम[2] कि था मेरे हाल पर,
मुझे सब है याद ज़रा-ज़रा तुम्हें याद हो कि न याद हो।
वो नये गिले, वो शिकायतें, वो मज़े-मज़े की हिकायतें[3],
वो हर एक बात वे रूठना, तुम्हें याद हो कि न याद हो।
कोई बात ऐसी अगर हुई कि तुम्हारे जी को बुरी लगी,
तो बयां[4] से पहले ही भूलना तुम्हें याद हो कि न याद हो।
कभी हममे तुममे भी चाह थी, कभी हममें तुममें भी राह थी।
कभी हम भी तुम भी थे आशना[5], तुम्हें याद हो कि न याद हो।
वो बिगड़ना वस्ल[6] की रात का, वो न मानना किसी बात का,
वो नहीं-नहीं की हर आं[7] अदा, तुम्हें याद हो कि न याद हो।
जिसे आप गिनते थे आश्ना जिसे आप कहते थे बावफ़ा
मैं वो ही हूँ 'मोमिने-मुब्तिला'[8], तुम्हें याद हो कि न याद हो।

मोमिन

1.पहले 2.दया, कृपा 3.कहानियाँ 4.बयान 5.प्रेमी, परिचित 6.मिलन 7.निश्तर 8.प्रेम के दुख से ग्रस्त

Wo jo hum mein tum mein qaraar tha, tumhe yaad ho ki na yaad ho ,
Wahee yaanee waada nibaah ka, tumhein yaad ho ki na yaad ho.
Wo jo lutf mujh pe the peshtar, wo karam ki tha mere hal par ,
Mujhe sab hai yaad zara-zara, tumhein yaad ho ki na yaad ho .
Wo naye gile, wo shikaayatein, wo maze-maze kee hikaayatein,
Wo har ek baat pe roothhna, tumhein yaad ho ki na yaad ho.
Koee baat aisee agar huee ki tumhaare jee ko buree lagee,
Tau bayaan se pahle hee bhoolna, tumhein yaad ho ki na yaad ho.
Kabhee hum mein tum mein bhee chaah thee, kabhee hum mein tum mein bhee raah thee,
Kabhee hum bhee tum bhee the aashna, tumhein yaad ho ki na yaad ho.
Wo bigadhna wasl kee raat ka, wo na maan-na kisee baat ka,
Wo naheen-naheen kee har aan ada, tumhein yaad ho ki na yaad ho.
Jise aap ginte the aashna, jise aap kahte the baawafa,
Main wohee hoon 'Momine-mubitla, tumhein yaad ho ki na yaad ho.

The pledge which was tacit between us, you may remember or may not remember (it),
(I mean) The pledge of holding hand till eternity, you may remember or may not remember.
All those pleasures bestowed on me, all that compassion on my plight,
I remember every bit of if, you may remember or may not remember.
Those strange grudges, those complaints, those interesting stories,
That getting angry at everything, you may remember or may not remember
When expecting to hear from me something unpleasant to your heart,
Then forgetting about it before I could utter, you may remember or may not remember.
There did exist mutual love between us, there did exist a common path between us,
We too were quite close to each other, you may remember or may not remember.
That annoyonce of yours on the night of union, that not agreeing to anything,
That graceful 'No, No' of yours, you may remember or may not remember.
Whom you used to proclaim as a lover, whom you used to hail as the devoted one,
I am the same lovelorn 'Momin', you may remember or may not remember.

'Momin'

देर लगी आने में तुमको, शुक्र है फिर भी आए तो,
आस ने दिल का साथ न छोड़ा वैसे हम घबराये तो।
शफ़क़[1], धनुक[2], महताब[3], घटाएँ, तारे, नग़मे, बिजली, फूल,
उस दामन में क्या-क्या कुछ है, वो दामन हाथ में आए तो।
चाहत के बदले में हम तो बेच दें अपनी मर्ज़ी तक,
कोई मिले तो दिल का गाहक, कोई हमें अपनाए तो।
क्यों ये मिहन-अंगेज[4] तबस्सुम, मद्दे-नज़र[5] जब कुछ भी नहीं,
हाय कोई अनजान अगर इस धोके में आ जाए तो।
सुनी-सुनाई बात नहीं ये अपने ऊपर बीती है,
फूल निकलते हैं शोलों से, चाहत आग लगाए तो।
झूठ है सब, तारीख़ हमेशा अपने को दोहराती है,
अच्छा मेरा ख़्वाबे-ज़वानी थोड़ा-सा दोहराये तो।
नादानी और मजबूरी में कुछ तो यारों फ़र्क करो,
इक बेबस इन्सान करे क्या, टूट के दिल आ जाए तो।

अन्दलीब शादानी

1.सूरज की लाली 2.इन्द्रधनुष 3.चन्द्रमा 4.उतावला करने वाली 5.दृष्टि में

Der lagee aane mein tumko, shukr hai phir bhee aaye tau,
Aaas ne dil ka saath na chhodha, waise hum ghabraaye tau.
Shafaq, dhanuk, mahtaab, ghataaein, taare, naghme, bijlee, phool,
Us daaman mein kya-kya kuchh hai, wo daaman haath mein aaye tau.
Chaahat ke badle mein hum tau bech dein apnee marzee tak,
Koee mile tau dil ka gaahak, koee humein apnaaye tau.
Kyon ye mihin-angej tabassum, madde- nazar jab kuchh bhee naheen,
Haai koee anjaan agar is dhoke mein aajaaye tau.
Sunee-sunaaee baat naheen ye, apne oopar-beetee hai,
Phool nikalte hain sholon se, chaahat aag lagaaye tau.
Jhooth hai sab, taareekh hamesha apne ko doharaatee hai,
Achchha mera, khawaabe-zawaanee thodha-sa dohraaye tau.
Naadaanee aur majbooree mein kuchh tau yaaron fark karo,
Ik bebas insaan kare kya, toot ke dil aajaaye tau.

You took time in coming, thank God at least you came,
Hope never left the heart, even though I did feel nervous.
Redness of sun, rainbow, moon, clouding, stars, songs, lightning, flowers,
What all is there in that hem, only let that hem come into my hands.
In exchange of love, I am even willing to sell all my wishes,
Let me meet a buyer for my heart, let someone make me her own.
Why this kind smile when there is no real intent in the eyes,
God save the gullible one, who may get cheated by this deceit.
This is no hearsay, it has happend to me,
Inflamed by love, flowers emerge out of the flames.
It is a sheer lie that the history always repeats itself,
Ok, let it repeat even a bit of my dream of youth.
O, friends! undustand the subtle difference between immaturity and compulsion,
What a helpless person can do if the heart becomes mad in love.

'Andleeb' Shaadaani

शबे-मयख़ाना[1] भी जब तुझपे ग़राँ[2] गुज़रेगी,
ज़िन्दगी तू ही बता दे कि कहाँ गुजरेगी।
तूने इक बज़्म[3] को रौशन तो किया है लेकिन,
उम्र ऐ! शमा, तेरी बन के धुआँ गुज़रेगी।
ज़िन्दगी तेरे लिए मैनें बहुत कुछ खोया,
ये न समझा था कि बे-नामो-निशाँ[4] गुज़रेगी।
आज पी लेने दे जी लेने दे मुझको साक़ी!
कल मेरी रात ख़ुदा जाने कहाँ गुज़रेगी।
उनसे कह दो मुझे ख़ामोश ही रहने दे 'वसीम'
लब पे आएगी तो, हर बात ग़राँ गुजरेगी।

वसीम बरेलवी

1.शराब खाने की रात 2.बोझिल 3.महफ़िल 4.बिना नाम और चिन्ह के

Shabe-maikhaana bhee jab tujhpe gharaan guzregee,
Zindagee too hee bata de ki kahaan guzregee.
Toone ik bazm ko raushan to kiya hai lekin,
Umr, aye shama! teree ban ke dhuaan guzregee.
Zindagee tere liye maine bahut kuchh khoya,
Ye na samjha tha ki be-naamo-nishaan guzregee.
Aaaj pee lene de, jee lene de mujhko, saaqee!
Kal meree raat khuda jaane kahaan guzregee.
Unse kah do mujhe khaamosh hee rahne dein 'Waseem',
Lab pe aayegee tau, har baat gharaan guzregee.

When the night of the tavern too will weigh heavy on you,
O, Life! you only tell me where thou will get spent.
You have illuminated an assembly, agreed, but
O, candle! your life will end up in smoke.
O, life! I have lost a lot for you,
Had not thought that you would go unnoticed, unnamed.
Tonight let me drink, let me live, O, barmaid!
God only knows where my next night will be spent.
O, Waseem! tell them, " Let me remain silent",
If it comes on the lip then every world would become unbearable.

Waseem Bareilvi

प्यार तुम्हारा भूल तो जाऊँ लेकिन प्यार तुम्हारा है,
ये इक मीठा ज़हर सही, ये ज़हर भी आज गवाँरा[1] है।
हाँफ़ गये पतवार, सफ़ीने[2] चलते-चलते चूर हुए,
ये है भवंर तो ऐ मल्लाहों! कितनी दूर किनारा है।
हम तो एक अनोखी ज़िद में अपनी जान पे खेल गये,
तुम ही बताओ उजड़ी रातों! क्या जीता क्या हारा है।
ओ बेरहम मुसाफ़िर! हँसकर साहिल[3] की तौहीन[4] न कर,
हमने अपनी नाँव डबोकर तुझको पार उतारा है।

क़तील शिफ़ाई

1.मंजूर 2.कश्तियाँ 3.किनारा 4.बेइज़्ज़ती

Pyaar tumhaara bhool tau jaaoon lekin pyaar tumhaara hai,
Ye ek meethha zahar sahee, ye zahar bhee aaj ganwaara hai.
Haanf gaye patwaar, safeene chalte-chalte choor huye,
Ye hai bhanwar tau aye mallahon! kitnee door kinaara hai.
Hum tau ek anokhee zid mein apnee jaan pe khel gaye,
Tum hee bataao ujdhee raaton! kya jeeta kya haara hai.
O, beraham musaafir! hanskar saahil kee tauheen na kar,
Humne apnee naaw dabokar tujhko paar utaara hai.

I can forget your love, but then this love is yours,
This may be a sweet poison yet this poison is acceptable to me today.
The boats have run out of breath, totally exhausted by this marathon sailing,
O, boatmen! if this is the whirlpool then how far is the shore.
Possessed by some strong ego, I had put my life at stake,
O, ravaged nights! you only tell me who has won, who has lost.
O, heartless traveller ! do not insult the shore by laughing,
I have drowned my own boat in the process of taking you across.

Qateel' Shifaai

दोनो जहान तेरी मुहब्बत में हार के,
वो जा रहा है कोई शबे-ग़म गुज़ार के।
वीरां है मयकदा, ख़ुमो-साग़र[1] उदास हैं,
तुम क्या गये कि रूठ गये दिन बहार के।
इक फ़ुर्सते-गुनाह[2] मिली वो भी चार दिन,
देखे है हौंसले हमने परवरदिगार[3] के।
दुनियाँ ने तेरी याद से बेगाना कर दिया,
तुझसे भी दिल-फ़रेब[4] हैं ग़म रोज़गार[5] के।
भूले से मुस्करा तो दिए थे वो आज 'फ़ैज़'
मत पूछ वलवले दिले-नाकर्दाकार[6] के।

फ़ैज़ अहमद फ़ैज़

1.शराब का प्याला और घड़ा 2.पाप करने का अवकाश 3.भगवान के 4.दिल लुभाने वाले 5.संसार के कालचक्र के दुख 6.अनुभवहीन दिल

Dono jahaan teree muhbaat mein haar ke,
Wo jaa raha hai koee shabe-gham guzaar ke.
Weeraan hai maikada, khumo-saaghar udaas hain,
Tum kya gaye ki rooth gaye din bahaar ke.
Ik fursate-gunaah milee wo bhee chaar din,
Dekhe hain haunsle humne parwardigaar ke.
Duniyaan ne teree yaad se begaana kar diya,
Tujhse bhee dil-fareb hain gham rozgaar ke.
Bhoole se muskara tau diye the wo aaj 'Faiz',
Mat poochh walwale dile -naakardaakaar ke.

Having lost both worlds in your love,
Someone is going away having spent the night of sorrow.
The tavern is deserted, the pitcher and the goblet are mournful,
With your departure the days of spring too have turned their back.
The time granted for sinning was four days only,
This much for the magnanimity of God almighty.
This world has made me oblivious of your memory,
The worldly woes are far more captivating than you.
By mistake she did smile today, O, 'Faiz'!
Do not ask the turmoils of (my) inexperienced heart.

Faiz Ahmed 'Faiz'

कहीं शैर-ओ-नग़मा[1] बन के, कहीं आसुओं में ढल के,
वो मुझे मिले तो लेकिन मिले सूरतें बदल के।
ये वफ़ा की सख़्त[2] राहें ये तुम्हारें पाँव नाजुक,
न लो इन्तिक़ाम[3] मुझसे मेरे साथ-साथ चलके।
ये चिराग़े-अंजुमन[4] तो हैं बस एक शब[5] के मेहमाँ,
तू जला वो शम्मा-ऐ-दिल जो बुझे कभी न जल के।
न तो होश से तआरुफ़[6] न जुनूँ से आशनाई[7],
ये कहाँ पहुँच गये हम तेरी बज़्म[8] से निकल के।

ख़ुमार बाराबंकवी

1.कविता और गीत 2.कठिन 3.बदला 4.महफ़िल के दिये, 5.रात 6.परिचय 7.दोस्ती 8.महफ़िल

Kaheen shair-o-naghma ban ke, kaheen aansuon mein dhal ke,
Wo mujhe mile tau lekin mile soortein badal ke.
Ye wafa kee sakht raahein, ye tumhaare paaon naajuk,
Na lo intiqaam mujhse, mere saath-saath chal ke,
Ye chiraaghe-anjuman tau hain bas ek shab ke mehmaan,
Too jala wo shama-e-dil jo bujhe kabhee na jal ke.
Na tau hosh se taaruf, na junoon se aashnaaee,
Ye kahaan pahoonch gaye hum teree bazm se nikal ke.

Sometimes in the form of poetry and song, at times in the form of tears,
She did meet me but only after changing faces.
These difficult tracks of faithfulness vis-a-vis your delicate feet,
Do not take revenge on me by keeping pace with me.
These earthen-lamps in the assembly last only for the night,
You should kindle that candle of heart which does not go off once kindled.
No more I am aware of myself, no more I am at home with madness,
Where have I reached after leaving your assembly.

'Khumaar' Baaraabankvi

मुझे सहल हो गई मंज़िलें, वो हवा के रुख़ भी बदल गये,
तेरा हाथ हाथ मे आ गया कि चिराग़ राह में जल गए।
वो लजाए मेरे सवाल पर कि उठा सके न झुका के सर,
उड़ी ज़ुल्फ चेहरे पे इस तरह कि शबों के राज़[1] मचल गए।
वो बात जो वो न कह सके, मेरे शेर-ओ-नग़मों में आ गई,
वही लब न मैं जिन्हें छू सका क़दहे-शराब[2] मे ढल गए।
मेरे काम आ गईं आख़िरश[3] यही काविशें[4] यही गर्दिशें।
बढ़ीं इस क़दर मेरी मंज़िलें कि क़दम के ख़ार[5] निकल गए।

मजरूह सुल्तानपुरी

1.भेद 2.शराब के प्याले में 3.अन्त मे 4.घुमक्कड़पने की आदतें 5.बुरा समय 5.काँटे

Mujhe sahal ho gaee manzilein wo hawa ke rukh bee badal gaye,
tera haath haath mein aa gaya ki chiraagh raah mein jal gaye.
Wo lajaaye mere sawaal par ki utha sake na jhuka ke sar,
Udhee zulf chehre pe is tarah ki shabon ke raaz machal gaye.
Wo baat jo wo na kah sake, mere shair-o-naghmon mein aa gayee,
Wahee lab na main jinhein chhoo saka, qadhe-sharaab mein dhal gaye.
Mere kaam aagayeen aakhirash yahee kaawishein, yahee gardishein,
Badhheen is qadar meree manzilein ki qadam ke khaar nikal gaye.

Destinations became easy to reach, behavior of winds too changed favourably,
(Ever since) Your hand came in my hand, the earthen lamps got lit on way.
She felt so ashamed at my query that (she) could not lift her head once bowed,
The tresses flew on her face in such a way that all secrets of nights went berserk.
The feelings which she could not utter, became vocal in my couplets and songs,
Those lips which I could never touch, melted in (my) cup of wine.
In the end these very aimless wanderings and bad times came to my rescue,
For the distance to my destination increased to the extent that all thorns embedded in my feet got consumed.

'Majrooh' Sultaanpuri

तंग आ चुके है कशमकशे-ज़िन्दगी[1] से हम।
ठुकरा न दें जहाँ को कहीं बेदिली से हम।
लो आज हमने तोड़ दिया रिश्ता-ए-उमीद[2],
लो अब कभी गिला न करेगें किसी से हम।
उभरेगें एक बार कभी दिल के वलवले[3],
गो दब गये हैं बारे-ग़मे-ज़िन्दगी[4] से हम।
गर ज़िन्दगी में मिल गए फिर इत्तफ़ाक़[5] से,
पूछेगें अपना हाल तेरी बेबसी से हम।

साहिर लुधियानवी

1.जीवन की ज़द्दो-ज़हद 2.आशा से रिश्ता 3.गुबार, बोझ 4.दुख भरी जिन्दगी का बोझ 5.अचानक

Tang aa chukein hain kashmkashe-zindagee se hum,
Thhukra na dein jahaan ko kaheen bedilee se hum.
Lo aaj humne todh diya rista-e-umeed,
Lo ab kabhee gila na kareinge kisee se hum.
Ubhreinge ek baar abhee dil ke walwale,
Go dab gaye hain baare-ghame-zindagee se hum.
Gar zindagee mein mil gaye phir ittfaaq se,
Poochheinge apna haal teree bebasee se hum.

I have become fed up with the tussles of life,
I may kick the world (someday) caring two hoots (about it).
Look, today I have broken all relations with hope,
From now onwards, I will hold no grudge against anyone.
Someday these turmoils of heart will give vent,
Even though we have been weighed down by the woes of life.
If by chance we happen to meet in life again,
I will ask about my plight from your helplessness.

Saahir Ludhiyaanvi

ग़मे-आशिक़ी से कह दो, रहे-आम[1] तक न पहुँचे,
मुझे ख़ौफ़ है ये तोहमत मिरे नाम तक न पहुँचे।
मै नज़र से पी रहा था तो ये दिल न बद्दुआ दी,
" तेरा हाथ ज़िन्दगी भर कभी जाम तक न पहुँचे"।
नई सुबह पर नज़र है मगर आह ये भी डर है,
ये सहर[2] भी रफ़्ता-रफ़्ता[3] कहीं शाम तक न पहुचे।
ये अदा-ए-बेनियाज़ी तुझे बेवफ़ा मुबारिक,
मगर ऐसी बेरुख़ी क्या कि सलाम तक न पहुँचे।
जो निक़ाबे-रुख़[4] उठादी तो ये क़ैद भी लगा दी,
उठे हर निगाह लेकिन कोई बाम[5] तक न पहुचे।
उन्हें अपने दिल की ख़बरें मेरे दिल से मिल रहीं हैं,
मै जो उनसे रूठ जाऊँ तो पयाम तक न पहुँचे।
वही इक ख़मोश नग़मा है 'शकील' जाने-हस्ती
जो ज़बान तक न आये जो क़लाम तक न पहुँचे।

शकील बदायूनी

1.आम रास्ता 2.सुबह 3.धीरे-धीरे 4.चेहरे का पर्दा 5.छत

Ghame-aashiqee se kah do, rahe- aam tak na pahunche,
Mujhe khauf hai ye tauhmat mire naam tak na pahunche.
Main nazar se pee raha tha tau ye dil ne baddua dee,
“Tera haath zindagee bhar kabhee jaam tak na pahunche”.
Nayee subah par nazar hai, magar aah ye bhee dar hai,
Ye sahar bhee rafta-rafta kaheen shaam tak na pahunche.
Ye ada ye beniyaazee tujhe bewafa mubaarik,
Magar aisee berukhee kya ki salaam tak na pahunche,
Jo niqaabe-rukh uthha dee tau ye qaid bhee lagaadee,
Uthhe har nigaáh lekin koee baam tak na pahunche,
Unhein apne dil kee khabrein mere dil se mil raheen hain,
Main jo unse rooth jaaoon tau payaam tak na pahunche,
Wahee ek khamosh naghma hai 'Shakeel' jaane hastee,
Jo zabaan tak na aaye jo qalaam tak na pahunche.

Tell the sorrow of love, that it should not reach the open streets,
I fear lest this slander should reach my name.
While I was drinking (your beauty) from my eyes, the heart cursed me thus,
"May thy hand never reach the goblet throughout the life".
The eyes are glued to the emerging morning,
But alas! the fear also lurks that this morning too may gradually end up in the evening.
O, unfaithful one! may you cherish this coquetry of indifference,
But what sort of unfeeling is this, that even my salute is not acceptable to you.
(When she) Lifted the veil, then she put this embargo too,
That every eye can be raised but it should not reach up to the roof.
She has been getting news of her heart through my heart,
If I were to get cross with her, not even a message will reach her.
O, 'Shakeel'! life is that sort of a silent song,
Which does not come upto the tongure, hence not talked/written about.

'Shakeel' Badayooni

तेरे न होने से यूँ सोगवार[1] गुज़री है,
बहार जैसे शबे-इन्तिज़ार[2] गुज़री है।
वो शम्मा कैसे बताएगी मंज़िलों के निशाँ,
हयात[3] जिसकी सरे-रह-गुज़ार[4] गुज़री है।
मुझे हयात की मजबूरियाँ नज़र आईं
नज़र से जब कोई लोहे-मज़ार[5] गुज़री है।
सितारे डूब रहे है बिदाईयाँ देकर,
न जाने किस की शबे-इन्तिज़ार गुज़री है।
दिले-वसीम से हर शाम इन्तिज़ार के बाद,
बहुत उदास उमीदे-क़रार[6] गुज़री है।

वसीम बरेलवी

1.दुखभरी 2.प्रतिक्षा भरी शाम 3.जीवन 4.खुली सड़क पर 5.कब्र 6.चैन की मोहताज कामना

Tere na hone se yoon sogwaar guzree hai,
Bahaar jaise shabe-intizaar guzree hai.
Wo shamma kaise bataayegee manzilon ke nishaan,
Hayaat jiskee sare-rah-guzaar guzree hai.
Mujhe hayaat kee majbooriyaan nazar aayeen,
Nazar se jab koee lohe-mazaar guzree hai
Sitaare doob rahein hain bidaaeeyaan de kar,
Na jaane kiskee shabe-intizaar guzree hai.
Dile-'Waseeem' se, har shaam intizaar ke baad,
Bahut udaas umeede-qaraar guzree hai

In your Absence life has been so sad,
As if spring has been spent like the night of waiting.
How that candle will point towards the signs to destination,
Whose own life has been spent on the open street.
I did notice the vulnerabilities of life,
Whenever I happened to pass by a grave.
The stars are setting having said good byes,
God knows whose night of waiting has come to an end.
After every evening of waiting,
The hope for respite has passed very dejected through "waseem's" heart.

'Waseem' Bareilvi

तूफ़ान जब उटठा था, उस वक्त न था कोई,
एक भीड़ हैं साहिल[1] पे जब डूब गया कोई।
हँसती हुई बस्ती में रोने की सदा[2] कैसी,
शायद मेरे आलम[3] को पहचान गया कोई।
उस वक्त 'उमर' मुझको वो और भी याद आए,
जब फ़सले-बहार[4] आई, जब फूल खिला कोई।

उमर अन्सारी लख़नवी

1.किनारा 2.आवाज 3.हालत 4.बंसत ऋतु

Toofaan jab uthttha tha us waqt na tha koee,
Ek bheed hai saahil pe jab doob gaya koee,
Hanstee huee bastee mein rone kee sada kaisee,
Shaayad mere aalam ko pehchaan gaya koee.
Us waqt 'Umar' mujhko woh aur bhee yaad aaye,
Jab fasle-bahaar aaee, jab phool khila koee,

When the storm had struck,
No one was there then (to give a hand),
A crowd has gathered on the bank after someone has drowned.
In this laughing settlement, whose crying voice is this?
Looks as if someone has realised my (pathetic) state.
At that time 'Umar', I remembered her more than ever,
When the spring arrived, when a flower bloomed.

'Umar' Ansaari Lucknavi

दिल घड़कने का सबब[1] याद आया,
वो तेरी याद थी, अब याद आया।
आज मुशकि़ल था संभलना ऐ, दोस्त!
तू मुसीबत में अजब याद आया।
दिन गुज़ारा था बड़ी मुशकि़ल से,
फिर तेरा वादा-ऐ-शब[2] याद आया।
हाले-दिल[3] हम भी सुनाते, लेकिन
जब वो रुख़्सत[4] हुआ, तब याद आया।
बैठ कर साया-ए-गुल में[5] -नासिर',
हम बहुत रोये वो जब याद आया।

नासिर काज़मी

1.कारण 2.रात का वचन 3.हृदय का हाल 4.विदा 5.फलों की छाँव

Dil dharakne ka sabab yaad aaya,
Wo teree yaad thee, ab yaad aaya,
Aaj mushqil tha sambhalna aye, dost!
Too museebat mein ajab yaad aaya.
Din guzaara tha badhi mushqil se,
Phir tera waada-e-shab yaad aaya,
Haale-dil hum bhee sunaate, lekin,
Jab wo rukhsat hua, tab yaad aaya.
Baithh kar saaya-e-gul mein 'Naasir'
Hum bahut roye wo jab yaad aaya.

Recalled the reason behind the beating of heart,
That was your memory, I remember it now.
O, friend it was difficult to steady (myself) today.
In this predicament stangely you came to mind.
After a great difficulty (I) had managed to pass the day,
Again, your promise of the night came to mind.
I too would have told (her) the state of (my) heart,
When she had departed only then I remembered.
O, 'Naasir' after sitting under the shadow of the flooers,
I wept a lot when her thought came to the mind.

'Naasir Kaazmi

जो दे रहे हैं तुम्हें फल पके-पकाए हुए,
ये पेड़ तुमको मिले हैं, लगे-लगाए हुए।
ये क्या ज़रूरी है, ग़ज़लें भी खुद लिखी जायें,
खरीद लाएगें कपड़े सिले-सिलाए हुए,
ज़मीर[1] इनके बड़े दाग़दार निकलेगें,
ये फिर रहे हैं जो चेहरे धुले-धुलाए हुए।
हमारे मुल्क में खादी की बरकतें[2] हैं मियाँ,
चुने-चुनाए हुए हैं, सारे छटे-छटाए हुए।
ज़मीन ओढ़कर सोये हैं, सारी दुनियाँ में
ना जाने कितने सिकन्दर[3] थके-थकाए हुए।

राहत इन्दौरी

1.आत्मा, अन्त:करण 2.आर्शिवाद 3.अलकजैन्डर

Jo de rahein hai tumhein phal pake-pakaaye huye,
Ye pedh tumko mile hain lage-lagaaye huye.
Ye kya zarooree hai, ghazlein bhee khud likhee jaayein,
Khareed laayenge kapdhe sile-silaaye hue.
Zameen odh kar soye hain, saaree duniyaan main,
Na jaane kitne sikandar thake- thakaaye huye
Zameer inke badhe daaghdaar nikleinge,
Ye phir rahein hain jo chehre dhule-dhulaaye huye.
Humaare mulk mein khaadee kee barkatein hain miyaan,
Chune chunaaye huye hain, saare chhathe-chhathaaye huye.

These which have been giving you fruits all ripened,
You have inherited these trees in fully grown up state.
This is not necessary that the poems should be composed by ownself,
We will buy the ready made ones from the market.
Their consciences will emerge highly tainted,
Those very persons who have been roaming around with faces all washed and spruced.
In our country wearing the khaadi (Gandhian cloth) is very blissful,
All these chosen ones (political leaders) (infact) are the 'most-wanted' lot.
Under the cover of this earth, have been lying,
God alone knows how many tired alexander the 'greats'.

Raahat Endori

वो जितनी ख़ुदनुमाई[1] कर रहा है,
ख़ुद अपनी जगहसाँई[2] कर रहा है।
ज़रा सा जोश क्या दरिया में आया,
समन्दर की बुराई कर रहा है।
हमारे बल से मसनद[3] पाने वाला,
हमीं से कजअदाई[4] कर रहा है।
ज़रा हमने ज़ुबाँ क्या बन्द करली,
ज़माना लबकुशाई[5] कर रहा है।
दिखाया है किसी ने आईना क्या,
जो चेहरे की सफ़ाई कर रहा है।
नज़ारा देखलो ख़ुदग़र्ज़ियों[6] का,
दग़ा[7] भाई से भाई कर रहा है।

नईम अख़्तर

1.आत्म-प्रकाशन 2.सँसार का हँसना 3.ऐशो-आराम की वस्तुएँ 4.टाल-मटोल 5.बक बक करना 6.स्वार्थ 7.धोखा

Wo jitnee khudnumaaee kar raha hai,
Khud apnee jag hansaaee kar raha hai.
Zara sa josh kya dariya mein aaya,
Samandar kee buraaee kar raha hai.
Humaare bal se masnad paane waala,
Hum hee se kajadaaee kar raha hai.
Zara hamne zubaan kya band kar lee,
Zamaana labkushaaee kar raha hai.
Dikhaaya hai kisee ne aayeena kya,
Jo chehre kee safaaee kar raha hai.
Nazaara deklo khudgarzion ka,
Dagha bhaaee se bhaaee kar raha hai.

The more he is indulging in self-display,
The more he is making the world laugh at himself,
What a little fervour/ rise has done to the river,
That she has been talking ill about the ocean.
The one who had got the high seat through our mandate,
The same one has been dilly-dallying with us only.
I had stopped my tongue just for a while,
The world has become vociferous (since then).
Has someone shown the mirror to him,
(Perhaps) That is why he has been cleaning his face.
Come and watch the spectacle of selfishness,
Brother has been deceiving (own) brother.

Naeem Akhtar

काश! ऐसा कोई मंज़र[1] होता,
मेरे काँधे पे तेरा सर होता।
वो जो ठोकर न लगाता मुझको,
मैं किसी राह का पत्थर होता।
इस बुलन्दी[2] पे, बहुत तन्हा हूँ,
काश! मैं सबके बराबर होता।
जमा करता, जो मैं आए हुए संग[3],
सर छुपाने के लिए एक घर होता।
उसने उलझा दिया दुनियाँ में मुझे,
वर्ना एक और क़लन्दर होता।

ताहिर फ़राज़

1.दृश्य 2.ऊँचाई 3.पत्थर 4.सन्यासी, मस्तमौला

Kaash! aisa Koee manzar hota,
Mere Kaandhe pe tera sar hota.
Wo jo thhokar na lagaata mujhko,
Main kisee raah ka patthar hota.
Is bulandee pe,bahoot tanha hoon.
Kaash, main sabke baraabar hota.
Jama karta jo main aaye huye sang,
Sar chhupaane ke liye ek ghar hota,
Usne uljha diya duniyaan main mujhe,
Varna ek aur qalandar hota.

Wish, there was a spectacle like this,
That your head was resting on my shoulder.
If she had not kicked me (out of the way),
I would have remained a stumbling stone on (some) track.
At this (dizzy) height,I am very lonely,
Wish I was at par with all others.
If I were to collect all those incoming stones,
I would have had a house to shelter my head.
She ensnared me in worldly tentacles,
Otherwise there would have been one more
With an attitude,"To hell with the world".

Taahir Faraaz

चराग़ों को उछाला जा रहा है,
हवाओं पर रौब डाला जा रहा है।
मेरे झूठे गिलासों की चख़ा कर,
बहकतों को सम्भाला जा रहा है।
हमीं बुनियाद[1] के पत्थर हैं, लेकिन,
हमें घर से निकाला जा रहा है।
जनाज़े[2] पर मेरे लिख देना, यारों।,
"मोहब्बत करने वाला, जा रहा है।"

'राहत' इन्दौरी

1. नींव 2. अर्थी

charaaghon ko uchhaala ja rha hai,
Hawaaon par raub daala ja raha hai.
Mere jhoothe, gilaason kee chakha kar,
Bahakton ko sambhaala ja raha hai.
Hum hee buniyaad ke patthar hain, lekin,
Humein ghar se nikaala ja raha hai
Janaaze par mere likh dena yaaron,
"Mohabbat karne waala ja raha hai"

Earthen lamps are being thrown high,
In order to intimidate the winds.
Leftover wine of my tasted glasses is being offered,
In order to steady the ones who are staggering.
I who has been the foundation stone(all along),
Am being thrown out of the house.
O, friends! let this be inseribed on my bier,
"The one who used to love is departing".

'Raahat' Indori

दयारे-नूर[1] में, तीरा[2] शबों[3] का साथी हो,
कोई तो हो, जो मेरी वहशतों[4] का साथी हो।
मैं उससे झूट भी बोलूँ, वो मुझसे सच बोले,
मेरे मिज़ाज[5] के हर मौसमों का साथी हो।
मैं उसके हाथ न आऊँ, वो मेरा होके रहे,
मैं गिर पड़ूँ, तो मेरी पस्तियों[6] का साथी हो।
वो मेरे नाम की निस्बत[7] से मौतबर[8] ठहरे,
गली-गली मेरी रुस्वाईयों[9] का साथी हो।
करे कलाम[10] जो मुझसे, तो मेरे लहजे[11] में,
मैं चुप रहूँ, तो मेरे तैवरों[12] का साथी हो।

'इफ़्तख़ार आरिफ़'

1. प्रकाशमान क्षेत्र 2.अन्धेरा 3. रातें 4. डरों 5. स्वभाव, मूड 6. गिरावटों
7. सम्बन्ध 8. विश्वस्त 9. बदनामियों 10. बात 11. बात करने का ढंग, टोन

Dayaare-noor mein, teera shabon ka saathee ho,
Koee tau ho, jo meree wahshaton ka saathee ho.
Main usse jhoothh bhee boloon, Wo mujhse sach bole,
Mere mizaaj ke har mausamon ka saathee ho.
Main uske haath na aaoon, wo mera hoke rahe,
Main gir padoon, tau meree pastion ka saathee ho.
Wo mere naam kee nisbat se moatbar thhehre,
Galee-galee meree ruswaaeeon ka saathee ho.
Kare Kalaam jo mujhse, tau mere lahje mein,
Main Chup rahoon, tau mere taiwaron ka saathee ho.

In this well-lit territory, let the darkness be my companion,
Let someone be there to share (all) my frights.
Even if I were to tell lies to him, he should tell truth to me,
Should remain by my side during my ever changing moods.
I should be out of his reach, yet he must remain belonging to me,
If I were to fall, then he must share all my dejections.
He should remain totally confident of things related to my name,
In all walks of life, he should stay by my side during all my infamies,
While talking to me, he should talk in my tone,
(And) If I were to remain silent, then he should be able to understand
the meaning of my frowns.

Iftkhaar Aarif

गाँव लौटे शहर से, तो सादगी अच्छी लगी,
हमको मिट्टी के दिये की रौशनी अच्छी लगी।
बासी रोटी सेंक कर, जब नाश्ते में माँ ने दी,
हर अमीरी से हमें ये मुफ़लिसी[1] अच्छी लगी।
आसमाँ के चाँद तारों में कहाँ ऐसी चमक,
हमको अपने घर के बच्चों की हँसी अच्छी लगी।
जिसमें अब भी गुनगुनाते हैं मेरी बहनों के गीत,
जगमगाते रास्तों से वो गली अच्छी लगी।
दे ना पाई बाल-बच्चों को जो रोटी, क्या हुआ,
सुनने वालों को तो मेरी शायरी अच्छी लगी।

हसन काज़मी

1. गरीबी

Gaaon laute shahar se, to saadgee achchhee lagee,
Humko mittee ke diye kee raushnee achchhee lagee.
Baasee rotee seink kar, jab naashte mein maa ne dee.
Har ameeree se humhein ye muflisee achchee lagee.
Aasmaan ke chaand taaron mein kahaan aisee chamak,
Humko apne ghar ke bachchon kee hansee achchhee lagee.
Jismein ab bhee gungunaate hain meree bahnon ke geet,
Jagmagaate raaston se wo galee achchee lagee.
De na paaee baal - bachchon ko jo rotee, kya huya.
Sun-ne waalon ko to meree shaairy achchhee lagee.

On return from the city to the village , (I) liked (its) simplicity,
I relished the brightness of the earthen lamp.

When (my) mother roasted the leftover *chapatti* and gave me in the breakfast,
I preferred this penury to all the riches (of the world).

Where is such brightness in the Moon and Stars of the sky,
I get more delight in the laughter of children at my home,

The lanes in which the songs of my sisters still hum,
Those lanes are preferable over all the brightly-lit roads.

Agreed, it could not provide bread to my children, so what?
Nonetheless, my poetry was enjoyed by the listeners .

Hasan Kaazmi

Index (poet wise)